ENERGY TRANSITION
AND THE LOCAL COMMUNITY

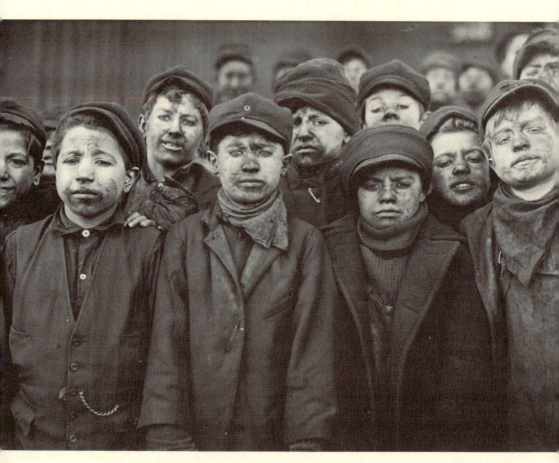

Breaker boys. (Photograph courtesy of the National Archives)

DAN ROSE

ENERGY TRANSITION AND THE LOCAL COMMUNITY

A Theory of Society
Applied to
Hazleton, Pennsylvania

UNIVERSITY OF PENNSYLVANIA PRESS
Philadelphia
1981

This work was published with the support of the Haney Foundation

Library of Congress Cataloging in Publication Data

Rose, Dan.
   Energy transition and the local community.

   Bibliography: p.
   Includes index.
   1. Hazleton (Pa.)—Economic conditions. 2. Human
ecology—Pennsylvania—Hazleton. 3. Community
development—Pennsylvania—Hazleton. I. Title.
HC108.H47R67   330.9748'32   80–52808
ISBN 0–8122–7792–9   AACR2

Printed in the United States of America

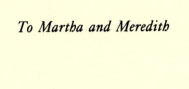

To Martha and Meredith

CONTENTS

ILLUSTRATIONS

PHOTOGRAPHS

FIGURES

TABLES

PREFACE

It is difficult for authors to discern all the reasons why they write a book, but I did have two conscious concerns. First of all, I was anxious about the contemporary energy crisis and its long-term effects on my life, my career, and my family. I set out to understand it, using some of the central ideas current in anthropology and other disciplines.

My second concern was professional. I happened upon a puzzle and a challenge in the course of my anthropological fieldwork in 1974. The puzzle was why a community in the depressed anthracite coal mining region of northeastern Pennsylvania should have full employment in 1974. The challenge became not to describe, but to explain, this anomaly. I felt that description, which is the goal of ethnography, was insufficient —an explanation that could form the basis of a theoretical model was needed. My concern was not simply to understand a community, for American communities have been studied extensively. Rather, I sought to understand what occurred within a community as it responded to strong exogenous forces that were being played out within it. Ethnography is a method that was developed to provide descriptive information on social realities never before documented. Ethnography cannot, however, provide the explanatory power or the generalizations that were demanded in order to address the questions: why did the region around Hazleton, Pennsylvania, have full employment and how was this achieved? My aim was to write a long essay, a discourse that would set up an explanatory model of social forces, to show how these forces developed, and then to explain the region's economic picture and its specific, emergent social organization as it responded to these forces.

This order, in fact, became the logical organization of the book. Chapter 1 describes the model, chapter 2 sketches its operation through time, and chapter 3 applies the model to the Hazleton region, thus unifying both the synchronic and diachronic dimensions. The book was written to explain puzzling social phenomena generated by ethnographic methods, but the book is not ethnographic, that is, descriptive and analytical, in execution or intent.

Ethnography, like many of the methods of science, is close to the natural history phase of a discipline. Complementary to the descriptive is the theoretical, that scientific mode by which we explain previously unrelated phenomena. Although theory and description develop together, we are undoubtedly in an increasingly theoretical phase in the evolution of science. While such a moment can be decried on several grounds, the best justification for theory remains its attempts at constructing explanatory models, and this book is weighted in that direction.

I wanted specifically to explain why a certain group of men organized themselves in the way they did. The men were business people, small manufacturers, large merchants, and professionals from Hazleton, a small city in eastern Pennsylvania. It is an area that flourished in the days when coal was king—in this case, anthracite coal. Their effect on the landscape surrounding Hazleton was obvious when I first drove the roads of that mountainous area in the winter and spring of 1974. I observed the ravages of 125 years of coal mining and I spoke to the people: those who had worked the mines, their children, the descendants of Tyrolean tinsmiths, Italian-American farmers, the elderly of Anglo-American descent, unemployed young people, the affluent business people, doctors, ministers, coal mine owners, and others. Although the domination of coal was visible everywhere on the horizon and in the acidic streams draining the mountains, the talk on everyone's lips was of the efforts of a group of men who had changed the region from a depressed Appalachian community into a place enjoying full employment in 1974. There is a fundamental anthropological theme addressed here, that of social organization. The group that succeeded in its tireless efforts at economic revitalization was an emerging piece of social organization. I felt strongly in 1974, and that feeling grew in later years, that it would advance our scientific understanding of American society to explain the dynamics of its presence, to understand the reasons why it was formed, and to describe its accomplishments in the region.

The emergence of the group of men who called their organization CAN DO (Community Area New Development Organization) was an occurrence within the world economic system of the 1970s. Models of underdevelopment or dependency were not particularly relevant to Hazleton because they are applied to less developed societies. There is, as far as I know, no adequate non-Marxist theory that explains why certain areas within a capitalist country should be severely depressed.

In developed, capitalist societies a combination of public welfare and private initiatives is the preferred strategy for regional redevelopment after severe decline in a particular economic sector. The men of CAN DO learned to manipulate this model perhaps better than any other anthracite community. In this book I have refrained from telling their story in great detail because they told it themselves in a monograph that was funded by a grant from the federal government. Chapter 3 offers the abstract framework of their self-organization and their strategies for successful economic redevelopment. I have avoided excessive detail because I do not want to obscure the scaffolding on which their organization and effort were built. I feel ambivalent about my choice, though, because I have repressed detail in favor of a conceptual scheme.

The first chapter develops a model that was designed to account for the social organization I discovered in 1974 while surveying the greater Hazleton area. The model is firmly grounded within an anthropological view of the world. For unification I have relied on general systems theory modified by the use of recently formed ideas from biology and several other scientific fields. General systems theory is now so widely accepted in contemporary scientific thought that I have felt no need to lay out either its history or its major conceptual domains. Both tasks would have been redundant to the large existing literature, and would have required diversions from the task of clean model building. A word should be said about model making, however. Models can be realistic, predictive, precise, or general. I take the model constructed herein to be qualitative rather than quantitative, and to be realistic in that it takes into account many variables. The model seeks to explain the local community in terms of its place within the modern capitalist world-system and its local ecosystem. If the model is sufficiently general it can be applied, with proper adjustments, elsewhere in the world. There is a critical dimension ignored by students of world-systems, a dimension that is undeniable today: the local community is related to world and local ecosystems. The local community is particularly closely related to its immediate environment—it depends on freshwater sources, it affects local climate, it has a direct relation to other natural resources. The social organization of the local community is a function of environment and economy and, I claim, can only be fully understood within this double structure.

There is behind this volume an ethic that is not readily apparent. During the 1960s anthropologists and members of the American Anthropological Association were concerned about their role in non-Western countries. Of all the sciences, anthropology inhabits a niche that is peculiarly a world niche. It deals largely with the social organization of peoples on the subnational levels outside the West, and it has in the past had an overwhelming interest in description of previously undocumented peoples. It was considered proper to describe these peoples in the ethnographic present, a rhetorical style that often omitted the effect of westernization on them. The description was meant to reveal the people as they were organized before contact with the West.

This strategy was devised neither maliciously nor naively, but so that a universal history of humanity could be written and explanatory theories could be constructed based on adequate scientific description. Most anthropologists were indeed Boasians, because adequate description became the prime concern in the fieldwork experience. This phase of anthropology has now encountered insurmountable difficulty as the last of the aboriginal groups and peasants have become socially extinct or have been incorporated, with varying success or failure, politically, economically, and linguistically into the nations within whose boundaries they fall. The role of anthropologists in colonialism and its aftermath and in the terrible light of the Vietnam War prompted ethical questions, and with the heightened awareness of ethical dilemmas came associated concerns. One of these was whether anthropologists were to be disinterested scholars or advocates of what they perceived as their native friends' best interests. Given the spirit of modern science and the endlessly different real-life situations, there can be no resolution to the problem.

Whether or not anthropologists should be advocates for their subjects was a subset of the whole question of the extent of the anthropologist's professional responsibility. These questions are now largely pre-empted by the political realities of the 1970s and 1980s. Increasingly, anthropological fieldwork is constrained or facilitated by the host country. The ethical question has become once again dominated by concern with expediency, now political in nature.

While I have no ideological commitment, I have made numerous practical political ones. As a means of realizing my socialized urge for relevance, I have been politically active while engaged in fieldwork, have made the results of my research available to elected officials, and have lobbied with them to advance my research priorities. It is obvious that within the climate of citizens' rights and access to redress for grievance under the law in the United States, political involvement here has a very different character than it does in other countries. I am reminded of Sartre's remark that Americans who seek to change the system do not find it contradictory to work from within, while the European intent on substantive social change attempts to effect it outside the established institutional structure. I think this observation is generally true of us in the United States, unless one is an Afro-American or Native American, and even their almost total exclusion from civil status has been ameliorated by protest and by increasing legal and economic enfranchisement during the last two decades. It still makes me angry that groups in this country must lobby and manipulate the mass media, if they can, for civil rights; it bears witness to the incompleteness of the privilege of citizenship conveyed by the modern nation state. On the other hand, it also suggests a system resilient enough to respond to evolving libertarian demands.

The concern with humans and natural systems is not far from the central concern of sociocultural anthropology, the social organization of human life. Natural systems framed within social organization can be visualized as a medium that affects directly the social organization of other humans. I do not wish to push the view of ecosystem as medium too far, but a homely illustration may help me make the point. If I establish a residence on a stream in a region where water is relatively scarce, near the headwaters, and others take up residence downstream, then my quantitative or qualitative modifications to the flowing body of water directly affect my downstream neighbors. If I consume the water, leaving little in the stream bed and thereby curtailing the quantity of flow, I have intervened in my neighbors' life chances insofar as they are a function of water quantity. One can discern here the rudiments of a social contract even more complex than that celebrated by Rousseau, for by manipulating resources to my advantage over my neighbors', I may deny the most elementary life chances to them. To overcome the terrific advantage and personal power my upstream position gives me, a social contract must be established for relative access, or we must establish procedures for bargaining. Otherwise I may find that my neighbors have, in the absence of established norms, raised an army to capture the headwaters of what is also their stream. Despite the crudeness of the story, I think the message is clear enough. One of the counters in the organization of society, one of the media that binds one human to another or keeps us apart, is the natural world—a watering hole, a wallaby for supper, iron ore deposits, acid rain, petroleum reserves, damaging effluents, or hegemony over upstream water supplies.

To tie up the loose threads from my homily, let me say that I have made an effort to contribute to a relevant human systems ecology both within and beyond anthropology, and inside and outside the United States. In the last analysis, my concern is a humanistic one, and this book represents but a small part of that effort. I am a committed social scientist, but I should clarify that I have no partisanship with a capitalist or socialist ideology, unless perhaps it is an unconscious one. I believe the modern world-system to be totally determined, a product of necessity. Capitalist and socialist political systems are merely different political strategies to achieve industrialization. Contemporary industrial society is another human ecological adaptation—it is a complex of technological means that allow us to feed ourselves. There is very slim chance that we can de-determine this capitalist industrial historical epoch. Our contemporary system is determined completely by our biological overproduction, our ignorance of its causes and implications, and our lack of political mechanisms to address associated economic, political, and social problems. If, as a species, we knew what we were doing, perhaps we could intervene in the system and from our knowledge produce a political agenda worthy of the highest collective aspirations. Perhaps we could achieve a more benevolent relationship with our life support system, a medium in our social organization that we are simultaneously building up and degrading. Our current efforts are creating fluctuations in natural systems, in social systems, and in our social relationships that we may be unable to dampen before catastrophic consequences ensue. These are some of the dimensions of our contemporary ecological transition. We need a theory of intervention in human ecological processes, and at present we have none.

This book has grown out of those debates of the 1960s, and I chose in my dissertation fieldwork and in my later work to make relevant the discipline of anthropology, at least that part of sociocultural anthropology with which I was familiar. I chose to work in the United States, but not among Native Americans, and to work toward a human systems ecology that can contribute to policy formation. I want to advance knowledge of human system-ecosystem relations so that humans may be understood as not just a part of nature in a naive naturalistic sense, but as a product of natural processes, and to comprehend humans as intervening in the processes that give rise to their evolution. Humans are by far the most unstable elements of contemporary natural systems and are now the most volatile agents for change, perhaps in this solar system, certainly in terrestrial and marine ecosystems.

ACKNOWLEDGMENTS

I have been urged by colleagues to put this model of ecological anthropology into print, and I appreciate their encouragement. Jon Berger went through the original field experience with me; it is rewarding to work with a tireless field person, and we learned much from one another. Robert Douglas has provided the perspective of the regional scientist on more than one occasion, and we have had students in common, much to my benefit. Brian Spooner has offered thoughtful and very helpful criticism, particularly on an early draft of the first chapter. I am indebted to his always useful proddings. Without the inspiration of Ian McHarg and the great freedom to explore he encourages, this book would never have been written. Special thanks are due Ben Miller for his extensive criticism and friendship.

During the spring of 1978 I asked a number of anthropologists to address one of my ecology seminars. I benefited immeasurably from the array of ideas presented there, and I would like to express my thanks to each of the participants. Richard N. Adams advanced the theoretical work on energy and social power which he presented in his presidential address to the American Anthropological Association in 1977. Alexander Alland analyzed sex roles in ritual performance and Frederick Bredahl-Petersen demonstrated the effect of advanced technology on the North Atlantic ocean ecosystem. Michael Harner's vivid accounts of human sacrifice complemented Marvin Harris's theoretical discussion of the evolution of human population and the resulting pressure placed on natural and sociocultural systems. Bernard James applied general systems theory concepts to the management of complex bureaucracies, and Dean MacCannell noted the changing form of human settlements and contemporary trends in the way Americans conceptualize themselves. Laura Nader reported on her recent involvement with federal energy policy makers and continued to urge that we study a vertical slice when examining highly stratified societies. Brian Spooner presented a systems account of the effects of land tenure reform on the ecology and social organization of Iran. The model I constructed in this book owes most to the work of Adams. Naturally, all errors and omissions of fact as well as problems of interpretation are entirely my responsibility.

My research assistants Mark Kocent and Laurie Berk, though not always working on this project, have been supportive beyond paid responsibilities, and my graduate students have pushed me into domains I would not have entered otherwise. Three students wrote papers during the course of a semester on topics related to the history of Hazleton and the anthracite coal region: Rick Seeley on the development of the infrastructure, Ethan Seltzer on population and textiles, and Michael Udell on the railroad system and the price of anthracite in the nineteenth century. I have benefited from their efforts and have incorporated prose from Seltzer's paper.

The Ford Foundation made funds available to the University of Pennsylvania's Department of Landscape Architecture and Regional Planning, stimulating the early involvement in Hazleton and the development in the department of an applied human and biological ecology. After the Ford Foundation stimulus, the National Institute of Mental Health provided a training grant to the department that underwrote my original Hazleton fieldwork. For the last stages of writing, the dean of the Faculty of Arts and Sciences, and the provost of the University of Pennsylvania generously made financial support available to me.

John Szwed has been a friend for a decade and has given me the benefit of a continuous rereading of America; his vision is a constant reminder that there are other visions than the one presented here. Most of the issues and ideas presented in the book have been touched upon by John Bennett; there are echoes of his work throughout, for he has anticipated most of the problems of ecological anthropology. The people of Hazleton who offered their cooperation and hospitality deserve more thanks than I can give. Although I have been critical of the region, I admire the people who make it their home. Dr. Edgar Dessen, the Andy Deisroth family, Theresa Zogby, Joe Yenchko, and especially the Webster family have my gratitude.

The book was further encouraged and made more possible by the kind efforts of John McGuigan and Anne Toffey.

ENERGY TRANSITION AND THE LOCAL COMMUNITY

THEORY

In fact, the problem of how to transmit our ecological reasoning to those whom we wish to influence in what seems to us to be an ecologically good direction is itself an ecological problem. We are not outside the ecology for which we plan—we are always and inevitably a part of it.

Herein lies the charm and the terror of ecology—that the ideas of this science are irreversibly becoming a part of our own ecosocial system.

Gregory Bateson (1972:504)

The central thesis of this book [*The Ecological Transition*] is that the best case for the existence of something called cultural ecology can be made on the grounds of public policy. Research data that has significance for shaping environmental policies (mostly physical, but always including some social) can be obtained from something less than a comprehensive human ecological science or theory, which does not yet exist in any event. . . . In its bare essence, our definition of cultural ecology is therefore a study of how and why humans use Nature, how they incorporate Nature into Society, and what they do to themselves, Nature, and Society in the process.

John Bennett (1976:2–3)

Human ecological studies within complex societies have only relatively recently been attempted. For the United States they are nearly nonexistent at present. This book, growing out of anthropological research techniques adapted to the United States, seeks to contribute to a human systems ecology. The demand for such a study has increased with rising world population and mass migration, worsening oil shortages, massive ecological degradation, uneven economic development and decline, and scattered small-scale wars.

This book develops an empirical study undertaken in Hazleton city and in southern Luzerne County, Pennsylvania, part of the nation's only major anthracite coal mining region. The original field research was initiated in the winter and spring of 1974, shortly after the first energy crisis. In 1973, months before the fieldwork, the petroleum-exporting countries inaugurated an embargo, then raised prices on crude oil. As a result, they sent oil-dependent countries into a series of shocks. The Iranian revolution of 1978 led to a subsequent shortfall in total world oil production and aggravated the already excruciating problem of world inflation. At the time of the Hazleton Study, as it was called, the author was becoming aware of a correlation between the fate of the coal industry and its users of an earlier era and today's oil industry and its users. Both coal and oil are primary, nonrenewable resources, and both have served at different times as the major energy source for the industrial nations.

Because there are underlying similarities between the two energy periods—and both are reflected, although differently, in the organization of social life in Hazleton—nineteenth- and early twentieth-century regional history is reviewed. Special attention is given to population, infrastructure, and energy. The focus of the historical overview is upon those social formations that arose first with increasing coal production and then its decline. The final sections concentrate on the region after World War II, when the anthracite mines were all but closed and the shift to an oil- and hydroelectric-based economy was fully realized in the United States. On the local level, organizations, institutions, and social activities changed drastically to accommodate and control as best they could the conditions that evolved in the region, first around the mining of anthracite, and then around its demise and the subsequent small-scale industrialization within the area. Walter Rostow captured nicely the early, uneven pace of development that the anthracite and similar regions experienced.

> The coming of industrialization to the United States poses sharply a problem to be observed in a good many other nations down to contemporary China, India, and Brazil; that is, the uneven regional pace of modernization within national societies. The problem existed and exists even within smaller national units; e.g., Britain, France, Germany, Italy. As we know, growth proceeds forward by sectors whose spreading effects suffuse the national market structure; but the various regions are unequally affected. Especially in early states of growth, some may be only slightly affected and left as quasi-traditional backwaters while growth proceeds rapidly in regional industrial enclaves. [1978:385]

The northeastern portion of the United States was the major platform for the Industrial Revolution in this country, and the Hazleton region was from the beginning an integral part of the vital energy supply (figure 1). The city is sited in the anthracite coalfields, directly above the Mammoth Vein in the Eastern Middle Basin. It is located at 41′01″ latitude and 75′54″ longitude. The southern end of Luzerne County is nearly coterminous with this coal basin. The whole anthracite area, representing all of the major deposits of this hard coal in North America, lies within a circumscribed 1243 square kilometer space. The anthracite fields lie on the western periphery of the megalopolitan corridor, a conurbation of 37 million people (Gottman 1961:7) stretching from Boston to New

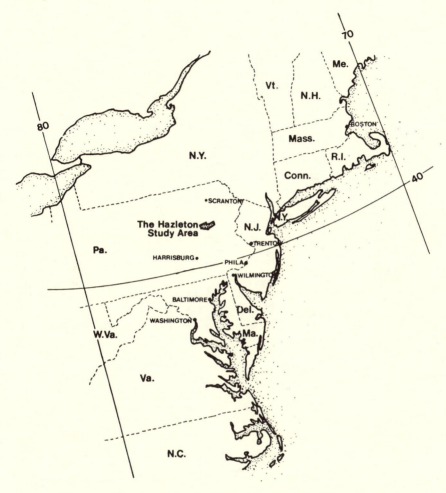

Figure 1. The northeastern United States (after Gottman 1961)

York, through Philadelphia and Baltimore, to Washington, D.C. Anthracite fueled the furnaces of New York City and Philadelphia tenements and homes during the last decades of the nineteenth century and the early decades of the twentieth.

Hazleton city was relatively accessible to the old manufacturing belt cities that were industrializing as the megalopolis was growing (D. Miller 1975:19). The remnants of this period are very much in evidence on the Hazleton landscape; upon entering the city one cannot miss the high mounded culm banks of the stripped coalfields on either side of the city. The Hazleton Study area included the city and adjacent coalfields, an agricultural valley, and the whole southern end of Luzerne County, 414

Hazleton, looking toward the southeast over the coalfields. The city of Hazleton rests on coal, and the people sometimes joke about the wealth buried under the city. The city is bounded on the east and west by mines, and many houses look directly over old mine strippings. In the city one is constantly visually reminded of the once flourishing economic base of the region. (Photograph by Ace Hoffman Studios, Wilkes-Barre, Pa., 1973, courtesy of CAN DO)

square kilometers in all. The population of more than 60,000 is distributed almost evenly between the city and the southern tip of the county (figure 2).

Until recently, southern Luzerne County, like much of the rest of the Appalachian Ridge and Valley Province, was isolated by its extreme physiography. The elevation shifts dramatically from 180 to 580 meters above sea level. Transportation in and out of the region before the interstate highway system was by tortuous roadways and expensively built and maintained railways. The valleys had been settled in the late seventeenth century by Connecticut Valley farmers, but they, like the Native Americans who knew the area before, never settled in large numbers. The great explosion of population came with the opening of the anthracite mines on a commercial basis in the 1830s.

The coalfields no longer produce significant tonnage, for there is no market demand, and the area has been in decline or severely depressed since the 1920s. The region has been a chronic problem to public policy makers and government agencies as a result of marketplace conditions, not exhaustion of the coalfields. The federal government and the state of

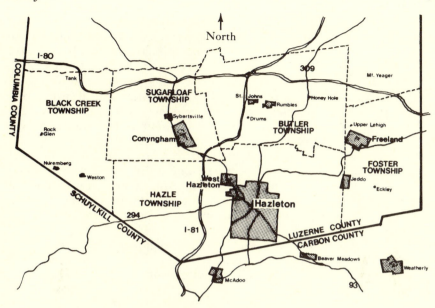

Figure 2. The Hazleton region

Pennsylvania have been called upon repeatedly to provide social welfare benefits and economic revitalization programs (Rondinelli 1975). The anthracite region is one of the better examples in the country of the public sector having to remedy the social and ecological consequences of private sector development and decline.

   This study has been designed to model the changing local-level social system and ecosystem as they respond to the evolution of the capitalist world-system (Barraclough 1978; Wallerstein 1979). This approach, because it calibrates the very large scale with the microscopic, omits much detail, but it can relate the ways in which local-level institutions emerge to adapt to the boom or bust developments of the fluctuating United States economy. The human ecological approach, focused in this study on energy, demonstrates positive relations between the macroscopic level, the local level, and the local ecosystem—where, after all, the world economy derives its resources, both human and natural, and affects the local ecosystem (Rose 1978, 1980). The local populations suffer or benefit accordingly. A developed theory of intervention is needed that will specify appropriate policies to address these complex relationships.

   In the course of their field studies and theory construction, anthropologists have focused attention on the formation of social groups, the role of individuals and their associations in the society—as entrepreneurs, for example—and the cultures or subcultures; that is, the perceptual, cognitive, procedural, and belief systems, the shared products of human learning employed by the people being studied (Goodenough 1966:257–59; 1978:79–86). How groups are stratified, the range of their activities, and the boundaries they erect or cross are also subjects central to this interest. For social anthropologists the very heart of the discipline has been social organization—the diverse ways people bond to one another, the structure of those bonds, and their order and disorders over periods of time. The Hazleton region was in fact a self-conscious, subcultural area as defined by local business and community leaders, and was organized as a part of the nation-state with similarities and regional differences. During the 1920s legislation was proposed in the Pennsylvania state legislature to break Luzerne County in two and to name the new county formed in the southern half Anthracite County. The bill mysteriously died in the legislature, but the old animosities that the Hazleton people felt toward Wilkes-Barre, the county seat, were very much alive in 1974.

The boundary between the Hazleton region and the rest of the county to the north was, in the minds of the local elite, an emotional one. It was economic as well, for the local community leaders were undoubtedly the most aggressive in the whole anthracite area—the northeast tier of the state—in working to revive their region after the demise of anthracite mining and the subsequent depopulation of the area. The community leaders, the subregional elite, were newly organized after World War II to meet these challenges, and they constitute the major operating unit or social group of this study. The theory and history drawn upon are intended to explain why the Hazleton business and professional men built institutions for economic recovery which became social innovations arising from a need to adapt to the new conditions they found when they returned from the war. The institutional features developed were the mechanisms used in organizing the people of the whole subregion to take action to secure their own employment futures.

Because the local community was successful at securing employment, this is a success story, albeit a mixed success. After 1974, the employment picture darkened as the Hazleton region once again began suffering from the effects of underemployment. Other monographs in the social sciences deal with devastation and exploitation in the bituminous coal fields (Caudill 1963; Erikson 1976). The Hazleton experience may have proved in some respects an exception and for that reason alone it is worth understanding.

ORIGINAL STUDY DESIGN

The original 1974 study of the region (Rose and Berger 1974) was based primarily on Julian Steward's *Theory of Culture Change* (1955) and Marx and Engels's *German Ideology* (1947). There have been criticisms that Steward's ideas about the "cultural core" in cultural ecology cannot be made operational. My efforts have been directed to prove the opposite.

Steward explained his very important notion of cultural core (akin to Marx's base) in an article originally published in the *New International Dictionary*:

> Elsewhere, I have offered the concept of *cultural core*—the constellation of features which are most closely related to subsistence activities and economic arrangements. The core includes such social, political, and religious patterns as are empirically determined to be closely connected with these arrangements. Innumerable other features may have great potential variability because they are less strongly tied to the core. These latter, or secondary features, are determined to a greater extent by purely cultural-historical factors —by random innovation or by diffusion—and they give the appearance of outward distinctiveness to cultures with similar cores. Cultural ecology pays primary attention to those features which empirical analysis shows to be most closely involved in the utilization of environment in culturally prescribed ways. [1955:37]

Putting Steward's ideas into practice was begun in Hazleton and was realized much more completely in the design and conduct of a subsequent study (Berger 1978; Rose, Steiner, and Jackson 1979). The Hazleton Study employed Steward's ideas for the following purposes:

1. To help realize a human ecology of complex societies by applying anthropological techniques in a fieldwork situation;
2. To create a holistic study of the social system that was directly and indirectly related to the ecosystem in systematic ways;
3. To create a holistic approach (theory and methods) by a focus on institutions directly involved in the exploitation of the environment.

It was thought that these aims would provide a much needed creative matrix for employing all the useful social sciences—history, sociology, political science, regional science, economics, and geography—as they were needed to solve specific problems, as well as the natural sciences, as they were required (Rose and Jackson 1978; see also Koopmans 1979:1–13). This goal, of course, has not been achieved, but the Hazleton Study and subsequent studies designed by the author were shaped by an intent to develop a holistic interactive human systems ecology. Although he was making another point, I agree with Wallerstein's observation:

> I do not believe that the various recognized social sciences—in alphabetical order, anthropology, economics, geography, political science, and sociology—are separate disciplines, that is, coherent bodies of subject matter organized around separate levels of generalization or separate meaningful units of analysis. [1979:ix]

I would add that this observation is especially true when these disciplines are linked by means of a specific research problem to the relevant natural sciences. These linkages of ideas in concrete tasks provide the possibility for developing a systematic human ecology.

A NOTE ON METHODS

The methods employed in the Hazleton Study were informed by a general goal of developing a systematic human ecology in the United States that would include the careful articulation of the natural and social processes. Steward again proved useful in proposing procedures for conducting research:

1. Analyze the interrelationships of the productive technology and the environment;
2. Identify the relevant environment as a function of the kind of knowledge that a cultural system had of its ecosystem; and identify the behavior patterns associated with the technology in using the environment (for behavior patterns, institutions were substituted);
3. "Ascertain the extent to which the behavior patterns [institutions] entailed in exploiting the environment affect other aspects of culture" (Steward 1955:41).

This body of directions served as the general guide for research and analysis. Steward's programmatic statement promised the identification of a core of human activities and institutions directly related to specific environmental factors. The interface, of course, is the current state of technology, equipment by which the social system exploits the resources culturally defined as relevant. The commitment to identify the core patterns of resource exploitation simplified the ethnographic task of documenting people and places by focusing on the nature-culture interface.

Perhaps more than other disciplines, anthropology has relied successfully on qualitative methods, mainly prose descriptions, in its numerous monographs. With the publication of Geertz's *Agricultural Involution*, however, human ecology acquired an interpretive basis. Anthropology's contribution to world scientific literature has been in the recording of peoples whose lifeways have recently been forever broken by the success of the capitalist world economy. The research tools have been aptly fitted for this mission, and much has been written about them. In the industrially advanced, literate societies, these methods have seemed redundant to the immense amount of historical documents and current written literature available, and the awesome hegemony of quantitative economics. A year's supply of town newspapers gives the kind of information that anthropologists struggle for months to accumulate. While this observation obviously raises the question of the fate of some of the methods—and perhaps of the whole field—of sociocultural anthropology, that is not the issue here. These methods and others are required in order to realize a human systems ecology. The place for qualitative research remains that of a complement to the quantitative within the field of anthropology and the other social sciences. What the qualitative can do is to capture the contributions of many approaches in an overall prose model. This is the very strength that allows it to articulate well with the policy sciences and policy makers.

The Hazleton Study must be understood within its institutional framework. When the study was undertaken early in 1974, the author had just joined the faculty of an ecological planning department at the University of Pennsylvania. The year before, a study team of faculty and students funded by the Ford Foundation had done a rather detailed inventory of the geology, soils, climate, hydrology, animals, plants, and some social factors of the Hazleton region. The data bases of the inventory were mostly compiled from published sources, but several pieces of the research were original. A household survey probing the social-economic linkages between households had been made and computerized, and a large sampling had been conducted in order to analyze water quality in area streams. A preliminary census analysis had been made employing age-sex pyramids and other graphic displays; crime statistics were analyzed, as were a local hospital's admissions by address. During the spring of 1974 this exercise was conducted again with slightly different emphasis and under the aegis of the National Institute of Mental Health. The author used these inventories and preliminary analyses to become acquainted with the regional ecology.

In addition to these inventories and data bases, a human ecological reconnaissance was undertaken. The objectives were to operationalize Steward's model and to become familiar with the whole landscape on a firsthand basis. The reconnaissance was conducted by a two-man team consisting of the author, an anthropologist, and a land planner trained in ecology and acquainted with the natural processes of the area. Both stayed with a local family descended from generations of merchants servicing the mining city. The hosts were exceptionally helpful and sponsored parties and dinners with many of the affluent citizens who were in positions of economic and political power. The sociable occasions became sources of information on the intricate workings of the local political economy and the status system. Those who attended knew the aims of the research and were more than helpful in their explanation of the community.

RECONNAISSANCE

The reconnaissance is an anthropological method for exploring regions that have never before been mapped or that have never fallen under European influence. It is a system for generating information, particularly concerning topography and settlement, vegetation and animal life, and human population. It was felt that the reconnaissance method would yield the kind of information that anthropologists need in order to conduct holistic studies of a place. In this case it also became a training ground for both anthropologist and ecological planner in the mysteries of each other's realms. Every passable road and lane was driven. Settlements and natural phenomena were mapped on topographical sheets and were keyed to notebooks; photographs were keyed to field notes and maps. The notebook contained architectural and settlement pattern sketches as well as interviews conducted with people in public places, stores, post offices, public officials' offices, banks, and homes.

The goals of the reconnaissance were, then, twofold: to map and understand at the most basic level the whole region as an interactive natural-social space; and to identify the cultural core, the interface between nature and culture. To achieve this, land use was identified as the locus of man-land relations.

Land use categories include, but are not limited to, residential, commercial, industrial, mining, public institutions, transportation, utilities, agriculture, and forestry. Also included are refinements of these and other categories, and in each category a breakdown was made by type. Farms, for example, were classified according to the primary crop grown, for example, as orchard or dairy. These more finely discriminated land uses were then mapped and keyed in their detail. The published inventories and the windshield survey from the road were complemented by open-ended interviewing. The interview, although open, was informed by a hidden agenda. Certain primary information was sought and additional subjects were then pursued. The nucleus of questions included:

1. Occupational history of the person interviewed and others that he or she knew in the area;
2. Historical sources of occupation in the region;
3. Major issues surrounding regional and personal employment;
4. Major issues of the environment;
5. Local perceptions of the trends in the local and national economy;
6. Local perceptions among the agriculturalists as to trends and issues.

Occupation-related questions were asked because occupation was related to employers. The businesses and industries that employed the populace were direct users of the natural resources, and thus were located in a cultural core that utilized the relevant environment. The format was not rigid, and a number of social issues came to light in the conversations: problems with the school system, organized crime, interethnic competition, changing recreational patterns, and a number of others.

The reconnaissance provided a wealth of direct information on the social organization of land uses. When factored into the other data bases it was a powerful resource for understanding the regional dynamics. Like all inventories, it provided a matrix of knowledge that indicated where specific institutions, natural systems, and critical issues might be probed in greater depth.

RESULTS

The most lasting result for the author was the beginning of a rapidly growing comprehension of the workings of the United States at the local level, where local includes a rather extensive subregion. The dependence of local systems on the larger system is an overwhelming reality. Social scientists studying communities have recognized this (Vidich and Bensman 1968), although local people have too often denied it on ideological grounds.

In order to make the results of the regional reconnaissance readily accessible and conceptually manageable, southern Luzerne County was divided into four human ecological subregions; rough categories of settlement were included:

1. Coal field complex
    Cities and towns
    Patchtowns
    New settlement

2. The mountain complex
    Uninhabited
    New settlement

3. Valley complex
    Farmsteads
    Corner crossroads
    Roadside strips
    New settlements

4. Creek complex
    Corner crossroads
    Isolated
    Seasonal
    New settlements

A breaker in the coalfields. Coal breakers situated at the mouth of deep mines were a familiar sight during the days of deep mining. The coal was brought out of the ground there and sorted, then shipped out in rail cars. The breaker boys during the years of child labor spent their days sorting coal in similar structures. (Photograph by the author)

A patchtown in the coalfields. There is new siding on the houses, and there are recent-model automobiles parked in front. The improvements to the houses reflect not only the pride of the people of the coal region in community and home, but the fact that the people are employed as well. (Photograph by the author)

The patchtown of Eckley. This town was once owned entirely by Eckley B. Coxe, descendant of the colonial proprietor of southern New Jersey. The movie *The Molly Maguires* was filmed here, and the houses have been painted black since that time. The companies actually painted the houses red, and remnants of company paint can still be seen on the rare houses that are poorly cared for. The Eckley houses are very tiny, and it is difficult to imagine raising a large family in them, though many have done it. (Photograph by the author)

Audenried. The village of Audenried witnessed many dramatic events during the period when the miners were attempting to organize themselves into unions. Today the village—partly destroyed by the movement of machines for the extraction of coal—still houses some of the poorest families of the coalfield. Like many patchtowns, it is difficult to say where exactly the town leaves off and the mine begins. (Photograph by the author)

Cory Webster of Rock Glen at a deer-hunting lodge on Buck Mountain. The mountains of the Hazleton region are heavily used by the local people and by outsiders who come to hunt deer in season. Hunting shanties and blinds are scattered throughout the mountains as are territories marked off by local hunt clubs for their own private use. (Photograph by the author)

The Conyngham Valley north of Hazleton. New houses are mixed with older farm houses. Farmers sell off an acre or two at a time to raise capital for farm improvements. Their activity has given the valley a strip effect: houses are built facing the roads with their backs to the fields. Many of the city and mountain dwellers build a house in the valley when they can afford it. (Photograph by the author)

New subdivision development in the Conyngham Valley. Affluence and a desire to live in rural surroundings motivates people to purchase these houses in new subdivisions. These settlements are entirely dependent on neighboring communities for the services they require. Although the houses are not a part of a country club, the illusion of that friendly atmosphere is fostered by the name of the settlement, Country Club Estates. (Photograph by the author)

Isolated dwelling in the creek corridor. The creek corridors, like the mountain areas, are marginal, and yet they sustain a number of land uses such as trapping, hiking, and hunting. The people who live along the creek are either well off and have large tracts of land or are relatively poor and live in badly deteriorated housing. (Photograph by the author)

The criteria for constructing these subregional complexes were established primarily from physiography, vegetation, and the complex of human uses associated with the area. Interviews, observer's choice, clusters of institutions, built structures, historical development, and ethnicity were factored into the model.

The interview data provided information on the folk models, that is, local people's cultural perceptions of their landscape. Some participant observation was also made of the working-class members' use of the mountains.

Traditional usufruct and ecological awareness were documented in detail and became important ingredients in the study. One of the major products of the interview process was information on the competition between various communities for the use of the environment. How and by whom the local resources were to be used were the issues involved. One particularly explosive example was the conflict between some members of the local working class and a second-home developer. The builder purchased a mountain where traditional hunting rights had prevailed. He headed off incendiary conflict by restoring use rights after learning of the hunters' resentment and threats of retaliation.

The results of the reconnaissance were summarized in a scratch atlas of settlements, subregions, and physiography. One page of that atlas is duplicated in figure 3. The greatest value of the reconnaissance spatialized into atlas form was that it forced acquaintance with the whole geographic space of the study site. Subregionalizing permitted comparison and contrast within the site and thereby heightened awareness of regional similarities and differences.

It must be emphasized that a major benefit of the reconnaissance was experiential, as any field ecologist will understand. The effects of human activity were everywhere on the landscape, and the processes were revealed in conversation and direct observation. This level of human experience, especially in relation to ecosystems, tends to be ignored by the social sciences in this country. The workings of the social system at the interface with nature—woodlots, strip mines, dairy farms, abandoned pastures, hunting deer, planting in one's new suburban yard—are virtually an uncharted territory.

These may seem trivial examples, but the Hazleton Study contributed significantly to the growth of understanding about the social organization of ecosystem dependence and resource use, bringing to life Steward's words. In documenting the three fundamental procedures of cultural ecology mentioned above, he explained, "The third procedure requires a genuinely holistic approach, for if such factors as demography, settlement pattern, kinship structures, land tenure, land use, and other key cultural features are considered separately, their interrelationships to one another and to the environment cannot be grasped" (1955:42). The discovery was precisely this interdependence; dairy farmers operating in the valley were organized by exchange patterns, and by such institutions as the Pennsylvania Farmer's Association, the Grange, church, and kin-

	Mountain		Valley	
	Coalfield	Mountain	Valley	Creek
Settlement Type	City Patchtown Shopping Center Industrial Park Suburb	Hunting Shanties	Farmsteads Corner Crossroads Roadside Strips Suburbs	Isolated Dwellings Corner Crossroads Seasonal Settlements New Settlements
Name of Settlement	Hazleton Freeland West Hazleton Twp. Hazle Twp.	Hazle Twp.	Sugarloaf Twp. Butler Twp. Foster Twp.	Black Creek Twp.
Population	Population 1970 U.S. Census 50,518		12,163	
	Total 62,681			
Schooling Income	Years of Schooling Patchtowns 9.6 years Hazleton 11.9 years		Valley Villages 12.4 years	
	Average Income Patchtowns $8,000 Hazleton $9,373		Valley Village of Conyngham $11,241	
	Majority of houses built before 1939		Majority of houses built after 1939	
Topography	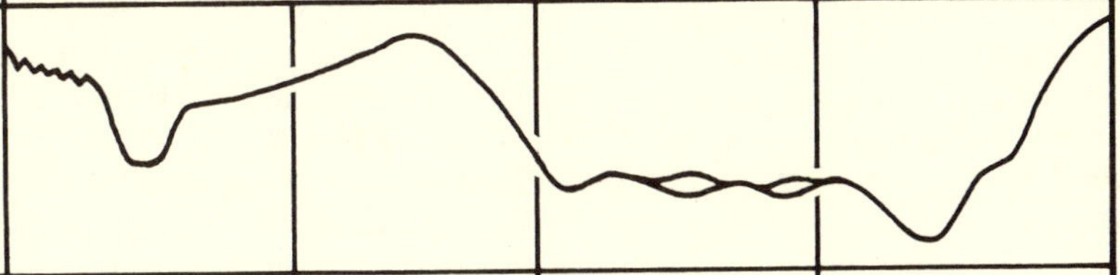			
Regions	Subregion 1	Subregion 2	Subregion 3	Subregion 4

Figure 3. Settlements, subregions, and physiography

ship. They were, in turn, institutionally and interpersonally connected with hunting associations composed of industrial and mining workers who lived on the mountain in patchtowns and urban centers. In summary, we found networks of relations between individuals who were members of trade associations, religious, political, voluntary, and civic institutions. The institutions were more often than not directly related to specific land uses. Thus land use and natural resources were linked through human associational life. The reconnaissance-interview method made it possible to work from the ecosystem up through the land uses to the institutional life associated with them, and then to the crosscutting associations that form the basis of North American communities.

The study generated two other insights. The first was that the local economy, based upon local land uses, was indeed a function of both the national and international system. When the oil-producing countries raised prices in 1973 there was a thriving second-home market in the region. A year and a half later, one of the new developments at the eastern end of the valley in the study area was in receivership. Rising energy and fuel costs destroyed the market for second homes in marginal areas. The second realization, linked to the first, concerned the formation of policy. Local policy, like the often remote functioning of the larger economy, is more often than not made outside the local system. Often such policy is made without adequate input from the locality, and without gauging the impacts that policy might have at the local level.

ECOLOGICAL TRANSITION AND CONTROL

Since the 1974 Hazleton Study, a handful of volumes and papers have advanced theoretical and applied human systems ecology. Brush's monograph on the human ecology of an Andean valley appeared in 1977, for example, as did a special number of the *American Ethnologist*. Notable contributions were made by Adams (1975, 1978) in energetics and control, by Bennett (1976) on policy and adaptation, by Harris (1977, 1979) on population growth as determinative in human production systems, and by Diener and others on a new evolutionary theory (Diener, Nonini, and Robkin 1980). Degraded ecosystems, especially those of the regions made arid by drought (Spooner and Reining 1979), received badly needed attention. Unfortunately there was no major review article during the 1974–79 period that sorted out the differences and synthesized the similarities in order to chart the directions that anthropological ecology was taking. Building on these advances and developments in other fields —notably chemistry, economics, and biology—I have attempted to incorporate the original Steward-based body of ideas with the later contributions, and then alternate between theory and the case study of the Hazleton site. This required further research in the region, additional data analysis, and additional interviewing.

Two themes emerge in this work: ecological transition and control. With the exponential rate of population growth since the eighteenth century and the maturing processes of worldwide industrialization, it is evident that we have been undergoing a continuous ecological transition in recent human history. Since then new relationships with nature have evolved with stunning rapidity and dramatic effects. We are developing new ways of feeding ourselves and new energies for constructing, heating, and cooling our built environments; for transporting humans and materials; for communicating; for storing, mixing, and retrieving information; for modifying physical elements and biological organisms; and for extending the life of our bodies in the face of almost intractable diseases.

Much of the world economic development in this century was accomplished with petroleum resources and their applications. The ecological transition that we face now—referred to as an energy crisis—is a result of the incipient exhaustion of petroleum reserves. This transition is strongly felt at the national and international levels. We need only witness the difficult political, social, and economic transition which Iran faced as a result of the massive exportation of oil and the sudden influx of nearly unusable wealth, or the recession which developed countries faced in the aftermath, beginning in 1979. The shift in energetic sources for the fueling of social systems is also evident at the most local level through such indicators as quality of life; access to various media; cultural creativity; political expression; and the expectations of citizens concerning their present and their future.

The concept of ecological transition has been used in the literature in at least two senses, the first described by Nash in these terms: The first sense of ecological transition widely held among anthropologists has three major dimensions—when humans emerged from their prehuman ancestors; the neolithic revolution when plants and animals were domesticated and urban places were established; and, finally, the industrial revolution, a revolution that has not yet run its course (M. Nash 1977a: 18–21). The second sense in which ecological transition has been employed by both Bateson (1972) and Bennett (1976) is rather more abstract. The transition results from being human, with our human skills in manipulating our symbolic apparatus. We have used powers of observation and thinking to describe and theorize about the natural world. Not content there, we have created an awesome technology for modifying the natural systems of the global ecosystem and the human body. The advances achieved in nineteenth-century metallurgy and railroading exemplify incorporation by humans of nature into culture, resulting in modification of natural and social systems. Twentieth-century developments in electrical engineering, in chemistry and biology, and in computer-related disciplines also illustrate these phenomena. Bateson seems to be arguing for and making illustrations of an ecology of mind—a science not yet fully developed—that would understand human thought as a part of orderly natural processes. It is a science that also understands the qualitatively different order the mind places on nature; the brain is a complex mechanism that makes new patterns with natural and social experiences of the world, and finds ways of imposing the new order on the world.

The description of ecological transition in this study will be closer to the first use. Human societies face ecological crises when population increases beyond the carrying capacity of the habitat, resulting in scarcities. An ecological transition may occur as environmental degradation challenges human ingenuity to come up with a more viable means of coping with deteriorating human system-ecosystem relations. An ecological transition occurs when one energy base of society is substituted for another because our relationship to the biosphere undergoes a fundamental transformation, and greater energy is required to run society. A transition may also occur when an old base runs out. In reality it is impossible to differentiate the first sense of ecological transition from the second, since humans have been forced to internalize through science and technology their knowledge of and manipulation of the natural world. We are undoubtedly approaching an ecology of mind, and if we put together Bateson and Bennett, our ecology of mind will be a science that will tell us how to better reorder the natural and social world, and will offer us intelligent choices for intervening in these processes. The goal can only be to achieve mutually productive, human system-ecosystem relationships that will free us, eventually, to move beyond what is now a critical threshold in these relationships.

Human systems ecology, a branch of science in its infancy, is the science of these relations and of self-conscious intervention to achieve a productive order. Reflexivity is implied by this statement, for when humans become aware of their dependence upon and fateful modifications of natural systems, then this awareness is itself a component in the relationship. Human ecological science develops with the Heisenbergian principle that the presence of observers modifies the phenomena under observation. Our theories about ecosystems change our behaviors toward them, and our intervention in either human systems or ecosystems is registered in the other.

Within the contemporary ecological transition the whole question of control is at the very heart of the matter. Is human society capable of controlling itself? This question undoubtedly underlies the search for control mechanisms, those sources of guidance in living systems that keep them successfully operating adaptively rather than maladaptively. Control does not mean a totalitarian political structure that achieves social guidance of a populace demoralized by means of physical terror and propaganda. It is a term that is used in many disciplines to isolate those features of a system that initiate or stop activities that maintain the structure or shape of the system within specific goal ranges. In its narrower definition control refers to the effective manipulation of physical elements by the system under consideration (Adams 1975:21). More generally social power accrues to those who can exercise physical control over resources of interest to others (Adams 1975:21, *et passim*). In our industrial societies labor, energy corporations, banks, and the federal government are the major interrelated loci of social power due to their exercise of direct physical control over the range of natural resources essential to our way of life. While these powerful institutional structures are central to the guidance of society by concentration of power and control at the highest levels of hierarchy, control mechanisms are dispersed through all system levels and in such impersonal structures as the market mechanism of the economy. Therefore, control is never perfectly centralized in complex systems and cannot be, for there are dynamic complementary and competitive sectors that necessarily evolve and accrue control functions (see also Flannery 1972). Thus emerging or existing control functions may or may not threaten the instituted order. While the loci of societal control in some basic sense reside in the brains of humans, it is more to the point to identify the unit of analysis as the institutions of society. It is human brains in symbolic communication with one another in institutional frameworks that regulate society (Geertz 1973:44–45). Interinstitutional relations of the whole society are emergents from the institution; that is, the collection of institutions (government, industry, education, health, welfare) in a society linked together in symbol-laden communications govern it.

Our conscious manipulation of the earth's ecosystems is incomplete. Humans cause changes without advance knowledge of—or concern for —consequences. Humans intervene for survival and for wealth production, but disaster often attends these pursuits (Eckholm 1976). It is the aim of human ecological science to address life on the planet and the parts people should play. A mature human system-ecosystem science would develop theories of human activities and their ecological implications and would establish bases for control with more rational strategies for adaptation and intervention.

This book attempts to wed theory and site analysis, to relate macroecological transitions to microecological adaptations. The significance of such a study lies in its demonstration of new social institutions that emerge in the face of rapidly developing technological, economic, and energetic sources. Its relevance is that, with the decline of inexpensive petroleum, much of the world faces an ecological transition of unprecedented proportions. It may help us to anticipate and to make communities more adaptive.

Some theoretical assumptions that underlie the case study presented here must be detailed. The most basic of these is that social systems, like all living systems, exchange energy with their environment. Books have been written about an energetics theory of society (Adams 1975; Cottrell 1955; and White 1949). Drawing largely upon anthropological theory, the foundation for the argument presented here is the assumption that energy is the essential input from nature that human systems require in order to exist.

Society is termed an energy conversion process (Adams 1975) that through human technological ingenuity transforms energy, matter, and information into food, fuel, or industrial material (see also Hall, Day, and Odum 1977:37–48; Odum 1971; Oettinger 1980:191–98; and Rappaport 1968, 1971). Through technology the social system incorporates energy and matter into the industrial production system. In the process, heat and wastes are ejected as the entropic byproducts. The production system, the first part of the energy conversion process, alters energy, matter, and information, and produces goods and services for members of society.

The energy conversion process encompasses the political economy, which is usually presented without considering the energy components of the system, but a larger model incorporating the political economy and the ecosystem is possible. The relationships between the environment and the political economy can be displayed as a compartment model in which the flow of energy leaves the ecosystem, is transformed by the energy conversion process, and then is discharged from the human system back to the environment as entropic wastes. The compartment model (figure 4) was designed in the spirit of Steward's cultural core, but with the addition of a one-way energy flow. Logically ordered as a flow of energy, the cultural core is made up of the relevant environment (ecosystem), energy, matter, information, technology, production, and control boxes in the model. In an energetics theory, the core institutions are a model of the political economy that includes production and consumption. In addition, the whole political economy of energy use and allocation is a guided process with varying degrees of control, including information management exercised through the system. In the United States the two sectors in which control is concentrated, the public and the private, corresponding to government and industry, are complemented by a third, the not-for-profit sector, which is exemplified in foundations and universities. This model translates roughly to a national system with its associated industries and its land base. But this image is increasingly complicated by the accelerating internationalization of capital and ownership patterns, by planet-wide rapid communications systems, by the growth of the multinational corporations, and by the international repercussions of environmental modification. In the compartment model, the controlling institutions are not merely guiding society, but are in vital connection with the biosphere and natural resources. The model portrays the political economy as an adaptive system that calibrates its energy intakes with entropic outputs and more or less pilots this whole energy conversion process. Economic theory, by and large, incompletely rationalizes this structure.

The energy conversion processes in society constitute a thermodynamic system far from equilibrium that requires great quantities of energy to maintain itself. It is a cybernetic process, with positive and negative feedbacks that constantly inform the control centers of the internal and external environmental systems, thereby making new adjustments as the demand arises. Prigogine calls these systems dissipative structures (Prigogine, Allen, and Herman 1977). If energy (or other critical) requirements are not met, the system can fluctuate widely and can collapse with catastrophic consequences. There is the possibility that it can stabilize at a lower level of inputs and integration, but it cannot revert to an earlier state. We cannot return to a nineteenth-century family farm economy powered by wind and the horse, for example, because living systems evolve through historically irreversible processes.

In addition to the two themes, ecological transition and control, there is a broad set of ideas that have been useful to this study. These ideas

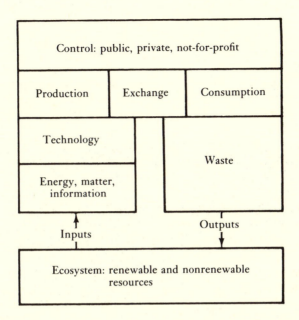

Figure 4. Model of the energy conversion process. For similar models, see Adams (1975:139,142); Daly (1977); Hjalte, Lidgren, and Stahl (1977:2); Rose and Jackson (1978:492–93); and Watt (1978:56–57).

are not restricted to general systems theory and cybernetics; they have been elaborated in the fields of biology and chemistry, among others. What makes them appealing is that they address system properties and behavior with theoretically developed concepts of control, irreversibility, energy, structure, fluctuations, evolution, learning, regulators, communication of information, linguistic modes in control systems, anticipatory systems, self-actualization, and self-organization. Mainly from contemporary biological theory, a picture emerges of dynamic, complex, evolving, self-replicating, stable systems, interacting with their environments by means of energy exchanges (Conant and Ashby 1970; Handler 1970; J.G. Miller 1978; Pattee 1977; Prigogine, Allen, and Herman 1977; and Rosen 1974). These dynamic concepts and others, with the impetus derived from the exploration of the cell from a variety of related scientific branches, have contributed to an epistemological revolution in biology that is spreading to other disciplines (Diener, Nonini, and Robkin 1980).

The exuberance and impetus for the impressive advances that biological research and theorizing have made, come, no doubt, from the hard-won realization that all living organisms are organized in homologous fashion. Mayr laid the responsibility for this realization at the feet of Darwin, who "implied, in fact, that all living organisms might be traced back to a single origin of life" (1978:48). Handler suggests that "the major questions concerning how to achieve the paramount manifestations of life had been solved, albeit empirically, when the first self-reproducing organized cell made its appearance on this planet" (1970:32). Arguments for employing the same language to describe cellular and social systems within the same framework have been made at great length (J. G. Miller 1978). Living systems have a number of characteristics in common:

1. They exchange energy/matter/information with the environment.

2. A guidance system or linguistically structured description of the system is read by an executor which cues the system how and when to operate. These are the control functions that are capable of conveying information on how to import, export, and assemble energy and material (Pattee 1977:260).

3. A living system is capable of self-assembly, or to phrase it differently, is autocatalytic and contains the information necessary for self-organization.

4. A system organized at a given level of complexity operates within a set of stated tolerances for inputs of energy, material, and information. It is termed a dissipative structure because its existence requires the incorporation and dissipation of free energy. "A dissipative structure can, indeed, be considered a giant fluctuation stabilized by exchanges of energy and matter" (Prigogine, Allen, and Herman 1977:38). With increased levels of input, the system can spontaneously achieve a higher, or more complex, level of organization.

5. These living systems, unlike physical systems, are evolutionarily irreversible, since they cannot revert to some former, lower-level state.

6. Living systems characteristically exhibit fluctuations; fluctuations can arise spontaneously from within the system due to its own internal dynamic complexity or can be induced by externally imposed fluctuations which must be coped with by reorganization of the system or the system will be destroyed.

In the social sciences, function has been usually defined as the way a system must continuously operate in order to sustain itself. A social system is both goal-directed and active, and the term function has been used to convey the activity and interrelatedness of the parts. Structure refers to the pattern of interrelationships between elements within a social system. Fluctuations are considered by Prigogine to be magnitude changes that can occur anywhere in the system. Change, however, can originate in the fluctuations, structure, or functions of the system. The arrows in the model indicate the intricate nature of interdependence within a system. Because they are each aspects of the whole system, a change in one feature, such as structure, will affect function and fluctuations. Prigogine, Allen, and Herman (1977:3, 39, 58) have diagrammed this as in figure 5. A change in the quantity of the oil flow, for example, into

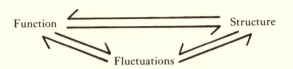

Figure 5. Structure, function, fluctuations (after Prigogine, Allen, and Herman (1977:3, 39, 58)

the industrialized countries affects the functioning of those industrial systems and leads to alterations in the structure of energy procurement or petroleum reliance. To give a blatant example, after the Arab oil embargo (fluctuation), the United States government established a Department of Energy (structure). Regulatory mechanisms undergo modification in cases of extreme fluctuation. These mechanisms may reorganize by evolving new structural features, reordering priorities, developing new tolerances, or finding and allocating new resources. If reorganization is not achieved by these means, innovative or already-competing regulatory mechanisms may replace those which prove ineffectual.

It would be stimulating to undertake a hermeneutics of biological theory, but it would fill more than this volume. It is appropriate to mention that ideas from biological theory, especially concepts dealing with the indeterminate nature of living systems, form a background for thinking about social systems. This background takes us beyond recent structural and functional analyses of society. The biological theories do not capture, however, the empirical realities of which societies are composed, particularly the economy and politics that make up the modern world-system. These theories do aid in the abstract formulation of system properties and their dynamic features. In human systems, multiple control mechanisms work competitively and in cooperation with one another. These mechanisms are widely distributed and differentiated, and are hierarchically arranged. Each mechanism controls its acquired portion of meaningful messages, energy and matter, personnel, goods and services, or capital. Institutional complexes, whether they are corporations or countries, compete for and come into conflict over scarce resources which they desire to allocate in their own interests. Institutions seek to maximize their gains and minimize their losses and to engage in asymmetrical exchanges favorable to themselves.

The fluctuations in the overall system, especially the fluctuations that result from an ever-shifting number of energy interdependencies with the environment, challenge human society to innovate new institutional forms in order to dampen the oscillations and impose the order necessary for successful operation. The theory being developed here recognizes that self-actualizing systems are creative and that they self-organize in nonpredictable ways. We are never assured, of course, of the outcomes of the plans we make. The making of plans as well as we can, however, is integral to our self-organizing. With regard to energy, we must try to insure an adequate supply and, ideally, its equitable distribution.

WORLD-SYSTEM

The choice of the unit of analysis in the social sciences has plagued many researchers; unlike physical data, human data are not discrete. Recently several social scientists (Orlove 1977; Schneider and Schneider 1976) have been linking their local-regional studies to the development of the capitalist world-system. Communities and regions, the units of analysis at the local level, have remained useful places for anthropologists and others to begin. These local-level social systems are poorly known, but it is now possible to explain the dynamics of local systems, not in terms of locally autonomous cultural factors or psychology, but in terms of the world-economy. Thanks to the very persuasive monograph and articles of Wallerstein (1974, 1979) which build upon Braudel's work, one can map the world in terms of regional development and follow chronologically the economic development of the capitalist world-economy. A double unit of analysis consisting of the locale and the world-system with which it particularly articulates is now available.

Under the inspired labors of Wallerstein, capitalist world-system analysis has become a minor academic growth industry. Among other sources there is a series, *Political Economy of the World-system Annals,* published by Sage. World-system analysis has its roots in Adam Smith's *The Wealth of Nations,* in Marx and Engels's *Communist Manifesto,* and in Bukharin's *Imperialism and World Economy.* The work on capitalist world-economy by contemporary academics is long overdue. I find at least one major problem with this literature, however. It is not at all materialistic: it does not deal with the prime materialistic basis of life, which is nature. The books and articles are written as if the capitalist world-economy was not a part of the life of this planet. Bukharin, who unfortunately came to a bad end under Stalin, did have a rudimentary theory of nature in the 1920s and it is reflected in his published works. It is strikingly contemporary in some respects, particularly in the realm of theoretical development. He knew that economic systems were constantly out of phase with natural systems, creating fluctuations, inducing structural instabilities, and producing further industrial growth (Bukharin 1969).

The contemporary world-economy seems well understood by economists and economic historians (Leontieff, Carter, and Petri 1977; W. A. Lewis 1978; Rostow 1978; Whitman 1979). It has been understood for some time, granting the difference in methods, in points of view, and, if the Soviet economists are included, in ideology. The particular historical developments that gave rise to the world-system and to the roles of specific countries and regions have been less than clear, however. Wallerstein has addressed the issues of emergence and has clarified a number of other problems along the way. The causes underlying the rise of capitalism have remained obscure (Macfarlane 1979:7–8, 195–96). Generally, the historians have been cautious, the anthropologists speculative, and the economists indifferent in offering explanations.

Leaving causality aside for the moment, it is useful to employ knowledge of the world-economy when studying local regions. The dual units of analysis help one to understand what controls can be exerted locally over the flows of such factors as information, energy, and capital, and what controls are exercised by distant markets, corporations, and governments. The question of control is thus critical in the indepth study of local-regional systems. The relative absence or presence of control over resources at the local level is an excellent indicator of the relative autonomy or dependence of the local people upon the world-system. These very relations of control and dependency underlie much of the surgent politics in the less developed countries. It is the commodities and resources of these nations that animate many of the interests of the developed countries in their internal politics.

The terms need some clarification. Wallerstein sets forth the definition of what he calls the *modern world-system,* or, synonymously, the *capitalist world-economy:*

> We take the defining characteristic of a social system to be the existence within it of a division of labor, such that the various sectors of areas within are dependent upon economic exchange with others for the smooth and continuous provisioning of the needs of the area. . . . [T]he only kind of social system is a world-system, which we define quite simply as a unit with a single division of labor and multiple cultural systems. [1979:5]

Again:

> The functioning then of a capitalist world-economy requires that groups pursue their economic interests within a single world market while seeking to distort this market for their benefit by organizing to exert influence on states, some of which are far more powerful than others but none of which controls the world market in its entirety. [1979:25]

In the capitalist world-economy, it is the economic system that is the major operational unit. The national systems are secondary, but are strengthened over time in the interests of those who manipulate the world economy. They are not the major source of dynamics in the system.

The idea that the world-market includes all national economies is central in world-systems theory. Every item manufactured in the world, once it enters the market place, is subject to the pricing mechanism. Socialist countries, although their ideology denies profit-seeking as the motive for exchange, produce goods that are priced on world-markets. The world-economy is thus a capitalist world-economy regardless of the political persuasion of a national government. Amin opened his *Accumulation on a World Scale* with this assertion:

One does not need to be an economist to know that our world is made up of "developed" countries and "underdeveloped" ones, that it is also made up of countries that style themselves "socialist" and of others that are "capitalist," and that all these countries are integrated, though to varying degrees, in a worldwide network of commercial, financial and other relations such that none of them can be thought of in isolation—that is, leaving these relations out of account —in the way that one can think of the Roman Empire and Imperial China, as they were unaware of each other. [1974:1]

Within the single all-embracing system, there are core and periphery nations. At the center of this system are the nations which have the most sophisticated agricultural specialization and the greatest industrial development. The great banks and corporations of the core control the sources of credit and the monetary flows. The peripheral regions, on the other hand, are sources of commodities, cheap labor, and markets. Increasingly, these regions are also debtors to the bankers in the developed core areas. The formulation of core and periphery areas enables the investigator to carve the world up through time into a geography of development and lack of development. The core has shifted several times, and Braudel (1977:82) dates the completed shift from England to the United States, particularly to New York, in the year 1929, remembered as the year that the world plunged into economic depression.

In addition to having examined the historical economic geography of the world-system, Wallerstein has untangled the temporal unfolding of the capitalist economy that began in the sixteenth century. He identifies four definite states—long-term cycles—from 1650 to 1965 (1979:1–36):

1. 1650–1730:recession and consolidation;
2. 1760–1810:agricultural capitalism;
3. 1815–1873:industrial capitalism;
4. 1917–1965:consolidation of industrial capitalist world-economy.

The growth periods are cyclical, typified by periods of rapid advance followed by stagnation.

Departing from Wallerstein, we may identify these cycles as major fluctuations that are constitutive of living systems far from equilibrium, that is, as dissipative structures. The world economic system can be considered a vast dissipative structure that exchanges energy with the biosphere; thus the world-system becomes the unit of analysis in human ecology. It is the major mechanism humans have evolved for adapting to the earth's ecosystem. In the search for wealth, the world-economy raises the planet's carrying capacity by stimulating industrial production—and associated science and technology—through capitalist market mechanisms. The dual control mechanisms in the market are the corporations involved and the national systems that redistribute capital in the form of services for their populations. The people of the various countries work within the structure and are the consumers of the products of the world economic system.

The corporations are the media through which energy is extracted from the environment and transformed into consumables. They are the institutions through which energy flows on the way to the consumers. The energy flowing through the world-system has been partially quantified thus:

> World energy use in 1975 amounted to roughly 260 trillion megajoules, not including energy in food and in dung, in wood, and in agricultural wastes burned for cooking and heating. The latter, largely untabulated sources may amount to two-thirds or more of energy use in the poorest LDC's [less developed countries]; they would add perhaps 15–20 percent to the global total. Of the tabulated energy use, 45 percent was supplied by petroleum, 32 percent by coal, 19 percent by natural gas, 2 percent by hydropower, and 2 percent by nuclear energy.... The dominance of the fossil fuels—more than 95 percent of the total for the world and for the United States—is overwhelming. [Ehrlich, Ehrlich, and Holdren 1977:393]

Drawing on the Study of Man's Impact on Climate (1971), Lovins portrays a picture close to that just quoted:

> Estimates of the present rate of man's global energy conversion disagree by $\pm 25\%$, but most people would agree on 8×10^{12} W [watts] as a round number. This is more than $20\times$ the energy represented by FAO-standard diet for the world's population. Thus global industry already uses about $20\times$ as much energy as is recovered from all agriculture and hunting on both land and sea, and gives everyone the equivalent of about 12 hardworking slaves (each 175 W 3600Kg-cal/day) or 50 slaves if we consider their work output in a 40-hour week (at 100% efficiency), rather than their food input in a 168-hour week. In density of power per unit of continental area, human energy conversion is now about ¼ as great as net photosynthesis and is roughly equal to the natural outward flux of geothermal heat from the earth's interior. [Lovins 1980:15]

Although Lovins hints to the contrary, only the corporately transformed fossil-fuel energy supply can sustain more than four billion humans (Cipolla 1975; McEvedy and Jones 1978) at the present level. It goes without saying that the distribution of energy per capita is unevenly allocated. The United States, as one of the core countries, captures an inordinate percentage of the total amount, 850 BTUs per capita, whereas India, in the semi-periphery, uses only 37 BTUs per capita (Luten 1971:116).

The scale of dependence on declining supplies of increasingly costly petroleum is the greatest challenge presently facing the capitalist world-system. The current ecological transition involves the development of substitutes for the petroleum energy basis of world industry. The fluctuations now confronting the established world order demand innovations that will directly affect the ecosystem, the industrial system, population growth, food supplies, living standards, economic growth, political stability, and other factors. The problem, phrased in economic terms, is whether the gross world product per capita can keep pace with the demands of world population growth, although both population growth rates and the energy demand of industrial countries are slowing perceptibly (Simon 1980).

International institutions such as the United Nations and the World Bank are presently formulating strategies to insure continued economic growth (Leontieff, Carter, and Petri 1977). Unless such strategies can be implemented, the world faces catastrophic consequences—starvation and warfare. These strategies depend upon the United Nations population projections, which forecast that the human population will follow the same sigmoid growth curve as animal populations do (figure 6). By 2025, according to the projections, the population growth rate will even off, and by 2075 world population may stabilize. Leontieff and other economists share the opinion that "this outcome would be achieved not through mass starvation, but through demographic change occurring at relatively high levels of economic development" (1977:4). The major tacit assumption of the economists has been that there is a secure energy supply and that industrialization and resultant affluence will lower population growth rates as it is thought to have done in western Europe. Will the energy resources and food supply be available to the less developed countries? The pressing question remains whether relatively inexpensive fossil fuels will be available, in the face of rising demand and uncertain geopolitical developments, for world industrial development and growth. Another question is whether some other comparable or less expensive energy source will be found as the result of new energy technology.

These considerations are critical for most local-level communities within the world production and consumption system. Local fortunes, families, life chances, community organization, industry, commerce, and agriculture evolve and devolve as the larger system fluctuates. Extraction regions, such as the anthracite counties, reflect very quickly and register deeply the movements of the larger system.

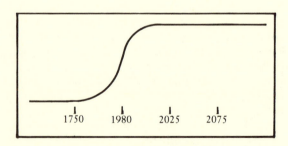

Figure 6. World population growth, 1750–2075. SOURCE: Leontieff, Carter, and Petri (1977)

FLUCTUATIONS

There is no limit to the type of fluctuations which may be considered, and no ecological equations can be structurally stable to all possible innovations. Because of this we have to expect a continuous diversification corresponding to this expansion into an area of unused freedom. . . .

[Energy] is merely one characteristic of the evolution, but a very important one due to its universality. [Prigogine, Allen, and Herman 1977:56, 59]

The work done to date on world-systems does not, unfortunately, establish an adequate theoretical basis for explaining the rise of the contemporary world-economy and the place of the local system within that economy. The descriptions are marvelous, but the causal mechanisms underlying the rise of the world-embracing capitalism remain elusive. Explanations are ad hoc or suggest that the system is motivated by avarice. Evolutionary anthropologists have pointed to the demographic transition—the long-term rise and then the explosive growth of world population—as the major cause of social evolution. The general argument is that as the population grows, the ecosystem is degraded. New efforts at intensification—greater efforts to extract energy—result, new technologies are developed, substitutes for existing necessities are found, and more energy is pumped into the system. The social system, then enjoying a higher level of energy production, organizes at a higher level of sociocultural integration. The population again expands beyond the carrying capacity of the new energy supply. Then the dynamics of degradation and intensification enter as before. This is, over the long course of human history, the dynamic of human social and cultural evolution (Harris 1977; Wilkinson 1973). Briefly stated, the increase in population requires a comparable increase in energy supply; the release of more energy stimulates, or at least permits, greater population expansion. In this synchronic model, begging all of the historical questions, the vital relationship is between population and energy, which interact dynamically to drive the evolving structure of human society. Wilkinson (1973) offers an explanation of the industrial revolution in England in these terms. (This view contrasts with the opinion of some that only population growth is causal.)

The model being developed relies on identifying the fluctuations within the presently constituted economies of the core area, suggesting the causal mechanisms that drive them, and suggesting an explanation for their behavior. No attempt is made here to wander through the intricate arguments and debates of the evolutionists.

In human social-economic systems, fluctuations foster uncertainty, or as Toynbee termed it, challenges (Prigogine, Allen, and Herman 1977: 57). Oscillations in natural habitats and social systems are the sources of demand for human response and human adaptation. Energy availability and variable use are only two of the sources of these fluctuations. The economies of the core industrial societies are sensitive indicators of critical fluctuations. There are well-known short, medium, and long cycles in the specific national economies. The short cycle corresponds to the familiar business cycle, while the lesser-known long cycle occurs over 50+ year periods (Forrester 1976:171–91). This long cycle is named the Kondratieff wave, after the Russian economist who formulated it in the 1920s.

Two characteristic phenomena of industrialized society are (exponential) economic growth and the peaks and troughs of the various cycles within the overall upward trend of industrial expansion (figure 7). The Kondratieff wave is the major oscillation considered, but other fluctuations in United States energy sources, the historical evolution of anthracite communities, political formations, and local migrations will be related to the wave.

In developing the model I have drawn on the work of economists and economic historians who have addressed the problem of long economic fluctuations in the world-economy. The question of whether or not long waves of forty to sixty years' duration even exist has been subject to much debate, and the timing and behavior of long waves has also been argued back and forth. There are only dangers for noneconomists entering the economist's realm, but I have done so in the interests of constructing a model that renders a local community intelligible. The model itself must be considered a heuristic for further research and for investigation as to its explanatory power.

Some of the problems with time series data in economics and of the ideas concerning the long-term fluctuations in economies reside severally in the nature of what phenomena are measured, the artifacts of statistical measurements themselves (patterns of data that could appear by chance alone), and the length of duration that might constitute an identifiable period. There are Kitchin cycles that reflect forty-month seasonal fluctuations, the Juglar cycles or business cycles that last seven to eleven years, the Kuznets cycles of economic growth that move in twenty-year periodicities, and the so-called long wave on which I am drawing here (see Barr 1979:675–718 for a bibliography of long wave literature). Despite the lack of agreement between various practitioners of long wave observation and theory, most notably Joseph Schumpeter and W. W. Rostow, I have

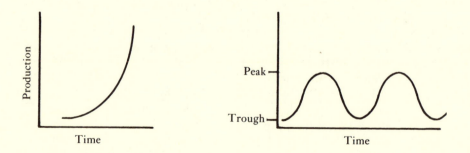

Figure 7. Exponential growth and economic cycles

employed the idea of the long wave in the model set forth to make sense of economic fluctuations as they relate to energy. In building a model of energy and long economic cycles, I have not sought to enter the treacherous waters of economic prediction and forecasting, a presumption I have no desire to assume. Rather, I view a model which incorporates the long economic oscillation as an analytic device which enables us to make more or less firm our expectations concerning the socioeconomic life of communities and the welfare of individuals.

The Kondratieff wave itself has a sinusoidal shape (figure 8) that in schematic form represents the major peaks and troughs, periods of growth and depression. The peak years—1810, 1860, and 1920 (Forrester 1976:103)—correspond to the periods of highest productivity. These are followed by periods of declining productivity and severe economic recession or depression. These correspond closely but are not identical to Wallerstein's stages in the evolution of Western economic development.

Kondratieff offered no explanation of the operation of the wave. He carefully analyzed wholesale price levels, rates of interest, wages and foreign trade, production and consumption of pig iron and natural resources, coal, and lead (Kondratieff 1935:105–15). His paper, written in 1926 and published in English in 1935, concluded on this note:

> In asserting the existence of long waves and in denying that they arise out of random causes, we are also of the opinion that the long waves arise out of causes which are inherent in the essence of the capitalist economy. This naturally leads to the question as to the nature of these causes. We are fully aware of the difficulty and great importance of this question; but in the preceding sketch we had no intention of laying the foundations for an appropriate theory of long waves. [1935:115]

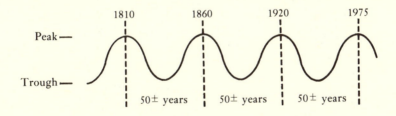

Figure 8. The Kondratieff wave. Forrester dates the peak of the fourth wave in 1975, when he was writing. Kondratieff, however, took the interest rates as a major indicator, and they had not peaked in 1975. The prime lending rates of the largest banks hit a record, breaking at 12 percent in 1974, but by the last quarter of 1980, this rate had been exceeded several times. The point here is that a precise date for the fourth peaking of the wave cannot be set with pinpoint precision. The temptation, which I will not resist, is to date the peak at 1974–79, in response to the steep price increases on oil in those years and the effects of the increase on the business climate, fears of recession, inflation, consumer prices, and interest rates.

Despite his careful qualifications and impressive scientific efforts, Kondratieff was banished to Siberia (Shuman and Rosenau 1972:29). He failed to reconcile his sober analysis with the prevailing Soviet dogma that predicted the imminent collapse of capitalist economies. He observed, rather, a self-correcting economic system that not only recovered from periodic depressions but continued to expand.

His analysis continues to stir controversy and misunderstandings, as well as respect, because there is no widely held theory of the causes of the fluctuations (Forrester 1976:181). Persuasively, the periods which he identified correspond closely to the subjective sense of economic good or bad times held by ordinary citizens. His views have received serious consideration during brief periods, including the 1970s. Forrester has attempted to address the question of causality in periodic economic fluctuations by computer simulation of long- and short-term economic behavior and to apply his results in the national interest. He observed in purely economic terms that

> A sufficient cause for a 50-year fluctuation lies in the movement of people between sectors, the long time to change production capacity of capital sectors, the way capital sectors provide their own input capital as a factor of production, the need to develop excess capacity to catch up on deferred demand, and the psychological and speculative forces of expectations that can cause overexpansion in the capital sectors. [1976:114]

Forrester figured that the Kondratieff wave could be accounted for in the processes of production and capital equipment acquisition, and in the relationship between the two major sectors, the capital sector and the consumer sector. Forrester is worth quoting at length, for he attempted to employ this causal analysis purely within an economic framework for policy and legislative purposes. He continued,

> Investigation of this long-wave mode is incomplete. Yet it is of sufficient potential importance that even preliminary hypotheses are worth serious consideration. Present symptoms of the economy seem consistent with the top of a Kondratieff wave when the top is viewed as a time of excess capital expansion [he was writing this in 1975]. New tankers are leaving the shipyards and going directly to anchorage. . . .
>
> If we are indeed in a condition of excess capital stock both at the industrial and consumer levels, the implications for business and economic policy are substantial. Under conditions of excess of capital plant, increasing the money supply will give little incentive to purchasing physical capital and instead may only feed speculative and inflationary forces. [1976:118–19]

The Kondratieff wave is used here to provide a base for relationships between the flow of fossil fuel energy and the long waves during the Industrial Revolution to the present. Once these linkages have been established, the remainder of the book will employ them as background to the analysis of the social organization of the southern Luzerne County anthracite communities.

The Kondratieff wave continues to be a powerful set of empirical observations. Its strength and persuasiveness derive from its being intuitively reasonable. It is also an attractive concept because it can be correlated with a wide range of societal phenomena (Forrester 1976; Rostow 1978; Shuman and Rosenau 1972; Watt 1978:60–61), including technological innovations, the aging of the population and workforce, public attitudes and expectations, consumer behavior, political preferences (liberal or conservative presidential choices), wars, and economic indicators (raw materials production, interest rates, wholesale price levels, consumer index, Gross National Product).

The Kondratieff wave can be used for economic prediction (Hartman and Wheeler 1979:70). In addition, the long wave has been built into a comprehensive model of postindustrial economies (Watt 1978). I have sought to use it to identify key oscillations in the system that force adaptive changes in the mechanisms that control the flow of energy through a system, and to treat these phenomena as a heuristic device for examining new institutional formations and microadaptations.

The Kondratieff wave, although it remains controversial fifty years after its formulation and has not been theoretically grounded by economists, will be useful for linking observations and for aiding in hypothesis formation. It has, for the purposes at hand, at least four major values:

1. It reflects large-scale fluctuations in core industrial economies (these are social systems far from equilibrium).
2. It temporalizes the phenomena under investigation.
3. It is a backdrop against which to view the rise or fall of local-level economies and communities.
4. It peaks with the high use of a given set of energy sources.

The argument that innovations will continue to increase world carrying capacity as they have in the past and that new energy sources will be found or exploited is not greatly favored among a number of academic writers. There is a very large literature, much of it futurist-oriented and written in a mood of pessimism, that calls for a powerful platform advocating world changes. Proposed changes include population reduction; invention and adoption of "soft" energy paths; a return to nonindustrial agriculture; and the creation of a steady-state economy (Brown 1978 and Ophuls 1977 have a bibliography of much of this literature).

The themes and theoretical concepts that have been introduced in this chapter can be joined to form a hypothesis that has guided the analysis of the data. Population growth, energetics, evolution, fluctuations, long-term trends in the economy of the modern world-system, and the themes of control and ecological transition constitute an interlocking body of concepts. The push for human evolutionary adaptation is ultimately biological. Population increase strains carrying capacity and induces scarcities. This problem has challenged humans at some unconscious and collective level to innovate a technology to raise agricultural and other production to meet increasing consumer demand. The human species has not been challenged to self-consciously and adequately intervene in its exuberant reproduction.

The biosphere is a set of interdependent, unstable ecological subsystems; human societies fluctuate; and there are continuous oscillations between the human system and the ecosystem. The systems and their relations are far from equilibrium. Humans, as part of an interdependent global system, must respond to the challenge of scarcities, severe ecological imbalance, variable energy supplies, and differential allocation, by evolving sophisticated political and economic control devices. Processes within the system underlie the continuing efforts to inaugurate new technological developments to insure energy supply. The industrial period—which may be dated from 1800, when good economic records first became available—has seen major fluctuations in the economic system, and major periods of an associated energy-technology complex. Within the Industrial Revolution the four periods have included horse-sail-canal; coal-steam-iron-rail; coal-steam-steel-oil-internal combustion engine; and then the hegemony of natural gas and oil and the internal combustion engine. These oil-based energies and technologies replaced steam and rail in transportation. Agricultural innovation has generally kept pace with development in the other sectors during the nineteenth and twentieth centuries. I suggest that there is an underlying relationship between the behavior of the economy as evidenced in the long wave, and the transition from one technology-energy complex to another.

There have been attempts to explain the behavior of the Kondratieff wave by referring to sources outside the economic system as well as within. Explanations of the wave have included population age structure; major capital investments that wear out slowly; and "the time it takes to get major new types of energy generating systems constructed in an entire nation. Historically this has taken 40–60 years" (Watt 1978:69). Earlier economists argued that the causes were gold discoveries; wars; major technical innovations; changes in financial institutions; or fluctuations in population growth (Forrester 1976:181). Forrester, however, proposes these economic processes as the underlying dynamic of the long wave:

1. Slow growth of the capital sector of the economy;
2. Gradual decay of the entire capital plant of the economy below the amount required, while the capital sector is unable to supply even replacement needs;
3. Initial recirculation of output of the capital sector to its own input whereby the capital sector at first competes with its customers for capital equipment;
4. Progressive increase in wages and development of labor shortage in the consumer sectors that encourage capital-intensive production and still higher demands for capital equipment;

5. Overexpansion of the capital sector to a capacity greater than required for replacement rate in order to catch up on deferred needs;
6. Excess accumulation of capital investment by consumers (housing and durables) and by durable manufacturers (plant and equipment);
7. Eventual failure of capital equipment users to absorb the output of the overexpanded capital sectors;
8. Sudden appearance of unemployment in the capital sectors;
9. Reversed change in relative costs to favor a more labor-intensive consumer production that further diminishes the need for new plant;
10. Rapid collapse of the capital sector in the face of demand below even the long-term average needed by the economy;
11. Spreading discouragement and slow decline of excess capital stock through physical depreciation (1976:183).

My position is closest to that proposed by Watt, although it goes beyond his model. The long Kondratieff wave in the advanced industrial economies is a critical fluctuation that responds to the periodic transition from one energy base and technology complex to another as a result of scarcity or replacement of basic energy sources in the core developed areas of the world system. Thus the Industrial Revolution has been evolving in a series of forty- to sixty-year increments between peaks in the wave. This evolution can be traced temporally along the long wave, and it is manifest spatially in the world-system in which core areas shift toward countries with high technology and energy capture.

The rise of the Kondratieff cycle is associated with the discovery and partial substitution of newer, less expensive energy sources, and with the installation of a new technological complex. The rising production is a result of the maximization of the energy potential of the new source. The fall in the wave is correlated with increasing energy costs, obsolescence, and a shift in capital from the expensive energy-technology complex to the less expensive, more efficient, higher-profit energy sources. Agricultural innovation continues apace of each major energy-technology innovative period, and is reflected in the United States in the dramatic plummeting of the percentage of people employed in agriculture in relation to the total number of the population. The ratio reflects the energy-technology intensiveness of industrial agriculture (Pimental et al. 1973).

Within the world-system, major fluctuations attend the supply and use of energy. The current ecological transition is most closely linked to energy supply. Because energy and its associated technologies change rapidly—within a forty- to sixty-year lifetime—the local areas linked into the system are terribly dependent on specific, sometimes obsolete, energy systems. These areas often suffer directly from energy-related boom or bust situations. The uncertainties in the energetics base are continuing challenges to local-level communities. These communities are often the operating units that must adapt—often painfully—to the obsolescence of the old and the installation of the new bases. The Hazleton region is such a place. The massive fluctuations attending the substitution of oil for coal in home heating from 1920 to 1950 were a dynamic process that devastated regional communities dependent on anthracite extraction and created inestimable personal suffering. The remainder of this study will place the Hazleton region in relation to the energy-ecological transitions that occurred from 1800 to the present. The Kondratieff wave will be used as a major indicator of the great fluctuations affecting the region. The regional-local fluctuations and evolutions within the anthracite area will be documented in relation to the control mechanisms that people evolved at various levels to meet the often obscure uncertainties induced far from the energy production regions that felt them most acutely.

EXTRACTION

The Industrial Revolution was fueled by natural resources which were extracted at unparalleled rates. The core countries of Europe and the emerging United States in the eighteenth and nineteenth centuries were pushed by scarcities caused by the demands of a rapidly growing population, were pulled by trade and its promise of profits and affluence in an expanding world-economy, and were industrially developed partly as a result of the highly articulated creative advances in science and technology. Anthracite coal was one of these resources in the United States, and it was relatively accessible geographically to the urban markets that could use it for industrial and home heating purposes.

Coal and mineral extraction sites, like the plantations of the mercantilists, demanded great quantities of labor. As a result, there were extensive migrations to the extraction areas, first by single men, and later by families. New communities grew up around the old or were started from scratch to accommodate the massive movements of people. This phenomenon occurred worldwide through the last two centuries, and continues today as new resource finds—such as those of Alaskan oil, Canadian tar sands, and Texas lignites—are brought on line. The problems of community formation and disintegration and the problems of labor associated with the development of energy resources are worldwide. They are also demanding for the laborers and their families who live in the communities, for the industries that require labor, and for the local, state, and national governments that often minimally provide necessary services.

Whole nations are becoming increasingly involved in the direct exploitation of—and dependence upon—their fossil fuel or nuclear resources. The oil-producing countries are the case in point. All national systems must accommodate the social implications of shifts in energy exploitation. These shifts deeply affect members of the nations' respective populations in terms of migration; services such as health and education; inundation of established communities by new migrants; labor unrest; ecological degradation; competition for scarce nonenergy resources such as water; and numerous other demands. The geopolitics of oil threaten the international balance of power.

The older core countries such as West Germany, the United Kingdom, France, and Japan face declining coal production within their borders (Cook 1976:237). Coal, however, is much more abundant than oil. Current anthracite reserves are estimated at 17.4 billion net tons (Blair, Cadwell, and Miller 1978:1–7). With major unexploited coal reserves in the United States, U.S.S.R., and China estimated at 6.5 trillion metric tons (Cook 1976:237) and with lesser quantities distributed widely, primarily in other northern countries, coal is available in large quantities in much of the world. The level of its use and distribution depends, of course, on its cost relative to other fuel sources. According to a recently released study, coal has a very bright future at costs per BTU falling below that of oil (Wilson 1980). What effects this projected future will have on the social organization of the anthracite region remains to be speculated upon.

ECOLOGICAL SITE-TYPES

From the perspective of human systems ecology, a coal mining community anywhere in the world coalfields represents a human ecological site-type. Ecosystem, industry, labor, community, and relevant political agencies are integrally related at the mine mouth or the stripping. Although there are endless local ecological and cultural variations in each of these communities in various regions of the world, there is a kernel of structural similarity in a site-type that renders it a reasonable unit of analysis. Similar challenges reappear in the coal extraction site-type. Exhaustion of the resources, for example, such as occurred in the Welsh coalfields, is the most traumatic (Rees 1978:69–77). A problem similar to that of these extraction communities, one which is of national concern, is that while the resource has been shipped away over a period of time, it is not as simple to move out the people. Communities, especially large ones, often just refuse to melt away or migrate en masse to new sources of employment, despite the chronic unemployment and ecological devastation that attend coal mining.

The problems in extraction site-types are not only formal. Nash amply documents the cultural struggle that the workers mount to maintain their cultural integrity in the face of dehumanizing laboring and living conditions (1979). Settlements and their inhabitants reflect cultural traditions, and sometimes these traditions are in direct conflict. King has commented, "Each human settlement, be it an Indian village or a European metropolis, is a cultural product. In attempting to understand such a settlement, it is essential to use a holistic approach which comprehends the geographical setting, the world view, values, and behavior of the inhabitants and their material culture" (1976:366). The practice followed in various countries by large corporations of establishing and owning houses in long rows or on a grid for workers may be unsuitable for traditional communal patterns or for kinship spatial relations. The industrial settlement pattern is probably spatially unsuitable for the cultures of the workers and their families in most cases. These site-types may well be characterized as arenas of continuing conflict.

My concern reflects that of the scholars working on human ecological policy and programs for the United Nations. Their work reflects an example of practical programs preceding the theoretical and methodological elaboration that often guides research. The authors write, "Among the important processes which should be included in an overall analysis of human settlements or ecological systems are flows of energy, materials, people . . . and information which includes both communication generally and decision-making" (United Nations 1975:15). Chapter 3 addresses this very ambitious call by the task force.

Other common features of this site-type include the life cycles and characteristic vulnerabilities of the communities. The life cycle of a mining town begins when the company initiates operations, recruits male laborers, and houses them, usually at its own expense. Successive phases include the maturation of community, the arrival of women, the beginning of familial and rudimentary community life, and the growth of services (Lucas 1971). The vulnerabilities register early and often lead to the demise of community; sometimes the settlement is totally obliterated. The major vulnerabilities of these communities include mine disasters, economic boom-bust situations due to nonsynchronous relations between producers and markets, high crime rates, serious abuse of alcohol, dissatisfaction of laborers over working and economic conditions, and lack of autonomy and of direct political representation. These sites are, without exception, developed by corporations with extralocal sources of capital; ownership remains offsite, in metropolitan centers. Technological change and resource exhaustion both take direct tolls on the local labor force, often by rendering labor obsolete. In the anthracite coalfields, the replacement of coal by oil for home heating and the replacement of workers by strip mining machinery lowered the demand for labor drastically. Today mining is no longer the major sector of employment in northeastern Pennsylvania, where once it held complete dominion.

Hazleton and its outlying towns form one complex of communities which evolved during a labor-intensive, coal extraction period and which has now lapsed into a costly social obsolescence. It is an example of the coal extraction site-type. The location of this type of community in the production process, arranged linearly from ecosystem through the marketplace where coal is consumed, can be diagrammed. The diagram (figure 9) suggests:

1. That there is a feedback loop between demand and supply, and that all components of the system are affected by this relationship, and that controlling mechanisms distributed throughout the whole production process attempt to manage the relationships in their own interest.

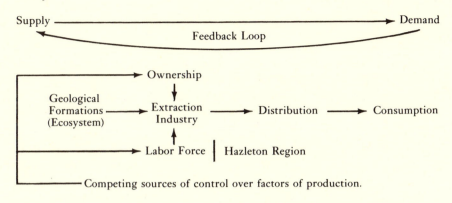

Figure 9. The coal community in the energy conversion process

2. That there is continuous competition between labor and manage-ment over control of the factors of production, and that the vicissitudes of this relationship underlie the historical and contemporary basis of a major form of conflict in United States and world mining regions.

3. That there is an indirect relationship between markets and ecosys-tems, but that a significant change in one will affect the other. Nations, the United States in particular through the Environmental Protection Agency (EPA), have become deeply involved in regulating this relation-ship by setting standards for air and water quality. Although regulations are not modeled in figure 9, mine reclamation and state environmental quality agencies are controlling functions directly affecting mining re-gion ecosystems.

4. The arrows between geological formations, extraction industry, distribution, and consumption represent the flow of energy in the energy conversion processes. This is an adaptation of the compartment model presented in figure 4. In this case the flow of energy is that of anthracite. These and other flows, such as capital, labor, or welfare services, can be quantified using neoclassical economics as needed and as data are availa-ble.

5. The extraction industry can be understood as a mechanism that generates a settlement pattern. Writing about the southwest, the cultural geographer Meinig explained: "Such mining districts came to have a more or less standard set of settlement components: an old town which bore the marks of many years of fluctuations as a mining camp; a small formal new town for the Anglo officials, engineers, and foreman; a sprawling unplanned workers' slum; and a new formally planned company-owned smelter town" (Meinig 1971:72). J. Nash reported similar patterns for Bolivian tin mining (1979:88). The particular configuration of the coalfield settlements—city and patchtown—are a function of the tech-nology and industry of coal mining at specific points in history. The

company town owned by the mining corporation is a most explicit example of infrastructure designed in the interests of an efficient and well-controlled industrial machine. These settlements in this human ecological site-type are depressingly similar the world over.

The creation by the United States of a cabinet-level Department of Energy in October 1977 reflects one nation's earnest attempt to increase its adaptive capability when faced with the difficult world and national dependence on uncertain petroleum supplies, and less-than-secured alternative energy sources. It has been noted that the establishment of the Department of Energy coincided with the massive fluctuations induced in the system by reliance on the uncertain and expensive oil supply from the Middle East. To insure numerous options, the department, a year after it was formed, opened a modest Division of Anthracite. A task force was charged with preparing a comprehensive report on the state of the industry. As is usual at these levels of government, there was a failure to take into account the vulnerability of the local communities to sudden changes and an equal failure to include the role of the local community in the growing energy problem.

REGION

In the winter of 1974, I was preparing for the Hazleton fieldwork by driving my jeep to the city for a preliminary interview with an influential citizen who was a building contractor, a member of the Chamber of Commerce, and the chairman of the Democratic Party organization of the area. Jon Berger and I left Philadelphia, located on the Fall Line where the piedmont drops to the coastal plain, and drove northward. It was a good thing that I drove the jeep. As the piedmont lifted to meet the Appalachian physiographic province where the anthracite coalfields are located, the rain turned to ice and then snow. The hardship of the winter weather and that particular storm suggested an irony. I was about to embark on a field situation with the methods and tools that had been traditionally applied to the most remote parts of the world, but I was taking these methods and tools to a marginal area of the United States, by all counts the most advanced industrial nation on earth. I must confess I enjoyed the irony—primitive methods/advanced society—mixed with the anticipation of the upcoming interview. The irony became less pleasant as I considered the way in which industrial development left ecological devastation and chronic unemployment in its wake as it moved on.

At the time of the first exploration and development of the anthracite fields in the early nineteenth century, the Appalachian Mountains were remote from the port cities of Philadelphia and New York. Hazleton is now only a little more than two hours away by car if one takes the Northeast Extension of the Pennsylvania Turnpike, but in the last century the elevation, steep slopes, and the dense oak-pine forests and difficult-to-navigate streams rendered the region almost inaccessible. As we left the turnpike, wound along the Lehigh River through Jim Thorpe, formerly Mauch Chunk, and crossed the mountains to Hazleton in the storm, I was reminded of the sheer physical problem of getting coal to markets. The impressive engineering achievements of the railroad companies, now largely of interest to industrial archeologists, are still visible from Highway 309. The abandoned track beds on steep grades snake around the mountains and penetrate the valleys through water gaps where the streams have broken through the mountain wall and drained into the next valley.

Anthracite coal beds underlie ten of the counties in northeastern Pennsylvania: Carbon, Columbia, Dauphin, Lackawanna, Lebanon, Luzerne, Northumberland, Schuylkill, Susquehanna, and Wayne. The fields are divided into the Northern, Eastern Middle, Western Middle, and Southern coalfields (figure 10).Well over 90 percent of the anthracite in the United States is found there. For the people of this region, despite the current low level of employment in the anthracite industry, the culture of the coalfield remains pervasive. It is a crucible that has made an oral and written tradition a collective memory, for all have shared memories of the difficulties and of the development of community life that established a real subculture in the region. For the anthropologist, it creates a desire to see a more highly developed cultural geography. The richness and diversity of social and symbolic life on the American landscape, especially in areas such as this, remain poorly understood.

The population of these counties now numbers more than a million, and nearly all immediate ancestors of the people residing there moved into the region during the great migration for work in the mines or in the provision of services related to mine operations. In 1914, the peak year of employment in the anthracite mines, more than 180,000 workers were engaged directly in mining. Anthracite was one of the major industrial drivers in the country at the time. Anthracite production reached a total of 99,445,794 tons in 1918, the most productive year. The great productivity of the mines was a major impetus for the eastern European migration, and coal operators recruited vigorously overseas to acquire a large, unskilled labor force. At present, the population of the area remains somewhat anomalous in relation to the rest of the country. In the coalfields there are more of the older working-age population, more persons sixty-five and older, more people of lower formal education, and a higher rate of "operatives" than elsewhere in the country. In addition, unemployment in this region is about a third higher than the national average (from the U.S. Census, 1970 figures).

Although the economy of the ten-county area was wholly dependent on anthracite and a few minor industries prior to World War II, the economic geography of the larger region extends to include the old manufacturing belt. Both the anthracite and bituminous fields of western Pennsylvania were located in the heartland composed of cities—from Washington, D.C., to Boston, and westward to Rochester, N.Y.—that were the platforms of development and growth during the American

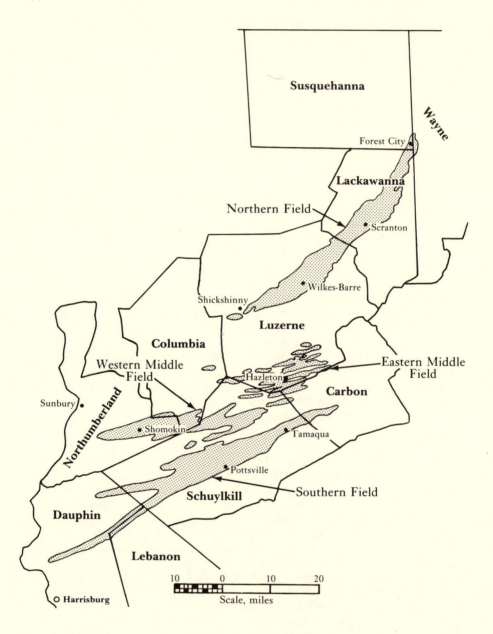

Figure 10. The anthracite coalfields of northeastern Pennsylvania

phase of the Industrial Revolution. It was these mines and these cities that gave the American industrial machine the momentum to overtake the British after 1873 (Wallerstein 1979:29, 31). These cities peaked during World War I. This was particularly true of Philadelphia, which was then the most balanced of the manufacturing cities in the country (Pierce and Barone 1977:114). As other sectors of the economy grew, the Northeast declined. These facts were already reflected in the figures Gottman analyzed in his massive study of the larger eastern region, *Megalopolis* (1961). Hazleton, the rest of the anthracite region, and Philadelphia have suffered the economic shifts associated with obsolescent technology and the closing of large manufacturing and transportation companies in earlier periods of economic growth.

Even the most cursory acquaintance with the coal mining regions in the country would leave the observer with the overwhelming impression that they are and always have been politically corrupt and incessantly turbulent, and that the people were subject to much suffering and misery. The politicians of the region, like those anywhere great concentrations of wealth are found, have been powerful and corrupt. They have often been singlemindedly devoted to their regions, but, like everyone else, have exacted a price for their involvement. At present organized crime, "the Mafia," is reported to be operating in the coalfields, and news reports of the gunning of mine owners' buildings in the coalfields east of Hazleton would not surprise readers in Philadelphia. The field investigation showed that the reports regarding organized crime activity in the Hazleton area are substantive. Even more significantly, a complete reading of all property ownership in Luzerne County revealed that the large coal companies have never paid local land taxes. The citizens have been left to foot the bill almost entirely for their own services.

The tax issue is minor compared with the intolerable conditions of the nineteenth century. By the age of twenty a man could have worked two-thirds of his life in a mine. The most notable rebellion against such conditions in the anthracite region came from the discriminated-against Irish. Signs at the collieries used to read, "No Irish need apply." Irish men reputedly formed a secret society, the Molly Maguires, who, among other acts of vengeance, killed mine supervisors who may have wronged one of their members. The Molly Maguire rebellion lasted thirty years and ended when a Pinkerton detective infiltrated the gang and finally gathered enough evidence to have ten of them hanged in the early summer of 1877 (A. H. Lewis 1965). This ended the rebellion, but the larger issues continued to be the conditions in the coalfields, with supervisors and company owners who had more to gain as their workers had less.

The structure of the industry in the United States contributed to the social problems. In this country, the states regulated coal mining, when it was controlled at all, whereas in Europe, when the industry was finally regulated, it was at the national level. Every state had its own regulations and standards; as a result these political units were easier prey to the interests of the owners than if the industry had been organized in the nation's capital. The conditions of child labor, interethnic conflict, periodic layoffs, reduction in hours worked, and reduction in pay kept the workers in constant turmoil. At the same time the industry grew dramatically.

The conditions that immediately preceded the rise of the Molly Maguires have been reported by Schaefer, an economic historian: "Between 1820 and 1865, the annual output of the Pennsylvania anthracite coal industry rose from 400 tons to 11 million tons. The number of firms increased from 1 to 313 and the number of employees grew from a mere handful to nearly 40 thousand" (1977:1). When this growth rate flattened out, the stresses felt by the miners increased and gave rise to the ill-fated rebellions in the coalfield. The constant oscillations of supply and demand, rising and falling prices, strikes, work stoppages, layoffs, and immigration of new workers exacerbated the structural weaknesses of the political economy. During the nineteenth and twentieth centuries, up to the stock market crash of 1929, there were attempts by various segments of the industry and its workers to develop institutional control mechanisms adequate to the challenges faced.

Culturally, the anthracite country greatly resembles the rest of the eastern seaboard of the United States. European populations have replaced Native Americans and established entirely new settlements and social systems. A closer look shows that the anthracite region, compared to the nearby cities, has relatively more eastern Europeans and relatively fewer English and western Europeans. What the Hazleton people call the "Slovak" and "Slovene" register their presence in the physical arrangement of the coal towns. The gold domes of their churches are silhouetted against the skylines of Hazleton, Beaver Meadows, and the other mining settlements. A list of the synagogues and churches is evidence of the continuing piety, community strength, and national origins of the area's peoples (see appendix). The mailboxes of the residents in the Conyngham Valley, immediately to the north of Hazleton and a part of the field site, display the German and English surnames of the first settlers to the mountain valleys. The old cemeteries have gravestones in them that carry the names that can be found on the mailboxes, so there is physical continuity in the region from the period of the first white settlers to the present.

The cultural geographers call the Pennsylvania area the Midlands (Zelinsky 1973:125–28) or the Mid-Atlantic. Zelinsky divides the Midlands into the Pennsylvania Region, and, to the north, the New York Region or New England Extended. There is a line separating the Pennsylvania from the New York Region on Zelinsky's cultural area map and in Kurath's word geography for the eastern United States (Kurath 1972:45); the anthracite region falls directly on this line. To the south of the anthracite counties in the Pennsylvania Region are cultural assemblages of farm and village that reflect William Penn's early settlement policy and the presence of the Quaker and German clients he attracted to settle in the area at the close of the seventeenth century. Immediately to the north of the anthracite counties there is a common housetype that extends north from just below the Pennsylvania border to the New York Finger Lakes district with its English and Scotch-Irish cultural heritages.

Hazleton is clearly located on a boundary. It is a cultural liminal zone, a region that belongs wholly neither to one core cultural area nor another. The reason for it is straightforward enough. The mountains were nearly impenetrable, a disincentive to the Native American populations as well. According to the *Handbook of North American Indians* (Trigger 1978), what is now the anthracite area in pre-Columbian times was a liminal place, underpopulated and never a core cultural area. An examination of the "Key to Tribal Territories" map (ix) represents most of the anthracite region as falling into the category "Poorly Known Tribes of the Ohio Valley and Interior." These exhibits merely serve to make the point that the region is and has been culturally marginal. A close examination of the contemporary interstate highway system, electronic and print media, and telephone network would reveal that the people of the region are less than completely marginal, however, and that they play an active and often prominent role in the life of the country.

The nineteenth-century experiences of the people and their role in the Industrial Revolution are very different from those of the people of English and Scotch-Irish ancestry who manned the mills of the fall line southwest of Philadelphia. Wallace, in a classic ethnohistorical study of the quality of life of the workers in the milling villages, portrayed Protestant workers and owners establishing the Protestant ethic in the workplace and in their daily lives (1978). The coalfields make the mill towns seem serene and beatific by comparison. This is accounted for partly by the harshness of life in underground mining, partly by exploitation by the mine owners, and partly by the sometimes violent nature of the melting pot that took the diverse Europeans and made them ethnic Americans.

The ethnic flavor of the anthracite area persists, and the investigator can still discern ethnic groups niched into the present political economy as they were in the nineteenth century.

The major division is between the old Protestant rural valley dwellers and the Catholic and Jewish urban dwellers of Hazleton city. The patchtowns in the coalfields still house descendants of the eastern Europeans who commute to work in industrial parks and Hazleton businesses. The Jewish community is composed of merchants and professionals, and members of the older Anglo communities are in the professions, and own the largest businesses as well as most of the farms. Italian-Americans and Tyrolean-Americans are in the building trades and food services; in addition, they presently own the coal mines to the east of Hazleton. Italians and their descendants and those of the eastern Europeans have moved successfully into city, state, and national politics.

Beneath the surface of the region one can feel stirring old hostilities and prejudices; the secret machinations of political patronage; fear of and anger at the Mafia for its involvement in mining and local public services;

and the old and enduring prestige systems surrounding those who are related by blood or marriage to the fabled mine owners. On the surface, however, the area is an anthropological field worker's delight—the people of Hazleton are open and cordial. There is the air of a small Midwestern town, where speaking to strangers—those who are white and well-groomed—and to neighbors is the cultural norm. In Hazleton the purchase of a newspaper will result in the vendor's saying, "Thank you, friend," without self-consciousness or effort. There is a strong sense of passion among the people for work, for community, for kinsmen and friends, and for achievement. The region bears the distinctive stamp of coal mining in the physical scars of its past and continuing presence, but the people transcend their geography.

One medium of prestigeful contact between the teenagers who can afford one is the automobile. To visit Hazleton is to witness the young driving up and down Main Street listening to their radios and observing one another. There is still an active if somewhat seedy rollerskating rink in the middle of the city, and the roads to the city are striped like any American city's with fast food establishments, shopping areas, gas stations, and auto service stores. Between the repressed and the spoken, and the unique and the common, Hazleton is both a city like other American cities and a place wholly set apart. The citizens have a deep awareness of these dichotomies and a vital sense of their place within them.

I pulled the ice-covered jeep up to the front of the builder's offices and we got out and went inside. Our host greeted us with surprise, saying that he had hardly expected us to make it in all that ice and snow. He took us to Gus Genetti's Tyrolean Restaurant, a meeting place of the Hazleton business people. After more than two hours of rather directed conversation he asked when the interview would start; we said that it already had been conducted. Our knowledgeable informant had been able to convey clearly much of the present dynamics of the city of Hazleton and its immediate hinterland. The interview had given us the kinds of guidelines we needed in order to direct our questions during the reconnaissance. Our informant had told us why Hazleton had full employment, a remarkable achievement for a depressed Appalachian region at that time. He said that after World War II the businessmen were forced to make a decision: They had to find jobs for their potential customers—out-of-work coal miners—or shut down their businesses and offices and leave. It was his point of view that provided the nucleus for my questions and subsequent research. How the bourgeoisie finds customers and insures demand was a locally formulated question and one eminently worth answering.

ANTHRACITE

The first geological survey of the state of Pennsylvania was undertaken by Henry D. Rogers, who had the distinction of being both a

professor of geology and mineralogy at the University of Pennsylvania
and the Pennsylvania state geologist. The survey was undertaken in the
1830s, the period of the greatest interest in Pennsylvania canal building,
and the time when the anthracite industry began emerging as a major fuel
source on the eastern seaboard. It was a decade of industrial beginnings
throughout the country in the wake of earlier successful English efforts.

Summarizing the geology of Hazleton region, Rogers wrote in 1838,

> The coal fields at the eastern end of the great middle region, will
> illustrate a very different structure, arising on the other hand from
> undulations of remarkable symmetry. The whole of this tract con-
> sists of rather high rolling table land, between the summits of the
> Buck and Spring mountains, the outer barriers of the coal measures.
> It is traversed longitudinally, or in a nearly east and west direction,
> by three, and probably in some quarters, four nearly parallel gently
> swelling ridges, dividing the region into about four very moderately
> depressed valleys. These valleys are so many almost regularly
> formed little coal basins, in which the coal measures, as a general
> rule, have a very gentle dip towards the interior of each basin, or
> away from the bounding ridges. The ridges contain broad, rounded,
> obtuse, anticlinal axes, having dips on both sides symmetrical, and
> expose across their summits, and on the upper portions of their
> acclivities, the conglomerate stratum which constitutes the forma-
> tion beneath the coal. Much capital may therefore be thrown away
> in explorations for coal upon these ridges, or in the tracts through
> which their anticlinal axes are prolonged towards the east and west,
> if due attention be not paid to the structure of the coal field contain-
> ing these lines of elevation. Some of the valleys on the other hand are
> richly supplied with coal, two or three of the seams which are those
> at the base of the formation, being of great thickness though the total
> depth of the coal measures, when compared with that in several of
> the other regions is materially less. [1838:76–77]

Rogers was informing an eager, tiny industry that it could, by employing the skills of a knowledgeable geologist, save on capital investments. Business people were in fact extremely anxious to develop the
lands, and in the Hazleton basins, one family name associated with Philadelphia and the University of Pennsylvania stands out, that of Coxe. The
Coxe, Markle, and Pardee surnames, in fact, were associated with the
Hazleton region from the beginning of the industry until World War II.
Because of mine ownership by families instead of by rail and banking
interests, Hazleton and outlying settlements remained an anomaly in the
anthracite country. While in the late nineteenth century the railroads and
their dummy corporations were controlling up to 96 percent of the anthracite industry, the Coxes, Markles, and Pardees owned large family
companies that withstood until the very end the monopolistic takeovers
of the line companies. Stories are still told in the patchtowns of the acts
of charity by a maternal Mrs. Coxe on behalf of poor mining families.

United States anthracites were deposited during the Upper Creta-
ceous and Upper Carboniferous geological periods (Petrascheck and Pe-

trascheck 1950), resulting from carbonification of woody plants accumulated in peat beds. Anthracite, composed of 95+ percent carbon, is
much harder than the more widely used bituminous. This quality is
attributed to geological activity—carbonification resulting from metamorphism. Coal metamorphism occurs under several conditions, as when
the weight of overriding sediments increases, by tectonic movements, by
rises in temperature resulting from depth of burial, or from closeness to
igneous intrusions or extrusions. These factors contribute to the widely
accepted classification of United States coals.

Most of the anthracite in Pennsylvania has been eroded away in
geological time, and only a minor portion of the vast original coalfields
remains. The middle and northern basins in the anthracite fields are
highly folded, making the coal often difficult and expensive to mine.
Costs are further increased by the thinness of the beds, which range from
a depth of a few feet to a rare depth of 114 feet in the Mammoth bed
(Ashburner 1884:1–32).

The geological structure of the particular anthracite formation is
expressed diagrammatically by Ashburner, the geologist who was specifically in charge of the anthracite area during the second Pennsylvania
geological survey. "The Pottsville conglomerate forms a rim around the
coal basins, and the Pocono sandstone and conglomerate an outer rim
with a valley included between them eroded out of Mauch Chunk red
shale" (1884:13) (figure 11).

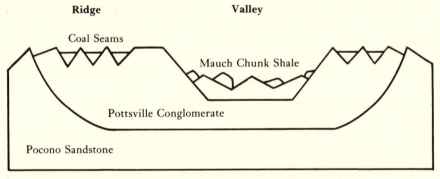

Figure 11. Schematic geology of the Hazleton region

Chemical and physical properties define anthracite and make for the
specific niche it has inhabited in the energy system. The high carbon
content makes it a very hard coal, easy to store, and resistant to deteriora-
tion. Anthracite's hardness and low content of volatile matter—the direct
result of metamorphism—cause this coal to require high temperatures for
ignition. It burns at temperatures unlike those of the more plentiful
bituminous. Boiler designs for steam making in coal-fired electrical generation plants must take into account which type of coal will be used,

since a given quantity of bituminous will produce more electricity than the same quantity of anthracite. The electrical power industries in the Northeast had to make hard decisions in their long-term planning during the 1950s and 1960s, and when they chose coal over oil, they chose bituminous. The anthracite industry, whose current viability could be assured if electrical generation corporations could sustain a high demand, continues to decline.

Because anthracite produces lower sulfur dioxide emissions when burned than does bituminous, industry leaders are guardedly optimistic about a potential upturn in demand. The Environmental Protection Agency (EPA) guidelines require that "scrubbers" be put on furnaces burning high-sulphur coal or oil. These may not be required for low-sulphur anthracite. For this reason, anthracite companies continue to look to the electrical power industry, the business most affected by EPA guidelines, for future market growth which could halt the continuing demise of the industry.

The cleanliness of anthracite turns out to be one of its major selling points today, as it was more than a century ago. This desirable quality partly accounts for its domination of the home heating market through the nineteenth century and well into the twentieth. John Holland, in a eulogistic treatise written in England in 1835 entitled *The History and Description of Fossil Fuel, the Collieries, and Coal Trade of Great Britain*, observed,

> A very striking contrast to the murky exterior of some of the large towns of this country, is presented by the appearance of the city of Philadelphia, over which, notwithstanding its thousands of coal fires constantly kept up, there is no smoke. The inhabitants mostly burn the anthracite, or stone-coal—a substance resembling the Welsh culm, the Kilkenny coal, and the blind or deaf coal of Scotland. These coals are difficult to kindle, which may have given rise to their name; but when once thoroughly ignited, they burn for a long time: they make a hot glowing fire, like charcoal, without either flame or smoke: but owing to their commonly emitting noxious vapours, they cannot be pleasantly used in dwellinghouses in this country, though they are in considerable demand among maltsters, dyers, &c.; more especially for the furnaces of steam-engines and breweries in those situations where smoke is a severe nuisance. [1835:344–45]

The "noxious vapours" of burning anthracite in the United States were largely avoided through the redesign of fireplace grates. Lehigh coal was the fuel which Holland regarded so highly, and this was mined mainly east and south of Hazleton. Some of this area is exhausted now, the empty depressions overgrown with small birch trees revealing where rows of coal company houses once stood. Another town, Upper Lehigh, bears the ravages of the declining industry; a former company town, it is now owned by those who live in the houses. An informant claimed that Upper Lehigh was established before Hazleton. It may be one of the oldest coal towns surrounding Hazleton. Lehigh is the name given to the coal of the Eastern Middle field. Holland noted it in 1835, and forty-two years later J. Macfarlane explained:

> Almost everywhere in America, the first branch of manufacturing business that is established, even in the smallest villages, is a foundary for the manufacture of articles made of cast iron. For this purpose, pig or ordinary cast iron must be melted, and for this work Lehigh coal must be used, if it can possibly be obtained. In the most remote parts of our country, in the States on the Mississippi River, on the Pacific coast, in the interior of our far Western Territories, all through the South, as well as in the more populous regions and large manufacturing cities in the Atlantic slope, Lehigh coal is one of the great necessities of manufacturing. [1877:-42–43]

The Lehigh basins for the most part are canoe-shaped. Hazleton was sited directly in the middle of one of these long, deep fields, and Macfarlane observed:

> The main or large coal seam of the Hazleton basin has a length from five to five and a half miles, and a maximum breadth west of Hazleton of nearly three-fourths of a mile. The lower seams are a mile wide, and much longer than the above. In this basin are situated some important mines at Stockton, and those of A. Pardee Co., at Hazleton. Hazleton village is one of the best looking of these mining-towns. It is situated directly on the coal-basin, the shales of which seem to afford a better soil than is usual in the anthracite region. [1877:39–40]

The siting of Hazleton, a function of roads, Indian paths, and proximity to the coalfields, was also a function of the value of the rich veins beneath it. It was observed that the basin

> . . . is remarkably free from faults or disturbances, to cause a waste of coal in mining, and the reader will observe, from the description, that, small as its area, it must have great depth. There is now a slope on the Big seam 800 feet in perpendicular depth below the surface. The full depth of the basin is estimated to be 1,500 feet. The Big seam is 30 feet thick, of which 18 feet is prime coal. Hazleton is a very small basin, but there is probably no more valuable coalfield of the same size in any other part of the world. [Macfarlane 1877:40]

Whether Macfarlane's opinion was correct is beside the point. However, it is important to note that the largest single operation in the anthracite region at present is in that basin. The Jeddo-Highland Coal Company, which purchased the old Coxe company, stripped 790,241 tons in 1975, and the Reading Anthracite Company stripped 563,390 tons during the same year; the two companies together accounted for 24 percent of the market share of current anthracite production (Anthracite Task Force 1977).

ECOSYSTEM

Ecologists of a generation ago developed a model for research that has been useful but antiquarian. It has been useful because it was broadly descriptive and because it was systematic. The ecology of North America, for example, was divided into biomes, and these were shown to be interactive communities of plants and animals (Shelford 1978). Examples include tundra, deciduous forest, desert, and coniferous forest. Biomes are named for the dominant species, particularly by the prevailing plant species of the climax phase when conditions are most stable. Hazleton falls within the northern and upland region of the temperate deciduous forest biome, as does the whole anthracite area.

North American ecologists were particularly antiquarian because they were intent upon reconstructing pristine conditions as they existed before "disturbance" by white settlers. For the east coast, the date usually was placed at 1600. Events occurring after that time were considered a disturbance and were systematically ignored. This formulation raised the nagging problem of determining the effect that Native Americans had upon naturally occurring flora and fauna, and the question was not resolved. The ideology of pristine conditions, with its misanthropic concept of "disturbance," has advanced our knowledge of what the country must have been like three and a half centuries ago. This ideology has also given some indication of the effects of industrial resource exploitation as registered in the number of animal species that are now extinct or near extinction. Attention, however, was diverted by these research priorities from the study of contemporary ecosystems and their intricate relationship with humans. One of the results has been the present lack of a human ecology sufficiently developed to model and explain human-ecosystem relations. Contemporary ecologists are much more concerned with human intervention in natural systems and take explicit account of some of these intricate relationships (Hall and Day 1977; Jansson and Zucchetto 1978).

Ecologists of the last generation also tended to ignore human domestication and modification of North American ecosystems. They were not concerned, for example, with imported exotic vegetation used to decorate lawns, domesticated field crops, policies for the extermination of carnivores, genetically engineered cattle, or domestic pets as components in an interactive system. Although these crucial elements of a human ecology remained for the most part outside the pale of academic ecology, the reinvented pristine ecology of North America provides a baseline to evaluate the environmental impact of mining.

The temperate deciduous forest biome receives between 28 and 40 centimeters of rain annually, and its northern boundary is marked by a mean temperature of $-10°C$ during the month of January. The biome is characterized by broadleaf trees that shed their leaves each fall. Oak, maple, and deer are the most abundant constituents. The deer have remained and provide for the working and middle classes of the anthracite region one of their most prized amenities. Deer hunting is widely practiced, and hunting clubs throughout the region enhance the pursuit of the sport. The commercial-size timber has been completely removed for housebuilding, for industrial purposes, and, in particular, for deep mining. The commercial stands were largely exhausted by the end of the Civil War, and have not recharged sufficiently in the ensuing hundred years to warrant commercial cutting. By the third quarter of the nineteenth century, the mining corporations were importing lumber from the South to meet the demand. Clearing of valley tracts for farming has further altered original conditions. Due to extensive timbering and clearing, there are no remaining pristine timber stands left in the ridge and valley province outside of public property.

Geologically, the areas that have undergone the greatest disturbance, of course, are in the coalfields. Here subsidence has been a major problem associated directly with the effects of mining on the local geological formations. The mountain soils are thin, having been eroded during glaciation, but the valley soils are deeper and richer. Farmers in the valleys produced foodstuffs for the miners during the nineteenth century and produce milk for the Philadelphia milkshed at present. Retired men have planted small Christmas tree farms on the edges of the valley above the apple orchards. A major amenity in the valley is wild blueberries, locally called huckleberries. These have become increasingly domesticated and represent a minor cash crop for those who tend them.

Wildlife in Hazleton is characterized by the removal of predators that are dangerous to humans and their domesticates. Five species of mammals predominate: short-tail shrew, raccoon, cottontail rabbit, white-tailed deer, and eastern chipmunk. Their habitat preferences complement those of humans, largely because they occupy numerous niches including farm fields and forests. A number of rare birds can be found, but most of them are transient, not permanent residents. Among these rare birds are goose, the bald eagle, the goshawk, the gyr falcon, and the saw-whet owl. The wild turkey is rare, but is a permanent resident of the area.*

On the area's dairy farms, the Holstein has replaced such breeds as the Jersey and Guernsey. The change has been due to increased demand for milk with low fat content. The major field crops of the area are grown for dairy cattle feed. Corn and alfalfa are planted instead of such historically important commercial grains as wheat, oats, or barley. Despite the advances of industrial agriculture and the prevalence of dairying in the Conyngham Valley, the area is underutilized in terms of its agricultural potential. The marginal lands formerly under the plow during the height of the coal period in the 1920s are now out of the hands of men, and, one is tempted to say, in the hands of nature.

---

*Taken from Hazleton: An Ecological Planning Study. Regional Planning 502, Department of Landscape Architecture and Regional Planning, University of Pennsylvania.

Mining has seriously harmed the quality of surface water. Creeks that run from the top of Buck Mountain in the Delaware River watershed have such high acidity that there is almost nothing living in them. The patchtowns and other settlements along the creeks emit sewage waste directly into the stream. Other mountain streams have been so completely modified by strip and deep mining that they have dropped underground, filling with acidic water the caverns left by the miners. Four tunnels drain Buck Mountain, where Hazleton is located, and the Jeddo Tunnel flows directly into a valley creek, severely limiting aquatic life.

The energy conversion process of the anthracite industry is visualized in figure 12.

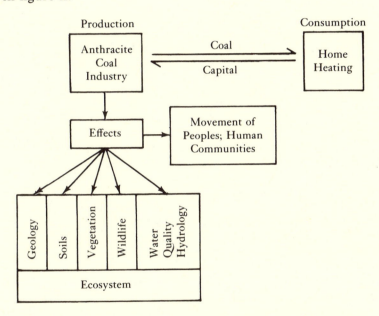

Figure 12. Energy conversion process in the anthracite industry

By means of boxes and arrows the diagram states relationships between the ecosystem, the production system, and the human communities that evolved over time. These flows represent the constant give and take and interdependencies established (the diagram shows one way to emphasize human demands). As in all ecosystem relations, a change in one crucial relationship has profound implications for the other components. The demand for anthracite was the key variable in the system of linkages. But the major point is that while anthracite mining bears a rather straightforward relationship with the geology, the mining enterprise affected directly and indirectly a much larger system.

THE MODEL

The local community or region such as the Hazleton area is located specifically in a world-economy, supplying specific goods and services. Each community bears definite relations to and dependence upon the development and evolution of demands in that economy. The evolving economy is characterized by a vast market, a partial guidance mechanism, on which anything humanly desired or made can be priced. As the economic system evolves it fluctuates. The fluctuations are due in part to the exploitation of new energy sources which fuel the economy or to the exhaustion of old ones. As energy supplies and technological apparatus are exhausted, certain geographic areas fall into decline. And as new energy technology evolves along with new resources, other geographic areas come into prominence. The economy ties all humans together in a single vast exchange network of energetic flows. The emergence of a world-system—of economic production, trade, communication, and diplomacy unifying the species on the symbolic and material levels—is a direct result of population expansion. The economy as an energy conversion process not only ties humans to one another but is the means by which energy is freed from nature, transformed into consumables, and distributed to consumers. The world-economy is a primary unit of adaptation for humans in the present period. And the economy is vulnerable not only to the changing demands brought about by the sheer quantities of humans but to human needs and desires. The economy is also vulnerable to the effect it has on the environment in the process of satisfying the numerical increases and symbolic-physical desires. The economy is the mediating mechanism between human life and the biosphere. Human life, the world-economy, and the planetary ecosystem are evolving together in a highly fluctuating, highly unstable complex of vital and vulnerable relations. The science that studies this evolution is called human systems ecology.

When catastrophe occurs anywhere in this web of relations, such as the exhaustion of vital energy resources, the autocatalytic features of living systems, distributed through the subsystems as well, activate to reorganize the system, to restore the interlocking integument of nature, economy, and humanity in new ways. Catastrophic events, termed punctuated equilibria in the evolutionary theory emanating from paleobiology (Gould and Eldridge 1977), are the sources of major, irreversible alterations in a living system. The punctuated equilibria provide for living systems those challenges to which the system responds by evolving toward increasing complexity. It seems to me that the most successful human communities maximize their access to the world-economy and attempt to anticipate changes that will affect directly community viability. Many communities are not so fortunate. The businessmen of Hazleton spend a good bit of time and thought attempting to respond to economic fluctuations which they perceive as international in scope.

The anthracite region is a set of coal extraction sites, and provides an example of an extraction industry in relation to its ecosystem. The coal mining communities are situated logically at the front of the energy conversion process. These communities bear the difficult burden of adapting to harsh conditions in the workplace, to a degraded ecosystem, and to the challenges of the world economy as the demand for the commodity, coal, changes. The local systems suffer the consequences wrought by the industrial machine. This machine simultaneously increases the carrying capacity of the earth for humans and degrades the ecosystem in the process.

As a result of the evolving, volatile economy, the local community is also in a state of continuing flux. As local places become more and more directly engaged in the international economic order—and they are—they will adapt means to articulate with it and shield themselves from it. The dialectic of an economic embrace and a cultural self-protection characterizes all the most vulnerable regions. In Hazleton I focus on the self-organizing control functions that emerged with changing energy and economic conditions after World War II. Particularly interesting are the ways the local community controls as best it can its double relation to the economy on the one hand and the ecosystem on the other.

HISTORY

Not a word was said. They were all hammering away, and nothing could be heard except these irregular blows, muffled and seemingly far away. The sounds were harsh in the echoless, dead air, and it seemed as though the shadows had a strange blackness, thickened by the flying coal dust and made heavier by the gases that weighed down on their eyes. Behind metal screens, the wicks of their lamps gave off only reddish points of light, and it was hard to see anything. The stall opened out like a large, flat, oblique chimney in which the soot of ten winters had built up an unrelieved darkness. Phantom forms moved about, dull beams of light giving glimpses of a rounded haunch, a brawny arm, a distorted face blackened as if in preparation for a crime. Occasionally, as blocks of coal came loose, they would catch the light and shoot off crystal-like glitters from their suddenly illuminated facets. Then it would be dark again, the picks would beat out heavy dull blows, and there was nothing but the sound of panting breaths, grunts of discomfort and fatigue in the stifling air, and the dripping water from the underground streams.

Emile Zola, Germinal, 1885

The construction of the evolutionary model has relied upon the dynamic concepts of energy, fluctuation, control, and transition. When the energy supply grows and fluctuates, new institutional means are required for guidance and control. As one energy basis of the system, such as oil, is exhausted and replaced by another, the economy registers the changes in forty- to sixty-year oscillations of the long wave. The Industrial Revolution, an ongoing ecological transition, responding to and stimulating population expansion, began in England in what was the developed center of the world-economy during the eighteenth century; it subsequently moved outward and expanded in the nineteenth. As an evolving dissipative structure, the world economic system had to keep acquiring new energy inputs or face catastrophic consequences. Famine and plague were two means by which the press of population had been checked earlier in Europe.

Two central areas—Germany and the United States—challenged

English industrial hegemony at the close of the nineteenth century (Wood-ruff 1973:683). In the twentieth century, the United States emerged as a preeminent world economic and political power and the expanding center of the world-economy was shifted across the Atlantic. The beginning of the relative decline of England in the core region can be placed in the late 1870s (Rostow 1978:52) with the onset of a world depression that lasted twenty years (Barraclough 1967:51, 59), while United States influence grew, peaking in the 1960s but thereafter eroding (Whitman 1979:528, 554).

The production of anthracite through the nineteenth century and its peaking and decline in the twentieth nicely fit the model. An examination of its emergence, growth, and decline shows that anthracite coal was one of the energy bases developed in the United States for industrial, commercial, and home uses. Its development is parallel to the maturing of the Industrial Revolution in the United States, particularly during the nineteenth century. The changing control structures reflect the massive changes attending the exponential growth of population in Europe and America between 1750 and 1900. The control structures in the anthracite industry included the owners of the industry, and their relationship to the political economy of the state, the country, and the international economy. They had difficult relationships with labor and with community life in the coalfields. Three forms of control have been identified as central, and they respond to the evolution of the world-economy in the nineteenth and early twentieth centuries. These control mechanisms are mine ownership, labor, and community. Responsive, of course, to new industrial markets, these are the three most prominent cybernetic features in the coalfields of the last century, since the political structures there were relatively weak. Much of the public sector services now expected of the national government were in the hands of the industrialists. Private businessmen inherited institutional forms from the privileges granted to the East India Company merchants by Queen Elizabeth in the opening moments of the seventeenth century.

The emergence of institutional control mechanisms initiated during the Industrial Revolution sets the stage for the evolution of these mechanisms in Hazleton.

The growth of the industry falls into five periods classified by the evolving social organization of the anthracite coal corporations (table 1).

TABLE 1
Evolution of the Social Organization of the Coal Corporations

	Period	K wave	Organization of Industry (Control)
1	1776–1820	Peak 1810	Search period by entrepreneurs
2	1820–1870	Peak 1860	Formative period: family, firm, and corporation
3	1870–1888	Trough 1890	Corporations form a combination to set prices
4	1888–1920	Peak 1920	Monopoly: interlocking directorates of banks, producers, rails
5	1920–		Decline and fragmentation of industry

These time periods are correlated crudely with the Kondratieff wave. Each of the first two periods extends ten years beyond the peak of the wave. The third period begins after the second wave and peaks at the beginning of the Great Depression of the nineteenth century. The fourth period begins at the bottom of the wave, in the trough of the Great Depression. The world-economy was poised at this point for a takeoff that occurred after 1920 as petroleum was applied to automotive engines and used for heating fuel.

The hypothesis was stated earlier that there was a relationship between the rise and fall in the basic energy sectors and the behavior of the world-economy as evidenced in the wave. Transportation is very closely linked to the energy basis of the system, and therefore is very responsive to changes in the type of energy developed. The first peaking of the wave in the industrial period occurred, according to Kondratieff, in the years just before and after 1810. In England the sources of energy for home heating and industrial power were coal and wood, which was increasingly costly. The energy for transportation, including canal transportation, was provided mainly by horses. By 1820, the canals had become, despite their scope, a bottleneck in the transportation of goods in the English countryside (Deane 1973). The steam engine, first developed to pump water from coal mines, had been successfully applied to the textile industry. As the transportation challenge faced the English inventors, they applied steam engine technology to transportation. The result was the railroad that helped England achieve its second economic boom, which peaked in the 1860s. In the United States, the second wave was propelled by the initial development of the canal system, and the rapid growth of the rail network in the 1850s. Intense growth and transition in the transportation sectors occurred after the shift from sail to steam on the seas. Four million net tons of goods were shipped from Europe, including Great Britain, in 1800; by 1910, 35 million net tons were carried. Europe and America accounted for 90 percent of world shipping by 1910, (Woodruff 1973:694, 695). Transportation sectors are the cutting edges in the harnessing of new energy supplies, and anthracite played its part in transportation development. The relevance of this observation for the current period is that as world petroleum reserves decline, transportation may be the sector of the world economy to bear the major consequences.

Anthracite production during this period reflects the growth of the world-system and the incessant demand for energy to drive it. In 1826 the Lehigh Coal and Navigation Company, franchised by the state as the first large commercial anthracite venture, shipped 31,000 tons of coal to Philadelphia at eleven dollars a ton. This was expensive fuel, and the costs were largely due to the difficulties of transportation from Mauch Chunk, down the Lehigh River, to the Delaware River, and into Philadelphia. Coal production trebled in three years as new industrial and domestic uses were found for it in rapidly expanding Philadelphia. Between 1830 and 1870 more anthracite than bituminous was mined, leading some observers to conclude that the early Industrial Revolution in the United

States was fueled by anthracite (Powell 1978). By 1842 one million tons were shipped at the dramatically lowered price of $4.20 per ton due to increased production, and the growth rate of anthracite use exceeded that of the population increase in the United States. In 1865, the anthracite coal production companies extracted 10,100,000 tons and retailed the fuel for $7.60 per ton. This was relatively high cost tonnage, and occurred at the peak of the long wave. In 1870 and 1880, as the depression deepened, prices plummeted. Anthracite coal prices rose as the Kondratieff wave did, and fell as the wave fell (Historical Census, United States Department of Commerce, Bureau of the Census, 1976).

NINETEENTH-CENTURY WORLD-SYSTEM

In the nineteenth century, the European economy expanded at exponential rates. Population increased, was exported, and helped to account for the European expansion of territory to include colonial subdivisions of the entire globe.

The push of European population growth, particularly the English population rise around 1750, may have triggered the Industrial Revolution. On a world scale, a regional population increase in Europe apparently gave rise to industrial innovation there. As Europeans colonized less technologically advanced nations, a demographic revolution was triggered that made the European population growth of the twentieth century pale by comparison.

There is evidence from historical demography that earlier population increases were similarly followed by periods of intensification. McEvedy and Jones (1978) have documented the successive westward push and cultural florescence of pulses of population growth from 1200 B.C. to 1800 A.D. They explain this population growth by saying:

> The wave-fronts represent rapid multiplication to high levels of density—high for the date in question, that is. There is an obvious correlation between these demographic surges and social advance: the first four waves mark the development of the classical culture of Greece and its spread through Italy; the next two the establishment of the feudal order in Western Europe; the final pair the appearance of the early capitalist society of the Netherlands and the beginning of the industrial revolution in England. [1978:31]

If population growth is the driving force in cultural florescence, then the world—numbering now more than four billion and rapidly growing—is an arena for intensification and necessary innovative processes. There are dissenters from the population push theory who have suggested that the rapid spurt of growth of English population around 1750 was the result of improved health care, which lowered the death rate, and of increased agricultural production, which provided better diets. The growing knowledge of agricultural production methods could, it is argued, have come to England from Flanders in the late seventeenth and early eighteenth centuries, for Flanders was an innovative country with intensive farming practices because of its own population pressures (Bairoch 1973:460–61; Grigg 1974:165).

The issue has not been resolved in favor of whether or not the Industrial Revolution was begun by population pressure or other causes. Concomitant and interdependent causes which have been cited are the agricultural and demographic revolutions. It has also been suggested that an organizational restructuring of the English social system was underway that laid the groundwork for a successful industrial takeoff after 1785 (Deane 1973). A cultural anthropologist might well say that a transformation of culture, ideas such as Baconian scientific method, preceded the change in material life, but the question of cause would remain. Most of the economic historians are dogmatically multicausal in their explanations, and most would agree that all the evidence is not in concerning the reasons for initial Western economic development. It is a challenge to human ecological science to explain the changing relationships with the ecosystem that occurred with the rise of industrial society and the global world-economy. The Industrial Revolution, and surely the events that led up to it, changed forever the way in which humans related to the earth's ecosystems. In the process, the systems themselves have been irreversibly altered, introducing new instabilities into the relationships.

Between the latter part of the 1700s and 1880, the English population had tripled (Deane 1973:223). With growth rates of this magnitude, technological innovation transforming the material world was the viable adaptive mode. In addition, wealth was gained from this material transformation. While wealth production was the intent, increased carrying capacity resulted. From the vantage point of human ecology it seems that capitalism was merely the economic scheme, together with its ideological rationalizations, that insured that exponential population growth did not force societies to debilitating diseases or other means for reducing their pressing numbers. Europe registered 110 million people in 1700, while two centuries later, in 1914, its population had increased to 450 million (Armengaud 1973:22). Largely through migration from Europe the United States population grew from 5 million in 1800 to 100 million by 1914 (Woodruff 1973:704).

The movement of peoples—particularly of those who emigrated from Europe in the nineteenth century and of those 10 million who were transported from Africa in the slave trade—was unprecedented in the history of the world. Up to 1845, 5 million had left Europe (McEvedy and Jones 1978: 31), but, between 1851 and 1920, 40 million Europeans emigrated, shipping between 20 million and 30 million to the United States (Woodruff 1973:701); the exact number is debated. The great migrations altered the world-system in one powerful way by introducing white European populations to continents that rapidly moved to industrialize as had the parent countries. An earlier colonial system gave way to a national system in world politics. Until the present the development of the land masses under European hegemony was accomplished in the interests of European investors.

Internal migrations within the European countries attended the industrialization processes. There was a massive shift from rural to urban. In England in 1811 one-third of the population was involved in agriculture; by 1831 this ratio had dropped to one-fourth; and by 1851 it had plunged to one-fifth (Deane 1973:192). It was an overall process that is now being prescribed by economists to stimulate international economic development (W. A. Lewis 1978). The planned cities of the United States were rapidly filling up, placing great demands on the hinterlands for supplies of food and raw materials. Philadelphia grew from a small urban place of 67,811 in 1800 to 161,410 in 1830, more than doubling its population in a generation and a half. By 1850 the city had grown sixfold to 388,721 (Warner 1968:51) and was a major manufacturing city. The demand for coal to make iron, to fuel train engines, and to heat the rapidly increasing number of homes made the nearby anthracite fields an opportunity and a resource that was not ignored.

The movement of peoples and the increase in trade to feed the growing populations—especially in the cities—required a network of relatively cheap and extensive transportation. After 1840 rails conquered the globe largely as a result of investment by London businessmen. By 1850 Europe controlled a landmass that was larger than itself (Deane 1973: 223). By World War I, the English businessmen and bankers had invested four billion pounds abroad, 40 percent of which was in railroads (Woodruff 1973:712). In the United States, railroad construction lagged for a few years behind that of England, but by 1840 the United States had half of the world's total rail network (Woodruff 1973:691). With this system rapidly expanding, the country was able to open its vast interior, again moving raw materials, goods, and people at unprecedented rates.

World trade grew as the infrastructure was built and fuels were made available for transport and domestic uses. By 1850, still leading the world in industrial productivity, England accounted for two-thirds of the world's coal production (Woodruff 1973:680). A decade later the United States was the world's largest economic power (Rostow 1978:75). Like population, world trade expanded exponentially. From 1750 to 1913, world trade increased fiftyfold (Woodruff 1973:658), and the world outside the north Atlantic was, for the most part, peripheral to the wealth generated by this world-system.

A number of critical inventions, beginning in the eighteenth century with innovations in textiles and iron in England, made this growth possible. It was in mining, manufacturing, and transportation that the key advances were made. Nef summarized their revolutionary effects:

> The phrase "industrial revolution" ought to be reserved for this unprecedented expansion, with its repercussions on every phase of economic, social, political, military, and intellectual history. The industrial revolution proper led the mining, the manufacturing, and the transport industries to dominate the economic life of nations, and brought a majority of all the workers in these industries to labor for wages away from their homes in establishments with more than a score on their payrolls. It made common for the first

time vast industrial enterprises with thousands, even tens of thousands of employees. It led to widespread replacement of manual labor by machines, to the regulation of work by machines instead of by the independent decisions of men. It made possible the construction of wagons, boats, airships, and even whole cities in iron, steel, glass, and reinforced concrete. . . . The industrial revolution harnessed much of the world's work to power, artificially obtained from coal, oil, and hydroelectricity, and perhaps eventually from atomic energy. It claimed for mechanically produced and transmitted pictures and sound a large proportion of the leisure of the greatly increased population of the world. [1963:293]

After the middle of the nineteenth century the Bessemer steel process gave new life to the railroads. In 1851 the Reading Railroad, which served the anthracite fields, perfected an anthracite-burning engine, and, as the Pennsylvania Railroad opened up the midwest by rail, it used the vast bituminous reserves of western Pennsylvania to fuel its engines. The Pennsylvania Railroad became the largest in the world (Binder 1974:126) with an abundant and relatively cheap fuel supply.

During the period peaking in 1860, the world-system expanded its trade based on an energy revolution that had transformed transportation. Two major transitions took place: (1) the core industrialized areas began to shift away from England as the United States and the other European countries caught up; and (2) increasing quantities of energy were pumped into the economic system as a result of the decline in the use of scarce wood and the increase in the use of abundant coal. This second transition was felt in the transportation sector. The rise of the second Kondratieff wave, peaking in 1860, was attended by the growth of railroads and by the maturing of canal transportation. It is as if the economic growth registered in a wave is partially a function of two transportation energy bases, one maturing, and a second one just kicking into operation. Baran and Sweezy discuss "epoch making" innovations, such as the steam engine, the railroad, and the auto, and they observe that "Each produced a radical alteration of economic geography with attendant internal migrations and the building of whole new communities; each required or made possible the production of many new goods and services; each directly or indirectly enlarged the market for a whole range of industrial products" (1966:219–20). The years 1820 to 1870 witnessed the explosion of transportation with the railroads, creating just these conditions.

1820–1870

The period extending from 1820 to 1870 witnessed a great growth in the demand for anthracite. Before 1820 there was little demand for anthracite in Philadelphia, but by 1865 it cost nearly eight dollars a ton, and the city depended on the fuel source to heat the row houses and to make commercial steam. English and Welsh miners, experienced and disciplined, moved into the anthracite coalfields; the English settled in Upper

Lehigh, the Welsh in what is now West Hazleton, among other places. English labor organizers followed and attempted—with mixed success—to organize the highly fragmented labor force so they could bargain for better working conditions and wages. The American West was opened by the railroads, and Hazleton was often merely a stepping stone for an immigrant's move elsewhere. Great mobility in and out, if not up within the coal industry, characterized the area (Berthoff 1965:261–91).

The industries' control extended to the infrastructure—especially canals and rails—to the labor force, to administrators and legislators at the state level, and to community life. Since industry itself was differentiated, companies bore different relations to these factors. Certain patterns emerge clearly, however. There were two major types of firms and, surrounding Hazleton, two major types of settlement patterns. The two types of companies were the large corporation run from New York or Philadelphia that emerged during this period and grew in strength and the family firm, whose size was a function of working capital and the richness and extent of coal land holdings.

Two major forms of settlement pattern developed: one was free, with individual property owners holding land in their own names, and the other was the company town, where every parcel was the property of the company (Aurand 1971:22). On the mountain, only Hazleton and Freeland were free towns (Roberts 1904:123). The company towns were called patchtowns and were built facing the mines; they tended to be small and isolated, made up of a row or two of standardized double houses, each half rented out to a family. After 1850 these settlements were linked by rail; before that they were linked by footpaths.

By 1850 there were patchtowns at Harwood, Cranberry, Eckley, and Drifton, all on Coxe coal land property. They were not charming little villages. Roberts, an early sociologist, a good observer despite his rather racist Social Darwinism, wrote in 1904,

> The dull monotony of a mining village is oppressive. Sixty double houses may often be seen uniformly built and placed in two or three rows; all of them with slanting roof over the kitchen; no porch; not the faintest attempt at decoration in any part of them; each block speaks of parsimony in its construction; the impression comes with irresistible force that these houses were built for rent. The homes owned by mine employees differ; they have a porch, and the windows and doors have something to break the monotony, while invariably there is a side door and a small porch. [1904:133]

Markle established a company in 1858, and in 1863 Pardee was the largest local coal company. In 1865 Markle created the patchtown of Jeddo, a small settlement that remains to this day. In 1946 the company that then owned the Jeddo houses sold them for varying prices from $400 and up depending on their condition. The houses were in company hands for eighty-one years. Despite the road system the isolation of these towns continues. During fieldwork in 1974, a Ford bus that had been converted into a general store made the rounds of the patchtowns selling groceries, household goods, and clothing. The towns remain without schools or hospitals and doctors, so the children have to be bused for education, and the ill have to be taken by auto or ambulance to the nearest clinic or hospital.

Hazleton mountain was more isolated than the other anthracite cities of Wilkes-Barre and Scranton, both of which are valley and river towns. Partially as a result of the difficulties of transporting goods to the mountainous area, the companies early provided all services and goods through company stores, company doctors, and even company lawyers. The pattern persisted, and in 1904 Coxe Bros. & Co. owned 850 houses (Roberts 1904:126).

In Luzerne County, 65 percent of the housing was owned or rented by companies. This was the highest such percentage in all the coalfields. Roberts calculated that the companies owning the houses made excellent profits on them, and that the Coxes received between 18 and 20 percent profit (1904:127).

On their properties the companies owned everything, and if a church wanted property, the company would grant them the privilege of building without alienating the plot. As well as recreation rooms, schools were sometimes set up in a company house, but the company again kept these structures under its ownership.

Between 1820 and 1870, Hazleton came into being. It was incorporated after 1840, and grew from 1,500 to 12,000 between 1850 and 1890. Socially, the free coal mining towns evolved local elites—upper classes that were made up of people who by Philadelphia standards would have been restricted to the middle class (Berthoff 1965). By 1855, Scranton had a modest relief program. Hazleton circulated a newspaper in 1866, and claimed enough property to warrant the establishment of a fire company by 1869. While the free towns were able to develop like towns anywhere in the country, they were constrained structurally by the major production system associated with coal. The company towns looked very different.

STRUCTURE

The company towns were constructed ostensibly to provide the services that the rest of the private sector was unable to offer due to the remote and underdeveloped nature of the region. This does not constitute an explanation, because the companies of the northern coalfields kept land for individuals who could purchase it for either house building or commercial purposes. The Coxe Bros. & Co. profits from rental suggest that many companies were willing to put up with the problems the patriarchal system imposed in order to maximize their profits.

The rent for the house is kept each month at the office, and if the company sees fit it can not only discharge the man from his work, but also evict him, which in many instances means departure from the town or village, every inch of which is owned by the company. This was done in several instances after the last strike on Hazleton mountain, and the evicted had to seek other shelter while their furniture was piled by the sheriff on the public highway. [Roberts 1904:122]

The larger and less personal the company, especially those owned by the rail companies, the less they were willing to maintain this oppressive system.

The structure of the company town is much more pervasive than a look at just the coalfields suggests. Among agrarian communities in the southern United States, there were company towns owned by individuals and families that paralleled the plantation system. They are common to extraction companies, to construction firms in areas without services, and to mineral mining concerns in all parts of the world. Migrant labor camps also resemble the company town. The larger corporations tend to do better in providing services and in making the transition from company-operated to merchant-operated towns than family firms.

In the coalfields, the family firm had two major features in addition to complete ownership of property. The workers were kept dependent, and, therefore, powerless, and all profits went to the owners, who set prices. The industrial family firms maintained all the privileges that had been granted by the English crown to the merchant firms dating from 1600 and Queen Elizabeth's legal charter to the 218 merchants and investors who made up the East India Company. Both wealth production privileges, including complete monopoly and broadly defined police powers over employees, were granted by the crown. Queen Elizabeth's charter stated

> ... that the said governor and company, so often as they shall make, ordain, or establish any such laws, constitutions, orders, or ordinances, in form aforesaid, shall and may lawfully impose, ordain, limit, and provide such pains, punishments, and penalties, by imprisonment of body, or by fines and amercements, or by all or any of them, upon and against all offenders. . . . [Henning, Foord, and Mathias 1949:217]

This was not so much a surrender of sovereignty by the state as an extension of privilege to those who would increase the state's wealth. The corporation of that period was in effect a tiny monarchy that acquired the mandate to trade for profit, share in the profits, and conduct any business it saw fit so long as it did not break the laws of the kingdom. This was indeed great license. The firm acted as a hinge articulating the nation with the world-economy. The firm was legitimized by the state, paid taxes to the state, and petitioned the state for privilege. The flows of goods and services it controlled, however, were priced and exchanged on the world market.

In the coalfields, the private family fortunes were made by the exercise of this legal hegemony. The family firms acquired labor as cheaply as they could, even personally recruiting laborers in Europe. They charged their miners for the oil they burned underground in their head lamps and for the powder necessary to blast the coal loose. Many laborers were remunerated according to what they produced, not the hours worked. And as in most of the factory systems of the period and since, the laborers were managed by a professional group of supervisors who were accountable to the company. These men were often unscrupulous and found numerous ways of maximizing their own gain, largely at the expense of the workers. They were often among the affluent of the coalfield free towns.

A social contract of asymmetrical exchange did underlie the arrangement between owner and worker for the owner's profits. The family firm provided minimal health care and death benefits, rented housing, and at times education. A company store system dispensed food, clothing, household necessities, and credit. A profit was made in each of these transactions. Coal costs for heating the miners' houses was deducted whether all the coal was used or not. Sick benefits were deducted from miners' paychecks whether or not the benefits were paid, and there were always additional costs. After 1866, the companies acquired from the state legislature the right to maintain their own police forces. The coal firms often acquired rights to maintain public roads, thereby reducing the public sector's responsibility even further (Aurand 1971:26). The Molly Maguire terrorism was suppressed entirely within the private sector. Aurand, a historian of the labor movement in the anthracite fields of the nineteenth century, explained, "The hanging of 20 men in the southern anthracite regions proclaimed a new order—the corporation-dominated society. By beating down labor in 1875, the corporation provided what neither labor union nor state seemed capable of providing: protection from and prosecution of criminals and terrorists" (1971:109). The corporations were themselves, however, an extension of the franchise that had been extended two centuries earlier, a charter by the state allowing the use of labor to transform natural resources into energy and useful products, thereby gaining wealth.

If the industrial bourgeoisie was indifferent to political involvement until after 1850 (Bergier 1973:404), they were nevertheless cosmopolitan people aware of international and national movements. Despite their often humble origins (Bergier 1973; Wallace 1978:45–58), they were the major entrepreneurs who through their efforts established the energy basis of society and altered human-ecosystem relations. The last of these great family firms in the United States include such giants as the present Ford Motor Company and the DuPont Chemical Company of a generation ago.

The coal region family firms with their company stores were in conflict with the merchants of the free towns. The merchants had their eyes on potential customers whom the company stores kept captive. A second set of competitors were the larger companies that after 1850 came to be dominated by the railroads. Labor, too, conflicted with the family companies, though the evidence suggests that the family firm was more successful at dampening conflict through repressive measures than the larger corporations. The large individual owners did not have an easy time of it, but great wealth often compensated those who were most successful at repressing the conflict.

After the Civil War, the large family firm operators were part of an industrial, political, social, and economic elite on the east coast. The Markles increased their control of production processes by establishing a bank in Hazleton with the Pardees. The Coxe family produced a state senator who conducted voluminous correspondence from the patchtown of Drifton. Thanks to the great efficiency of the anthracite railroads, he could be in Philadelphia, New York, Washington, or Harrisburg within a day's time.

Labor in the anthracite fields in the nineteenth century was irreconcilably fragmented for several reasons. Geology militated against unified labor organization. The anthracite coal basins are quite discrete, and each had its own set of operators. The basins were relatively difficult to reach. The lack of communication and rapid transportation made the coalfields, with their separate collieries and work forces, a fragmented social system. Another reason for the lack of unity among miners was their diverse ethnic origins. Thanks to inward-looking national churches, segregated settlement patterns, and linguistic and behavioral differences, the forces of social disparity were greater than those of social cohesion. The lack of integration was only one aspect of the continuous demoralization that miners suffered. Their structural relation to the powerful mine operators proved to be a source of continuing, violent conflict. Aurand explained,

> Deductions for mining supplies and for the company store, along with other features of the operators' system of paternalism, deprived the mine workers of nearly all freedom. Mine laborers tended to view people who were able to buy wherever they pleased as "a superior class of freeman." Denial of the right to choose one's physician and pay one's taxes continually ate away at the pride of the miners.
>
> In addition, the industry's payroll deductions reduced already low wages while the system of company paternalism, which the payroll deductions financed, further undercut the mine workers' pride. Indeed, the industry's reward system for anthracite mine workers appears on the whole to have been more of a studied insult than a reward. [1971:52]

Dependency on the mining companies, working conditions in the mines, and the endless, always-changing problem of wages plagued miners and their families.

The anthracite coalfields were perhaps the most dangerous places to work in the nineteenth century. The miners there suffered higher death rates than the bituminous workers. Workers and owners blamed each other for the conditions. The statistics on the coalfields kept by the state tell a terrible story. The ethnicity of the worker by occupation is recorded, for example, and the Polish, who were always underground, suffered the greatest death and injury rates. The death rate was recorded by thousand tons extracted.

Wages during the 1820–70 period fluctuated due to inflation, influx of cheaper labor in the form of new migrants, periodic, especially seasonal, layoffs, and actual wage reductions. The first strike occurred in 1842 against the low wages and the truck system. The truck system "was still another drain on the mine laborers' wages. Under the system workers received their pay in scrip, or store orders, rather than cash. Employees often complained that the scrip was discounted or that the store on which the order was drawn furnished shoddy goods at high prices" (Aurand 1971:48). This strike was staged largely by English and Welsh miners. After 1846, Irish and German migrants entered the coalfields. In 1848, an English union organizer was able to build a constituency and organize a strike, but the gains were shortlived for a number of reasons. The main reason may have been that not all of the coalfields were united in their striking efforts. Other companies could pick up the slack in production, and the strike remained less than effectual.

There were other strikes, but in 1867, after the peak of the wave, prices fell. The Civil War had ended and the demand for coal was not growing as rapidly as it had been. With the fall in prices, the operators cut wages. The shock of this move helped set the conditions for the emergence of the most successful labor organization to that date, the Workmen's Benevolent Association (WBA) of 1869.

The problem of calibrating supply with demand had already plagued the industry, and the state of Pennsylvania had inquired into the organization of the producers as early as 1834. The state wanted to know, in the public interest, whether or not the industry should be vertically integrated with the transportation companies owning the mines and creating thereby monopolies over the supply of heating fuel. Philadelphia had suffered a shortage of coal the year before, and it protested. Thirty-five years later the WBA diagnosed the problem of wages in the coalfields as a problem of overproduction, and they set about taking measures to remedy the situation. In theoretical terms, the fluctuations brought about by falling prices in the incipient economic depression in the late 1860s were addressed by the WBA union, a control mechanism. The union sought to control the fluctuations by establishing hours worked, wages, and quantity of coal produced. These moves, it was thought, would effectively manage the depressed market by limiting supplies, thereby driving prices upward. Because there was competition for control between the union and the owners, the owners diagnosed the situation in their interests and translated union efforts as a threat to their own means for manipulating the marketplace and profits. From the owners' perspective, it was labor that was driving up costs while coal prices fell. By laying off labor, the owners believed they would compensate easily for the shrinking profit margin. The WBA, being less powerful and less cohesive than the companies, was not successful. The continuing terrorism of the Molly Maguires was a rebellion that attempted through murders of mine supervisors and others to redress the growing stresses brought about by a downswing in the long wave. Both strategies by the workers—terrorism and striking—failed.

> The 1870 strike seriously weakened the W.B.A. Both the leaders and the rank-and-file realized that the goal of a regulated market was beyond their reach if one region remained working. The Wyoming region's failure to strike and the subsequent bitter feelings made a general strike improbable. [Aurand 1971:77]

Through the end of the nineteenth century, the attempt by the workers to establish a controlling structure that would meet their needs met with a series of failures. There were a number of strikes, but none that attacked the industry on the scale necessary to establish the workers as a unified body that could address their best interests against the owners.

The owners were successful at self-organizing. When the WBA threatened to achieve their demands, the owners pooled their local trade associations into the Anthracite Board of Trade. It became the social unit that made decisions for the industry, enabling them to concert their actions against the WBA. As a control structure, the owners had superior means, knowledge, skill, and capital to meet the challenge posed by the workers.

1870–1888

Despite the deepening world depression extending from 1873 to 1895, world production continued to expand. After 1880 refrigeration changed the flow of foodstuffs entering Europe; butchered rather than live animals could be transported. Emerging from the depression were new leading sectors, to use Rostow's phrase. The new technologies were electricity, chemicals, and the petroleum-fueled automobile. The world was quickly transformed after the Civil War, perhaps more deeply than before or since in history. The period after the Great Depression, culminating in the third peaking of the Kondratieff wave in 1920, has been called the Second Industrial Revolution. Its dominant features were the new uses of science. The payoff in scientific thinking occurred in the technologies used to exploit petroleum, the internal combustion engine, and the chemical industry. In addition, the electrical power industry, on which modern mass communications are based, also must be mentioned.

As the depression took hold, the family operators on the Hazleton mountain dug in so as to withstand the challenges of labor. The industry, however, was changing dramatically in ways not favorable to the family firm. The way had been cleared by the Pennsylvania legislature to allow transportation companies to own coal lands, and in 1873 the Lehigh Valley Railroad in one dramatic action purchased more than 30,000 acres of such land. This company's rail transportation facilities dominated the Hazleton fields and the Western Middle fields. Similar large-scale purchases in Schuylkill County by the Philadelphia and Reading Railroad in 1869 had contributed to the increasing vertical integration of the coalfields on the part of the railroads. By owning land and extraction companies, and by monopolizing rail transport, the railroads were combining to set prices. Ironically, this was the very strategy, if not the same means, that the WBA had attempted to use in order to include labor in the governance process. Unfortunately their bid had failed.

Declining prices—fallen from $5.39 a ton in 1870 to $2.34 in 1879—coupled with millions of tons of productive capacity never utilized, forced the industry to take measures to insure its viability. The overcapitalization of the industry was met, on the part of the producers, by a series of agreements among themselves to fix prices by limiting production. These were gentlemen's agreements which broke down as even the key companies overproduced. By 1879, the rail companies did not pay dividends on their stocks, and the number of days on which the miners worked plunged.

Not only did the number of work days decline, but the anthracite miners also saw their wages cut and witnessed the arrival of a new wave of eastern European immigrants in the coalfields. Ethnic conflict was given new dimensions. The merchants who had sometimes sided with owners, particularly when the workers were violent, were increasingly hostile to the company town–company store situation. The elites of the coal towns, which were rapidly becoming cities, were made of up lawyers, doctors, successful business people, clergymen, and others, who wished to expand their clientele.

At the bottom of the depression, respected coal companies and railroads went bankrupt; the newer immigrants acquired elected positions in local politics; merchants and the regional elite demanded more access to workers' incomes; and many workers maintained themselves with their own vegetable gardens.

Communities continued to mature as increasing attention was paid to education and the plight of children in the labor force. In 1879 Eckley Coxe opened the Drifton School of Industry, but it was not until 1895 that the state of Pennsylvania required that its children attend school. In 1884 Hazleton became the third city in the world to be electrified, as a result of its ample supply of the fuel needed to run the generators. Edison undoubtedly visited the city, and his name was used by the company, Edison Electric Illuminating Company, which he partly owned. The electrical development of the area made increasing amounts of power available to the mining companies, who soon grew to be the largest consumers. Another effect of electrification was that the textile industry turned to this source of energy and located where there was cheap electricity and cheap labor. The women of the coalfields were the cheap labor supply, and textiles moved into the region before the turn of the century.

COMMUNITY: 1888–1920

As the World Depression began to lift, the local communities in the anthracite coalfields diversified, expanded, and evolved new control mechanisms. New uses of energy were becoming available. Not only were there electric lights, but a trolley system was built in Hazleton in 1893. The more rapid mobility about the coalfields meant that the large family firms with their company stores were less isolated, and the businessmen continued to resent the unfair competition that the company stores enjoyed. The Hazleton Board of Trade, a precursor of the Chamber of Commerce, was established in 1896. The board attempted to diversify the economic base of the city and increase the growth of jobs and payrolls by recruiting new firms. The organization of the board reflected the growing strength of the urban-based businessmen, light manufacturers, bankers, and professionals.

By 1914 silk mills were the second largest employer in the region. By 1940 the Board of Trade had helped recruit close to thirty firms, many of them textile-related. The textile firms employed mainly women and helped stabilize the region during strikes, which were periods of great personal suffering—regional fluctuations that affected whole communities. The textile firms were, however, anything but benevolent. During the crippling strike of 1922, during which the anthracite industry lost most of its distant markets, the silk mills cut the women's wages almost in half. Their workers were captives with nowhere else to go, and in many of the households only one person had any income at all (Raushenbush 1924:39).

Twenty-six ethnic groups had migrated to Hazleton mountain and the other coalfields by 1900 (Roberts 1904:21). Jewish merchants walked through the patchtowns selling liquor and necessities, and served as bankers to the eastern European immigrants who often shared mutually intelligible dialects. Today the Jewish members of the coal communities are among the most notable community leaders and are established in both businesses and the professions. The eastern European emigrés rapidly adapted to the conditions of the coal communities. They bought property and formed those peculiarly effective American institutions, voluntary associations. The Slavic men would gather in a saloon, not to play the slots only, but also to discuss politics, and to encourage one another in gaining citizenship. Clubs would form—and in Hazleton today, clubs still are formed—at local bars. Hunting and fishing associations are examples of such organizations.

Despite the economic upturn, the coalfields remained in a turmoil. Crimes against persons were higher there than anywhere else in Pennsylvania. This can partially be attributed to the large number of single men, but also to the fact that there were over three thousand saloons in the larger region. This was the most saloons per capita in the state. It is estimated that the men spent $10,800,000 a year in the anthracite country on booze. Drinking became a medium of sociability and a temporary means of escaping the inhuman quality of life that the mines, marginal citizenship status, low wages, and a high injury and death rate conveyed. The per capita relief to the anthracite fields by the state of Pennsylvania was also inordinately high. It was three times that of the state average, twice as high as that of the bituminous fields, and eight times that of the agricultural communities. Fraud was reportedly widespread (Roberts 1904:299).

Beneath the turbulence, despite the hegemony of the large independent operators on Hazleton mountain, the foundations for community life were being established. Such foundations included the spread of the English language; the widespread desire for citizenship; the growth of mass transportation, newspapers, and the telephone; the emergence of community leadership among the urban business and professional community; and the growing solidarity of organized labor (cf. Gutman 1976: 43 on eastern European migrants and their adaptation to life in the industrializing United States).

The Second Industrial Revolution destroyed the large family firm, at least in the United States, as a viable capitalistic enterprise that would continue over many generations to provide economic security to a kin-based dynasty. Changing technology, inheritance laws, rational corporate behavior, and entrepreneurial skills for rapidly changing markets demanded more flexibility than families could muster. Kinship in the industrial machine became a vestigial mode of social organization. During the trough between the peaks of the long wave in 1860 and 1920, and in the upswing preceding 1920, the large family firms on Hazleton mountain were acquired by the railroads. The last of the firms to sell was Coxe Bros. & Co., also the largest independent firm in the anthracite region at the time. In 1904, for $17,440,000 (Anthracite Coal Commission 1938:403) the Coxe family sold its company and land to the Lehigh Valley Railroad. The historian Rowland Berthoff wrote,

> The Lehigh operators kept their sovereignty longest, most notably Ario Pardee of Hazleton and Eckley B. Coxe of Drifton. Coxe, profiting from the land speculation of his grandfather Tench Coxe, was the one-man upper-class of the isolated and, by his edict, saloonless village of Drifton, where he lived as an industrial feudatory, and leading Democrat, with his wife, as lady of the manor, visiting the sick and poor among their working people, who, it was said, "fairly worshipped" them. [Berthoff 1965:277]

No longer would the Lehigh independents be able to break strikes by refusing to negotiate with striking workers. The family companies had been able to shut out striking workers in the strike of 1887, and 5,000 workers had left the area. Those days were over.

By the late nineteenth century, though, the industrial bourgeoisie, such as the Coxes, were by no means isolated from public, even political, life. A more accurate characterization would describe them as fully developed members of a regional elite. Eckley Coxe might be lord of the manor as Berthoff suggests, and a leading Democrat. He was also a prominent mining engineer, had published scholarly papers, invented mining and other equipment, and served on state boards. The family never really followed the pattern of a rise from humble origins to great wealth. Eckley's great-grandfather had been a colonial proprietor in New Jersey, and his grandfather had served under Secretary Hamilton as assistant secretary of the United States Treasury. It is clear from an examination of the Coxe family in the nineteenth century that public life and the private accumulation of wealth through industry were not mutually exclusive.

The accumulation of wealth by the Coxe family, though exacted at great cost to the workers, flowed into causes that brought recognition and prestige to the philanthropic family member. The family firm was the engine of successful energy conversion processes but not as successful as the monopoly of banks, railroads, and coal companies that J. P. Morgan was able to establish in 1896. Nevertheless, large amounts of the money that was made by the family found its way to Philadelphia. Their money and their standing as an old Quaker mercantile family gave the Coxes legitimacy and power in the relatively closed world of the Philadelphia upper class. Eckley Brinton Coxe, Jr., was a philanthropist and nephew to mine owner Eckley B. Coxe. With his share of the Coxe family fortune he not only endowed the University Museum of the University of Pennsylvania, but also paid out of pocket for expeditions to Egypt, the director's salary, specific museum acquisitions, and maintenance of the physical plant. From 1910 until his death in 1916, he was president of the museum board. In his will he endowed the museum with most of the shares in its portfolio and its second largest endowment, which continues to provide funds to the present. The later industrial bourgeoisie were, at the turn of the century, firm members of regional elites who collected paintings and Eastern art, launched archeological expeditions to classical sites, and sent expeditions to collect photographs and artifacts of the vanishing American Indian. They also endowed museums in their respective cities to house collections. Those industrialists and that period have now passed, although the deep and abiding relationship between elites and images has not.

The third upswing of the long wave witnessed a new scale of industrial production that wove together the world-economy more intimately than ever before. Capital, transportation, and energy supplies, especially coal, were partially unified in the United States under the influence of J. P. Morgan, the Wall Street banker. The purchase of family firms in the anthracite region was minor compared to the scale of consolidation that was emerging in the oil and the railroad industries. In 1888 Morgan convened a number of railroad owners in an attempt to bring order to the industry and ameliorate the competition that threatened even the largest. By forming agreements, markets could be stabilized. The anthracite industry with its carrier railroads was but one segment of Morgan's much larger interests. But, from the perspective of the industry,

Morgan's machinations sometimes seemed to be directed at them. The agreements did not always work, although they were by and large successful.

By 1896, the need to develop agreements was ancient history. Morgan had, through purchases, acquired control of 96.2 percent of the anthracite-carrying railroads, and 90 percent of the industry was controlled by five of the eleven railroads serving the anthracite fields. The monopoly was formed not simply because the rail companies owned coal land or held companies that did, but because all coal was carried by rail. It was the sole source of transportation in and out of the fields. By hegemony over transportation, the rail companies could control markets and production. As late as 1936 ten companies controlled three-quarters of the production of anthracite:

> The Philadelphia and Reading Coal and Iron Company
> Glen Alden Coal Company
> The Lehigh Valley Coal Company
> The Hudson Coal Company
> Lehigh Navigation Coal Company
> The Pittston Company
> Coxe Brothers and Company, Inc.
> Jeddo-Highland Coal Company
> Hazle Brook Coal Company
> Scranton Coal Company.

Nine companies carried nearly all the tonnage in the same time period:

> Reading Company
> Lehigh Valley Railroad Company
> The Delaware, Lackawanna & Western R. R. Company
> The Pennsylvania Railroad Company
> The Delaware & Hudson R. R. Corporation
> The Central R. R. Company of New Jersey
> Erie Railroad Company
> New York, Ontario & Western Railway Company
> Lehigh & New England R. R. Company.

"The financial and other interests which control both the anthracite producing companies and the anthracite carrying railroads consist of New York and Philadelphia banks, investment houses, insurance companies and industrial firms, which are controlled by two principal groups" (Anthracite Coal Commission 1938:356–57). These were the controlling firms:

> *Morgan interests*
> J. P. Morgan and Company
> Bankers Trust Company (New York)
> Guaranty Trust Company of New York

The New York Trust Company
Drexel and Company
Markle Corporation
Girard Trust Company (Philadelphia)
The Pennsylvania Company for Insurances on Lives and Grant-
ing Annuities
United States Steel Corporation

Baker interests
First National Bank of the City of New York
First National Bank of Scranton
First National Bank of Wilkes-Barre

*Interests jointly controlled by the Morgan and Baker interests, or friendly to
them*
Allegheny Corporation and Chesapeake Corporation (to be merged)
Bancamerica-Blair Corporation
The Chase National Bank of the City of New York
Manufacturers Trust Company (New York)
Corn Exchange National Bank and Trust Company (Philadelphia)
Philadelphia National Bank
Insurance Company of North America
Virginia Coal and Iron Company.

These findings by the Pennsylvania Anthracite Coal Industry Commission echoed an old refrain. This monopoly had been intact nearly forty
years and had been the subject of scholarly work on the interlocking
directorates that controlled it before Morgan's death, as early as 1914
(Jones 1914). Although the Rockefeller oil interests had been successfully
broken up in 1911, measures taken by the federal government against the
anthracite monopoly were not as successful. The nagging problems of the
industry—production excesses, labor's legitimate demands, fluctuation
in market prices, high costs to urban householders, avariciousness of the
rail carriers searching for quick and incredible wealth—kept the situation
turbulent despite the controlling effect of monopoly. Questions by the
public about the high cost of anthracite, causes of labor unrest, and
conditions in the miners' workplace kept the national eye upon the Morgan interests and sustained efforts at breaking the monopoly. What no
one seemed to see until it was too late was the competition from other
fuel sources for the various categories of the anthracite market. It was not
the monopoly that destroyed the industry but coke and home-heating fuel
oil. The energy basis of the world-system and the United States was
imperceptibly shifting in the decades between 1890 and 1920. The surge
of petroleum-based industries, notably home heating and automobiles,
together with the railroad boom of World War I, launched the third
upswing in the long wave.

Between 1896, when Morgan acquired firm control, and 1913, there
was a rise in anthracite production from 54.3 million net tons to 91.5

million net tons (round figures). At $5.31 per ton in 1913 the anthracite industry generated $485,865,000 in retail receipts that were distributed back through the system of retailers, distributors, railroads, producers, banks, and laborers in the energy conversion process. Some of this money was collected in taxes at various levels. Peak production was in 1917, and after World War I, the industry emerged to face the competitive edge gained by the cheaper, more easily transportable, storable, and usable petroleum fuels.

LABOR

Periods of intensification have generally been followed by a lowered standard of living, and there is evidence that the quality of life for the urban—and certainly the extraction industry—workers in the nineteenth century achieved new lows (Harris 1979:67). It was not until the end of the century that state legislatures in the United States enacted eight-hour-day work laws. Men laboring in the mines worked ten- and twelve-hour days, and the same was true of the labor performed by many women in factories. The most onerous labor practice was undoubtedly the employment of children. They worked hours as long as their fathers and were paid poorly. In the mining communities it was not merely that children needed to supplement the family income, though it was needed more often than not; it was often, rather, because an adult man had been killed or maimed (table 2).

TABLE 2
Fatal and Nonfatal Accidents
in the Anthracite Mines
1916–21

Year	Fatal	Nonfatal
1916	592	25,610
1917	602	25,322
1918	626	22,268
1919	664	20,508
1920	512	21,659
1921	545	21,387

"That means that every year one mine worker in 270 is killed and one in seven is injured. Every miner takes as it were a Sabbatical year, when he must expect injury or death."
SOURCE: Raushenbush (1924:107)

Not only were adult men killed and maimed, but the breaker boys sorting the coal from the shale often fell into the machinery. One was killed almost every day; and they were sometimes younger than six when they went to work.

Photographers who captured images of the children in the coalfields and in other laboring activities did much to bring to the public arena an awareness of the abuses of child employment (Rosenblum 1977:12–13). Reformers and social scientists were also outraged at the abuses. Roberts reported,

> In the breakers of the anthracite coal industry there are nearly 18,000 persons employed as slate pickers. The majority of these are boys from the ages of 10 to 14 years. In an investigation conducted in an area where 4,131 persons wholly dependent on the mines lived, we found 64 children employed in and around the mines not 14 years of age. There were 24 boys employed in breakers before they were 12 years of age. [1904:174–75]
> No industry in the State is so demoralizing and injurious to boys as the anthracite coal industry. [1904:176]

Technological change and the unions had perhaps more to say in the last analysis than the reformers. Sorting was done by machine soon after Roberts wrote his monograph.

Although the strike of the miners on Hazleton mountain was broken by the family companies in 1887, the organizational strength of the miners continued to increase as the scale of control of production increased, as evidenced by the Morgan monopoly. In 1892–93, the United Mine Workers (UMW) entered the anthracite fields; the fields were eventually divided into three sections of the UMW. In 1900 and 1902 strikes were so effective that a commission was convened, and social scientists turned their attention to the problems of the coalfields. For the first time all the miners were organized within a structure that had the kind of clout necessary to win concessions that miners desperately needed from the companies and from the legislature.

Like so many organizational efforts, the UMW was shocked into being, in this case by events which occurred on Hazleton mountain in 1897. Miners had walked off the job at Audenried in protest against a supervisor, Gomer Jones, who was a particularly harsh manager. His threats of physical violence to the mine workers were met by an escalating confrontation between workers and management. Eastern European immigrants, the newcomers to the fields, refused for the first time to be intimidated and they marched in protest. Aurand gave the following account:

> At the Hazleton city limits the marchers met Mayor Altmiller, who refused to permit the men to parade through the town. The strikers then took a circular route and confronted Sheriff Martin in West Hazleton. Martin vainly tried to stop the march. Angered by their failure, Martin and his deputies took a trolley to Lattimer, where

they established a picket line across the public highway. When the marchers arrived in Lattimer the sheriff repeated his demand that the parade cease. Suddenly Martin either fell or was pushed aside and his posse fired into the unarmed strikers. The deputies fired with cool and deliberate aim, hitting some of the marchers in the back as they ran for cover. When the smoke finally cleared, more than 50 strikers, mostly immigrants, lay dead or wounded. [1971:139]

This event triggered wide acceptance for the union, and it grew in strength during the growth spurt of the economy before and after the war years. Again in 1922 and 1925 there were large and effective strikes, due in part to the failure of the companies to maintain wages at the level of the rapidly rising cost of living. But the strikes further damaged an extraction industry that was doomed by substitutions of other fuels to decline rapidly and disintegrate both the labor movement and the line companies associated with the railroads and banks.

An observer who spent four months in the region doing amateur ethnography during the 1922 suspension evoked the conditions, paraphrasing the miners with whom he talked.

They told stories of the mine fields where suffering and courage united in a heroism which was no less real because it was unspectacular and enduring. But they felt that after the stories had been told, no one would be any wiser. They accepted these things. They said that men accustomed to face death in routine darkness did not whine when there was no butter for their bread, and when the coffee grounds were boiled to their fourth weakness. They said that the women they married, and the women who were the mothers of such men, had that quality it takes to carry on. They had handled life without gloves and without perfume. They had seen limp bodies carried from the shaft to their own street, to be taken into some quiet little house. They never knew when it would be their own house. They knew their life was like that, was always to be like that. They did not ask much. They knew all these things. But they were not certain that others knew. [Raushenbush 1924:37]

Socially and culturally the most profound reality of the coalfields was the numerous national origins of its work force. The social divisions in the workplace and the spatial divisions of the communities kept these groupings at loggerheads for most of the last quarter of the nineteenth century and into the twentieth. By 1880 there was a definite hierarchy in the mine fields that was racist and oppressive but also rapidly changing. At the bottom of the hierarchy, deep in the mines, suffering the highest rates of death and loss of limbs, were the Slovaks, most recent Polish immigrants, and the Lithuanians. The contract miners were made up of experienced Poles and Lithuanians, while, outside the mines, Slovaks, Ruthenians, and Italians ran the machines and repaired them. The Irish had moved in significant numbers away from manual positions. The foremen and bosses were Irish, while the managers and supervisors were Welsh. Undoubtedly there are exceptions, but those who enter first tend to progress through the ranks as newer, less skilled workers are recruited. This should not be taken as a stereotype, for there are in the coalfields and other United States industries, countless exceptions to this general rule.

The coal mines of Pennsylvania were the largest sector of employment in the state by the third quarter of the nineteenth century, and the extraction industry had a voracious demand for unskilled laborers. Caroline Golab, in an important work on immigrants in the mid-Atlantic region focused on Philadelphia, explained that the mining companies were almost entirely dependent upon foreign labor. "The original anthracite mine workers were Welsh, Scottish, English and German, groups that were in the majority until 1875 when Poles and Lithuanians began to outnumber them. Slovaks, Ukrainians, Syrians and Italians (in that order) began to arrive after 1880" (1977:35). Two charts exhibit the relative numbers of foreign-born in the coalfields (tables 3 and 4). Golab found that, by 1910, "the Poles were the largest single group employed in the Anthracite belt" (1977:36–37). The Polish communities survive today in the towns which were settled around the years 1870–77: Shamokin,

TABLE 3
Foreign-Born Employees in the Anthracite Fields 1880–1900

Nationality	1880	1890	1900
Ireland	45,330	42,374	31,349
England	33,214	24,575	21,225
Wales		24,140	20,220
Germany*	20,686	28,534	24,086
Scotland	3,191	4,013	3,389
Total English-speaking	102,421	123,636	100,269
Poland†	1,925	15,142	37,677
Austria‡		9,226	17,876
Russia§		4,474	10,283
Hungary		9,931	13,534
Italy		4,234	9,958
Total non-English speaking	1,925	43,007	89,328
Total foreign-born	108,827	170,582	193,692

NOTE: The Pennsylvania Anthracite Region was composed of three "fields"—Luzerne County, the largest; Lackawanna County; and the "Schuylkill Field," which included Carbon, Dauphin, Northumberland, and Schuylkill Counties.
*Germany included a small portion of Poles from those provinces of Poland directly annexed by Germany.
†Primarily Polish persons from the Congress Kingdom of Poland.
‡Austria included Ukrainians, Ruthenians, Slovaks, Czechs, Slovenes, Slovenians, Servians, etc., and Poles from Galicia.
§Russia included Russians, Ukrainians, Lithuanians, and Poles from provinces directly annexed by Russia.
SOURCE: Golab (1977:36)

Shenandoah, Excelsior, Mount Carmel, Blossburg, and in Luzerne County, Nanticoke. People speak with coalfield accents in the twentieth century, and homemade ethnic delicacies can still be purchased in neighborhood grocery stores.

In the late nineteenth century workers in the labor force, divided by subdivisions of labor and ethnicity, were competing with one another for jobs, particularly during downturns in the economy. The integrative role of community institutions and organized labor emerged most powerfully in the twentieth century as the immigrants were more completely absorbed into the cultural, linguistic, social, economic, and political system of the evolving United States.

BEFORE AND AFTER 1920

The peak of the long wave after World War I in 1920 coincided closely with the apogee of the anthracite industry. After the boom of the war years, 99,445,794 net tons of anthracite were produced in 1918, and nine years later employment in mining peaked in the region. Anthracite was a major sector of the resource extraction industry in the United States, and its rapid drop in production was followed by numerous economic analyses attempting to explain the phenomenon (Anthracite Coal Commission 1938; Bakerman 1956; Hsiang 1947; Mead 1935; Raushenbush 1924; Strickler 1935). Analyses were attempted by members of the industry, graduate students at the University of Pennsylvania, and public officials who faced mounting social costs and declining tax revenues. They all concurred that competition from petroleum heating oil was a major cause of the decline, although a number of attendant factors were also advanced. The Anthracite Coal Commission of 1938 charted the in-

TABLE 4
Nationality of Workers in 116 Anthracite
Companies, 1905

Nationality	No.	%
Slavic and Hungarian	36,049	39.0
Italian	3,975	4.3
American, mostly of Slavic and other foreign parentage	25,905	28.0
Irish	6,351	6.8
Welsh	2,397	2.6
English	2,497	2.7
Scottish	289	0.3
German	4,003	4.4
Other	10,989	11.9
Total	92,455	100.0

SOURCE: Golab (1977:37)

crease of oil heating and noted that it expanded from 22 to 77 million barrels between 1926 and 1938, advancing more rapidly than new construction (1938:194, 242). This suggested how much more efficient oil heat was than coal, for many home and apartment owners were switching over. All major categories of anthracite coal use declined as petroleum and other substitutes advanced (table 5).

TABLE 5
The Decline of Anthracite Uses, 1919–36 in Millions of Net Tons

Year	Total Consumption	Consumed as Colliery Fuels	Remainder	Consumed by Railroads	Consumed by Mfg. Plants	Domestic and Commercial Consumption Amount	%
1919	86.4	9.6	76.8	5.0	15.3	56.5	65.4
1927	77.9	6.6	71.3	3.5	10.9	57.1	73.3
1929	74.3	5.3	69.0	3.3	9.7	56.0	75.7
1936	55.3	2.7	52.6	1.6	7.5	43.5	78.7
Percent Decline, 1919–36	−35.9	−71.9	−31.5	−68.0	−50.9	−23.0	

SOURCE: Anthracite Coal Commission (1938:177).

The decline of anthracite was attended by painful regional readjustments. Labor organization in the anthracite fields was crushed as the work force rapidly eroded. Community life was upset as men and their families outmigrated in search of work. The regional economy took a severe beating as the major source of employment died along with the service industries and the supportive infrastructure. Pennsylvania's overall decline as an industrial state was exacerbated by the demise of anthracite; it coincided with the erosion of those structures that gave rise to the Industrial Revolution in the United States: coal, steel, and rails. The overall effect on Hazleton was to strip off the extraction industry that had been the employment base, and the Hazleton region was moved from the front of the energy conversion process (ecosystem → energy/matter → technology → production) to the back of it. Hazleton was suddenly thrust into a depression, after 1929, dependent on a dying industry; a double blow had fallen. On Hazleton mountain the people were hit harder than others in the anthracite region, judging from the Works Progress Administration relief reports of 1936 (Anthracite Coal Commission 1938:79) (table 6). In a matter of two decades, Hazleton was moved from a highly productive extractive region to a region whose population was welfare-supported. The causes can be directly traced to the changing energy basis of the society, and of the core countries of the world-system.

TABLE 6
WPA and Relief to Coalfields by County in 1936

	Schuylkill	North-umberland	Luzerne	Lacka-wanna	Total Penn-sylvania
Average number of cases receiving relief	3,874	2,659	10,700	7,421	169,991
Average number of persons receiving relief	11,822	9,797	41,793	25,630	553,714
Percentage of population receiving relief	5.0	7.6	9.4	8.3	5.7
Average number of persons receiving WPA	9,589	5,249	15,663	10,716	273,795
Percentage of population receiving WPA	4.1	4.1	3.5	3.5	2.8
Total relief expenditures	1,230,718	943,332	4,065,823	2,516,645	63,443,715
Total WPA earnings	6,979,700	3,876,916	11,532,175	7,852,419	185,423,333
Average direct relief per person, monthly	8.62	7.98	8.13	8.23	9.58
Average WPA earnings per person, monthly	60.66	61.55	61.36	61.07	62.23

SOURCE: Anthracite Coal Commission (1938:79)

Generally speaking, population and employment trends in the city of Hazleton have reflected the changing production of anthracite. A rapid increase in the population from 1900 to 1910, coinciding with a rapid increase in the rate of coal production, almost doubled the size of the city (figure 13).* Hazleton's growth rate was still higher than that for the rest of the United States, its rate of natural increase was exceeded by in-migration, and the median age was below that of the country as a whole. There were more women than men in the population, although birth and fertility rates were lower than the United States average. The dangers of mining were reflected in the relatively high death rate.

Between 1910 and 1970 the size of the male labor force followed a trend similar to that of the total population. The total size of the labor force, male and female, is, however, inversely related to the birth rate; the more people working, the lower the birth rate and, in fact, the lower the absolute number of births (compare figures 13, 14, and 15). The birth rate could be expected to decline as more were employed if there was a surplus of females of child-bearing age in the population, if the work force was aging due to the lack of new job creation, or if the population at large was aging rapidly and reproducing more slowly. In reality it is probably a combination of all three, although regressing median age

---

*Figures are derived from the U.S. Census, and methods of analysis employ Shryock, Siegel, and Associates (1973).

against time yields a nearly exponential relationship in Hazleton (R^2 = .9601, T = 11.01, df = 5). This brings us to the first conspicuous lag.

The peak year for mine employment did not occur until nine years after the peak coal production year. This can be attributed to the steady decline of the mining industry. The mine operators began to respond to the plummeting demand for anthracite by shortening shifts and later responded by shortening the work week. This explains why skilled craftsmen remained in the community, in numbers, until at least 1950. The mines still produced, but on a reduced scale. The rate of attrition from the mines was lowered by shrinking employment opportunities. Hence, the rapidly rising median age, starting in about 1920, can be attributed to the out-migration of young people in search of work and to the retention of older, experienced workers in the community who had steady, but less, work. Add to this the depression and we come to the second conspicuous lag.

The total population of Hazleton did not reach its peak until about 1940, nearly twenty-three years after the peak of coal production (figure 13). This was due to older workers' keeping their families in Hazleton, holding the general belief that the anthracite industry would not totally bottom-out; it was also due to the depression. The depression made all places appear to offer the same opportunities (or lack of opportunities), and this checked the motivation for out-migration. For many of the immigrant miners, Hazleton was their first home. People left Hazleton not because they wanted to but because they had to. Evidence suggests that the depression induced some to return to Hazleton where at least they had family, friends, and all the coal for heat and cooking that they could pick. In fact, there appears to be a trend among those over the age of forty-five to return to Hazleton (figure 16).

The depression slowed population movement out of the area, and a wartime resurgence in anthracite production further blocked the dissolution of the community. However, the end of the war brought on a tremendous wave of out-migration, yielding, for the first time, a rate of natural increase overshadowed by out-migration (figure 14). It was at this point that employment in the textile and garment industries began to peak (figure 17). The importance of textiles in the region can be inferred from the fact that the out-migration was not larger, and it can be inferred from interviews. The employed females anchored some unspecified segment of the male labor force.

The textile and garment industries first came to the Hazleton area before the end of the nineteenth century and were composed largely of spinning, bleaching, knitting, and dyeing operations. The silk manufacturers were among the first to arrive, and the synthetic fibers were among the last. The garment industries were represented by numerous small cottage industry firms spread throughout the patchtowns as well as by a few larger factories in the cities of Hazleton and Freeland.

These industries were drawn to the region for several reasons. The area had a readily available, generally unemployed, population of females

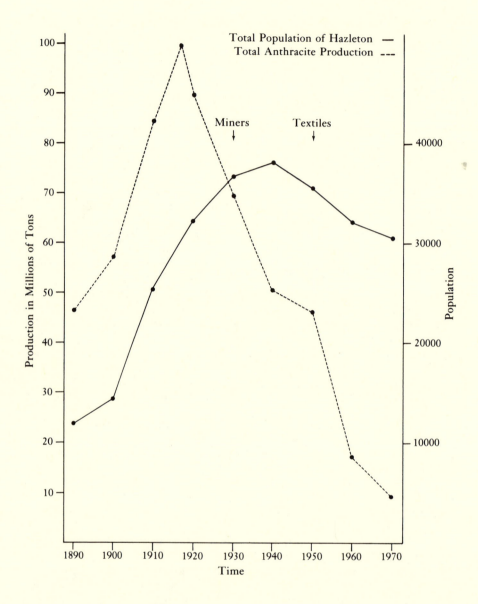

Figure 13. Hazleton population increase and total anthracite production, 1890–1970: *horizontal axis,* time; *left axis,* anthracite coal production in millions of tons; *right axis,* population. This graph shows the relationship of the population growth of Hazleton to coal production. The arrows for "miners" and "textiles" refer to the peak employment years for these two industries in the city. The methods of analysis are found in Shryock, Siegel, and Associates (1973).

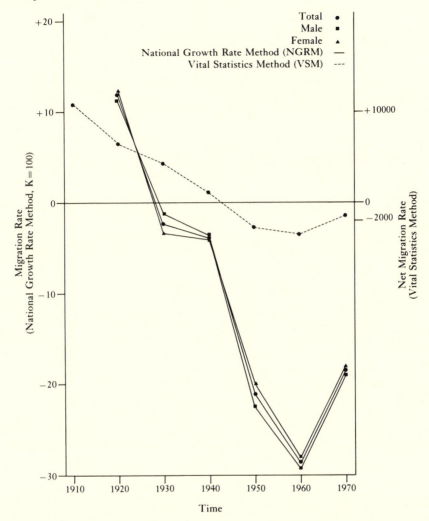

Figure 14. Migration and net migration rates: *horizontal axis,* time; *left axis,* migration rate via the national growth rate method (This method compares the growth rate of Hazleton to the growth rate of the rest of the country at a point in time. Values above 0 indicate a rate of growth exceeding the national average); *right axis,* migration via the vital statistics method. (This method compares the rate of natural increase in the community, births minus deaths, to the rate of population migration, the difference between natural increase, and total population growth. Values greater than 0 indicate that the rate of natural increase is less than the in-migration, whereas values less than 0 indicate that people are leaving faster than they are being replaced.) This graph compares the growth of Hazleton with the rest of the country and contrasts that growth with the dynamics of migration and natural increase in the community at the time. The methods of analysis are found in Shryock, Siegel, and Associates (1973).

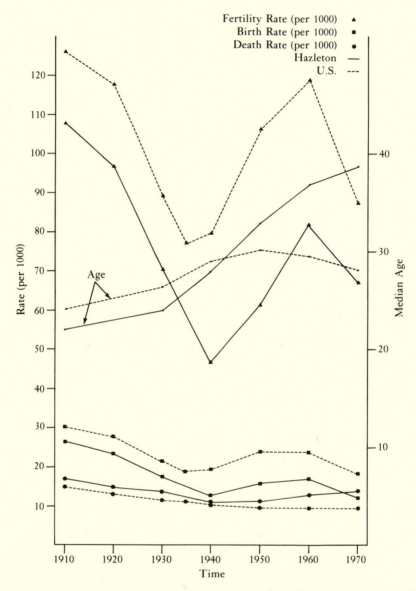

Figure 15. Birth, death, and fertility rates per 1,000 for Hazleton and the United States: *horizontal axis,* time; *left axis,* children less than 1 year old and deaths per 1,000, (birth rate, children less than 1 year old/1,000 general population; fertility rate, children less than 1 year/1,000 women ages 15–44; death rate, deaths/1,000 general population); *right axis,* median age for Hazleton and the United States, age in years. This graph compares several standard demographic indicators for Hazleton and the United States. Note especially the period from 1940 to 1970. The methods of analysis are found in Shryock, Siegel, and Associates (1973).

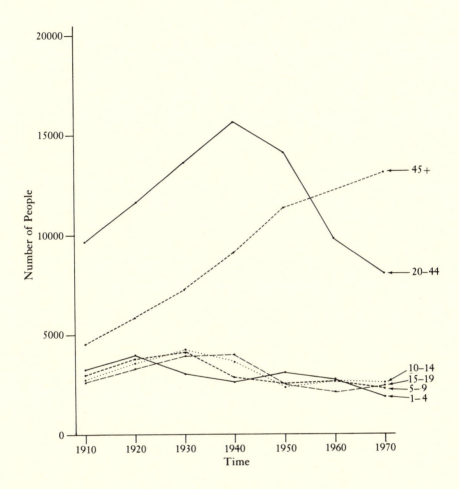

Figure 16. Age versus time: *horizontal axis*, time; *left axis*, number of people. This graph shows the dynamics of the age distribution in Hazleton over time. Note that those over age forty–five remain in the region, while those younger leave. The methods of analysis are found in Shryock, Siegel, and Associates (1973).

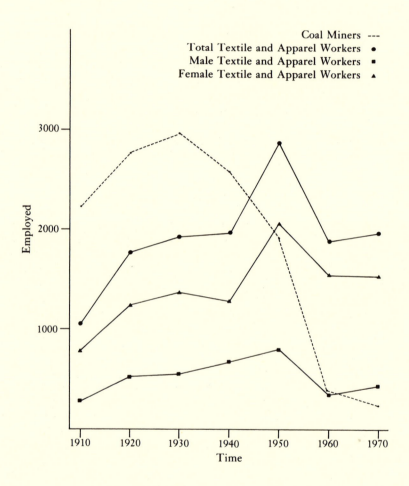

Figure 17. Number employed in textiles and mining, 1910–70: *horizontal axis,* time; *left axis,* number of people employed. This graph compares the number of people employed in the mines with the number employed by textile and garment trades. It also shows the predominance of female workers in the textile industries. The methods of analysis are found in Shryock, Siegel, and Associates (1973).

to which these industries had traditionally been attracted (Roscoe and Thuering 1958). A Bureau of Labor Statistics survey of wages revealed that Pennsylvania represented a veritable "sun belt" to the New England states, paying generally lower wages in all stages of clothing production (Bureau of Labor Statistics 1913). Hazleton was also convenient to major markets in New York City, and the rail transportation infrastructure offered cheap, efficient modes for the textiles and garment industries.

Efficiency in operation with the lowest possible overhead was the most important managerial and financial aspect of the textile and garment industries. These industries must maintain their ability to respond to rapid fluctuations in market tastes and demands on a seasonal basis. The convergence of conditions present in the coalfields made Hazleton a desirable location.

After the war, as more and more men became unemployed, the high, steady employment of women in clothing trades warned of imminent structural revolutions, long overdue since the decline of the anthracite industry. "Weekend husbands" became commonplace as men had to commute to other communities for work. Alternatively, women became the breadwinners, and their husbands began to take care of home and children (for similar conditions before 1850 in England, see Engels 1968: 162–65). The community, aging rapidly under the pressures for outmigration and facing increasing unemployment, was confronting the kinds of fluctuations capable of radically altering structure. In this case the end result threatened to be the near total depopulation of Hazleton.

The behavior of the long wave just before and just after 1920 resembles the rise and decline of anthracite during this same period. The wave, as evidenced in prices and interest rates, peaked in 1920. Just as a world depression followed the height of the wave in 1860, so a world-scale depression followed the peaking of the wave in 1920. (For an economic analysis of the causes, see Pinder 1976:328–29.) Furthermore, a major shift to the United States was occurring in the core-developed areas of the world-economy, and this added other fluctuations to the system, particularly in capital flows.

As with the second peak of the wave in 1860, two energy bases and two transportation modes, one new and one maturing, pushed the growth from the trough to the peak of the third wave. The two energy sources were coal and petroleum-derived gasoline; the transportation sector included the maturing mode, rails, and the newcomer, the gasoline-using automobile. During the rise of the wave the use of energy for rails, as registered in horsepower gains, increased 56 percent. The exponential growth, however, during the same decade was registered in the 833 percent gain in horsepower by the automobile. The shift in sectors from rail and coal energy sources to auto and petroleum energy supplies caused a massive dislocation that attended the shift of the developed economies to the United States. According to my hypothesis, the social order and the economic system of the modern world which had been created by rail and coal were giving way to the petroleum energy base.

New transportation structures, new settlement patterns, new control mechanisms, and new cultural forms evolved to meet this technological challenge.

The public sector in the twentieth century was very different from that of the nineteenth. The wealth that had been poured into the social system through the exploitation of coal and oil was taxed by the federal government, which was thus strengthened and grew in scale along with the industrial base. As a result, the twentieth century has witnessed a shift toward a service economy that was able to redistribute wealth widely through society. O'Connor has commented on this phenomenon. "But most important, there was a steady expansion of state expenditures and an increase in the number and variety of state economic functions. ... The evolution of the state budget as an increasing source of monopoly profits has gone hand in hand with the development of the state bureaucracy as the administrative arm of the giant corporations" (1974:113). The use of the control mechanisms in the public sector by the controlling interests in the private sector is partially explained by the energetics-based model. The growth of the public sector evolved as a response to the greater energy pumped into the system, and one of its major functions was to dampen the fluctuations brought about by the surge of energy inputs and the massive social and economic dislocations that this industrial process produced. Whole sectors of the economy have been rendered obsolete in the industrializing process, and new sectors have emerged that partially replace them. The anthracite industry remains one of the best examples, although one could cite the railroads in this country, the steel industry in France, and, perhaps, the American auto industry.

New public sector controlling institutions that directly affected anthracite country emerged during the rise of the third wave. The Interstate Commerce Commission and the Federal Trade Commission were two federal level agencies that, with Senate committees and subcommittees during the 1920s, regulated or altered aspects of the industry. Numerous commissions were convened that attempted to diagnose the ills of the industry in the public interest; examples include the 1902 U.S. Anthracite Strike Commission, the 1920 U.S. Anthracite Commission, the 1922–23 Federal Coal Commission, and the 1937 Pennsylvania Anthracite Coal Industry Commission. The Sherman Anti-Trust Act also served to dismember partially the anthracite industry after World War I.

A student of this period, James Weinstein, has shown how the largest corporate leaders formed an association they called the National Civic Federation (NCF):

> [It] ... took the lead in educating businessmen to the changing needs in political economy that accompanied the changing nature of America's business system. In its membership the National Civic Federation originated the principle of tripartite representation that was later to become a feature of various government boards and agencies. The Federation was organized in three nominal divisions, representing business, labor, and an undefined public. [1968:7]

The membership was composed of the top leaders of the labor organizations and the business community. Names such as Andrew Carnegie and John Mitchell of the United Mine Workers were included among bankers, other industrialists, and labor leaders. Not only did the NCF act as an educational vehicle for businessmen, but it actively wrote legislation and met with the highest government officials on matters of concern to its members. It sought to intervene and to anticipate more radical demands on the nation's political and economic systems; the strategy was to sponsor reforms in the capitalist system based on a consensus of the heads of the largest business and labor organizations. The point Weinstein made is that it was in the interests of the largest corporations, big labor, and a public they could identify to have the modern affluent state and its economy run with a minimum of turbulence from either the right or the socialist left. The interests of those controlling large banks and industries involved maximizing the efficiency of the system by writing the program for the control mechanism in the public sector. They were effective in accomplishing this in the matters of the Federal Trade Commission, workmen's compensation, and the Commission on Industrial Relations. Despite their successes, there were long battles, both within the private sector—especially among the large and small businessmen— and between the private and public sectors.

The uneasy relationship between the private controlling interests and the public controlling mechanisms was clearly evidenced in the anthracite industry. These relationships between public and private control over the energy conversion processes continually raised the question of civic responsibilities. The private sector in the United States sponsors profit making innovations and develops energy production; the national government, representing the citizens, must insure adequate care for the population. When the private sector fails, the public must step in with a remedy. During shifts in the energy sources this is particularly critical. At present the relations between corporations and government are intensifying, and corporations are dominating (Haefele 1979). I would argue that the swing toward industry as a more controlling voice is a function of the profound changes in the energy bases as a result of the incipient decline in world oil availability.

After the failure of the stock market in 1929, and the worsening economic situation, the federal government attempted to support the citizens by establishing a Works Progress Administration (WPA) during the Franklin D. Roosevelt administration. It was one of the first American efforts at large-scale planning, and, in this theory, the direct result of a major energy transition.

> The liberal planning impulse began with national goals that went quite beyond adequate profits, and included full employment, rising mass consumption, even public educational standards, health, nutrition. In this view the purpose was not simply the rescue of faltering industrial or economic sectors, but a broad national advance. [Graham 1977:25]

National wealth production made such an effort possible and even necessary, especially during the steep downturn of a highly developed economy.

The public sector at all levels was called upon during the demise of anthracite to respond to the deteriorating social conditions in the coalfields. The Pennsylvania Anthracite Coal Commission of 1937–38 not only initiated a major analysis of the ills plaguing the industry, but proposed a reconstruction of the region that sounded much like a contemporary body of ideas. The commission members borrowed the major outlines from the British, who had already faced similar problems in their coalfields; they urged that the coal operators that remained be regulated in the interest of steady employment for the workers, that new industries be attracted to "trading estates" (industrial parks) in the region, and that surplus workers be transferred in orderly fashion to other parts of the country where employment could be had. Public-private cooperation was central, if not explicitly recognized, and was considered essential to the success of regional economic recovery. Although the commission called for a complete reconnaissance of the region to establish its needs and future possibilities, it was never conducted. The new industrial development they prescribed, however, was implemented through other state and national mechanisms after the hiatus of World War II. The commission included in their list of proposals

> The establishment of local development boards in each of the important communities or sections; these boards to consist of local representatives of the business, labor and professional groups, and to cooperate with the state commissions in both the planning and the carrying out of plans affecting their particular localities. . . .
>
> In attempting to establish new industries in the areas where they are found to be needed, nothing should be done which would injure outside areas by attracting established industries therefrom. This would be merely "robbing Peter to pay Paul." But new industrial enterprises are being constantly started in Pennsylvania, and it would be perfectly proper to encourage these new enterprises to establish themselves in the anthracite areas. Indeed it would be a vast social gain if newly established plants and industries could be directed away from the larger cities of the State.
>
> The encouragement needed would, in some cases, almost certainly involve some financial incentive. This might take the form of favorable taxes, free or low cost land sites, and even monetary loans for reasonable periods. Also the possibility should be considered of having community factory sites, properly equipped with power, water and other conveniences, which could be let at low rentals to small manufacturing enterprises. [Anthracite Coal Commission 1938: 640–41]

In the 1950s the state legislature in Pennsylvania made it possible to acquire cheap money for industrial expansion, and many of the funds went to the anthracite region. Despite the rather embracing proposals of the commission, a much more modest public effort was made, largely through financial incentives.

Local development boards—although not called that—were in fact established in the coal region communities, and chapter 3 documents how those were organized and what they achieved in one particular case. These local boards, incorporated as nonprofit community organizations, were then able to manipulate both the private and the public sectors as their resources for controlling the flows of energy, material, messages, and employment, in their areas. They became local, miniature controlling mechanisms at the community level.

By 1940, the institutional frameworks of the public sector that emerged in the postwar period to aid in the growth spurt that attended the fourth rise of the long wave were largely in place. These were further elaborated after World War II in response to the petroleum energy sources used to generate the postwar prosperity of the 1950s and 1960s. Coal no longer employed significant numbers; in order to adapt to changing conditions in the private sector, the anthracite region had to explore relatively recent institutional structures established by the public sector.

OIL

A large sudden increase in oil prices would have serious indirect effects. It would exacerbate inflation, place further strains on the international monetary system, and sharply contract the demand for goods and services, further reducing national income. In short, the economic consequences would likely be a major recession, or possibly even a depression. [Stobaugh and Yergin 1979:5]

. . . although petroleum supplies somewhat more than half of the world's present consumption of industrial energy, and has been responsible for a large part of the development of the world's industrial societies, still it represents only a brief epoch in the longer span of human history. [Hubbert 1977:637]

The rise from 1900 of the use of oil for auto, truck, bus, airplane, and train engines helped push the economy to new levels of prosperity in the first decades of the twentieth century. By the post–World War II period, petroleum sources energized the takeoff of industrial production that gave the Western world its greatest moments of material affluence. This was the period of the fourth Kondratieff wave in the two-century growth frame of the Industrial Revolution. The changes that attended the introduction of petroleum into the world-system were unprecedented in an already rapidly developing world. As a result of the automobile, cities were completely redesigned and simultaneously packed more fully and expanded further than could have been imagined a century ago. With petroleum the world was no longer unified only by trade and the rather slow transmission of messages. The world economy was fueled by a common source, inexpensive oil. Interdependence was further intensified by a common dependence on diesel fuel and gasoline. The challenge to Hazleton, a city and a way of life built during the heyday of coal and rail, was to adapt to the new energy base or suffer, after World War II, even more massive depopulation and social disintegration.

The growth of horsepower in the transportation sector reveals the massive inputs of energy that fossil fuels offered the society (U.S. Census). In 1890 all primary movers in the United States, including work animals, factories, mines, railroads, merchant ships, sailing vessels, farms, windmills, and electrical generating plants, produced only 44,086,000 horsepower. Twenty years later, by 1910, the amount generated by the primary movers had more than tripled. Exponential growth of horsepower mirroring petroleum energy developments was linked to an economy that suffered from boom and bust fluctuations. By 1970 the total horsepower of these movers had accelerated to more than 20 billion with automobiles accounting for the astronomical amount of more than 19 billion. It has been indeed the age of the internal combustion engine.

By 1976 world production of crude petroleum had expanded to produce 2,863,518,000 metric tons (United Nations 1977:183). One of the more knowledgeable and accurate scientists in the petroleum field has placed these numbers in perspective.

> The systematic depletion of this stock pile (of oil) began in Rumania in 1857 and in the United States in 1859. Subsequently, the annual production rate from 1880 until 1973 increased exponentially at a yearly constant rate averaging 7 percent per year, and doubling every 10 years. The cumulative production has also been doubling approximately every 10 years so that the quantity of oil produced during the decade 1960 to 1970 was approximately equal to all of the oil produced from the beginning of oil production in 1857 to 1960. [Hubbert 1977:636]

Figures such as these indicate that the growth of the world-system was fueled in the last two decades by increasingly available quantities of oil.

The control mechanisms in the oil industry have always been highly concentrated. The U.S. government, under the aegis of the Sherman Anti-Trust Act of 1890, was able in 1911 to disassemble Standard Oil, a complex of American companies that in 1880 controlled from 90 to 95 percent of refining capacity in the country. But despite anti-trust actions during the 1920s the oil companies moved to integrate vertically, and, with the oil embargo of 1973–74, they integrated horizontally as well through the purchases of coal lands and coal companies. In the 1970s the Organization of Petroleum Exporting Countries (OPEC) and the Seven Sisters—the seven largest oil-producing corporations—began to dominate international production, distribution, and, therefore, prices of oil. The reason OPEC is the largest figure in the world energy picture is that it is a cartel that accounts for 90 percent of world exports; and Saudi Arabia, the most important member, accounts for 30 percent of this production and has 34 percent of its reserves (Stobaugh and Yergin 1979:-31). OPEC raised the price of crude oil sharply in 1979, an increase of 42 percent bringing the cost of a barrel of oil to an $18 to $23.50 range. Shortly after this increase, the U.S. prime interest rate climbed beyond 20 percent, breaking all previous record highs for two centuries. The increase in the interest rates in the United States fits with the Kondratieff wave and is another indicator that it is peaking in the 1970–80 period.

With Canada, the United States has been the highest per capita consumer of energy in the world. Although this country produces more than half of what it consumes in oil, it imports such vast quantities that the nation has become something of an international villain. The bill for oil imports into the United States in 1978 amounted to $39.2 billion. The imbalance in trade that U.S. oil imports induce has contributed to the serious weakening of the dollar, traditionally used as an international currency. The competition for oil between the superpowers U.S.S.R. and the United States is about to become more heated, according to Central Intelligence Agency (CIA) reports; one of the most difficult problems anticipated by business leaders, high ranking government officials, and academics is that there will be increased competition among the developed countries of Western Europe and the United States for declining supplies. This potential conflict could unravel alliances, disrupt trade, and lead to instabilities that are too massive to easily contemplate. For the United States the situation continues to deteriorate. Between 1970 and 1976 production of domestic supplies fell at an average rate close to 18 million metric tons annually (United Nations 1977:184).

The world-system has received two staggering shocks during the 1970s: the first was the Arab oil embargo of 1973–74, and the second was the OPEC price increase of 1979. These were two challenges to the energy bases of the world-system and, in political terms, to the security of the West. There have been many results, although few long-term remedies have been successfully enacted by the oil-dependent developed countries. One rather weak control mechanism that was triggered by the embargo was the annual economic summit meeting convened by the noncommunist industrialized countries: Canada, the Federal Republic of Germany, France, Italy, Japan, the United Kingdom, and the United States. Member nations of the 1979 summit held in Tokyo issued a communique that included the phrase, "We are agreed on a common strategy to attack these problems. The most urgent tasks are to reduce oil consumption and to hasten the development of other energy sources" (*New York Times,* 30 June 1979). Despite the expression of laudable sentiment, there is little evidence that there is a unified attack on the problem, which is to find and install a safe, inexpensive petroleum substitute. By way of stop-gap measures, inducements are offered to corporations in the attempt to extend the petroleum reliance by developing synthetic fuels from tar sands, shales, and coals (see Stobaugh and Yergin 1979:101, for the emergent relations between companies and government in these operations). There is no coordinated, unified attack on critical problems associated with a change in the energy basis of world societies. France, for example, continues to firm up an energy policy that relies on nuclear reactors, thereby hoping to unhinge its economy from a reliance on imported fossil fuels (Zaleski 1979:849–51). Countries such as the United States cannot pursue this path. The major reason is that the general public has misgivings and that vocal anti-nuclear groups oppose a nuclear strategy.

A growth industry in articles, books, and reports by business and government has been one response in the United States to the shocks of increased oil costs and incipient scarcity. Reserves of fossil fuels, and alternatives, especially the synfuels, are being discussed, and some of the implications for society are gingerly explored. The most definite state-ment to date has emerged from the Harvard Business School in the form of a comprehensive four-year analysis conducted by Stobaugh, Yergin, and others (1979). Not being discussed to any extent are the implications of a major energy transition for human communities. The potential for warfare between opposing superpowers contending for scarce oil, for severe strain between allies among the developed countries, or for a world depression that would be even larger in scale than those following the two previous peaks in the Kondratieff wave, has not been the subject of serious public debate. While none of these events seems necessary, they do seem highly probable. Although second guessing these possibilities lies beyond the scope of ethnographic reporting and theory building, they are of moment to the student of human communities who seeks to understand the humble role of community economies and social organi-zation within the world-system.

Hubbert in a convincing, disinterested analysis (figure 18) has pro-vided a chart that shows the peaking of oil production in the late 1990s. Taking into account the political realities of the troubled Middle East, Stobaugh and Yergin predict a turbulent period confronting the world before 1990, when the actual decline of oil supplies would otherwise set in. Hubbert concludes, "Hence, if the world petroleum industry un-dergoes an orderly growth and decline in the future, the peak in the production rate will probably be reached in the 1990-decade and children born in the 1960s will see the world consume most of its oil during their lifetimes" (1977:637). One can only conclude from the best analyses being made at present that the energy basis of the contemporary world-system is giving out. New adaptive strategies are being evolved by the world industrial machine and its associated political entities that will self-organize to meet the challenges. The fluctuations attending this transi-tion promise to be of a high magnitude, involving, as a result of their centrality in the energy base of the system, the whole world and its peoples.

From 1985 to 2000 energy resources available to the United States will not match previous supplies. In his analysis of this time period, Hayes concluded,

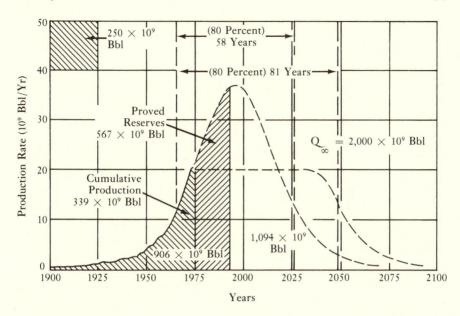

Figure 18. The Hubbert estimates of the complete cycle of world oil production. SOURCE: Hubbert (1977:644)

The facts point to the inescapable conclusion that exponential growth of energy supply is coming to an end in the United States. Energy and gross national product have risen 3 to 3 1/2 percent a year since 1940, and a decrease in the energy growth rate to less than 1 percent a year by 2000 will occasion some fundamental national problems for which we have no precedent. The involuntary conservation brought on by higher prices and decreased supplies will be exceedingly painful for an unprepared American public. [1979:239]

This diagnosis points to the new ecological challenge that faces us all: our successful adaptation to the planet as a species in a period of painful transition.

Hazleton was studied close to the peaking of the fourth long wave. The subsequent analysis documents the emergence of local control mechanisms that evolved during the rise of the wave. These mechanisms enabled them to adapt themselves and the relevant public and private institutions to meet the local impacts of the shift from coal to oil. Their experience illustrates what many communities during the period could do and what many in fact did. The strategies employed by the business and professional people of Hazleton mountain should be useful in understanding the scope and the limitations that communities have in adjusting themselves and their local economies and environments to the larger movements of the world-economy.

Drifton in 1979. Drifton is the coal mining village where the Coxes made their home. Contrast the houses of the miners on this street with the doctor's house. (Photograph by the author)

The doctor's house in Drifton in 1979. The contrast between the doctor's and miners' houses indicates the extreme stratification found in coalfield society. The doctor's house was obviously palatial by the standards of the tiny patchtown house. (Photograph by the author)

Child labor in hard coal country. Child labor as a national problem included children working in southern knitting mills and newsboys in New York City. The photographer Louis Hine visited the anthracite region in 1911, and these pictures and others were used to reveal the abuse of children in coal country. These boys lived like men—gambling, smoking, and drinking—and were often considered not as children but as severe social problems. (Photograph by Louis Hine, courtesy of the National Archives)

Anthracite deep-mining operation during World War II. The war years cast a false sense of well-being over the mining communities. Wartime production hid the fact that anthracite as a fuel was in a deep decline despite the war. Associated with breakers such as these are the railroads and electrical energy. The fortunes of both the railroads and the power companies in the anthracite areas were all too closely linked to the fate of coal use. (Photograph courtesy of the National Archives)

Sorting coal during World War II. The increase in mechanization had helped put the children out of the labor force, but some tasks still require a human touch. Photographs like this one were used in Washington D.C. as fact-finding material to discover the sources of labor unrest that plagued even the wartime effort. (Photograph courtesy of the National Archives)

Fern Glen. In this patchtown the local school was turned into a knitting mill (far right). Women walk to work from their homes nearby, and when they have problems with their children the proximity to home allows them to deal with their domestic demands while holding their jobs. The local knitting mills have done much to stabilize the population in the region. Before the paved roads were put in, these patchtowns were remote from shopping and medical services available in Hazleton, now one-half hour away by automobile. (Photograph by the author)

3

COMMUNITY

The frenzied pace of life in industrial towns, characterized by sudden and unpredictable stops and starts, reflects the linkage of human lives to machines and to the fickle demands of a distant economic market place. Every human community has a specific character, identity, a certain manner of existence, in which its long-term residents also partake, accepting as their own its problems and virtues. In the evolutionary development of human kind, each new type of community—primitive, rural agricultural, urban industrial, suburban, etc.—is a crucible in which forms a new kind of human being and a new kind of social conscience.

MacCannell (1977:208)

Beyond their multiplicity, the processes of re-creation and renewal possess one common characteristic: they operate both on the social universe and on nature, their actors are both men and their gods.

Balandier (1970:110)

It has been said that it takes a crisis to produce great leadership.

CAN DO (1974:37)

THE COLLAPSE OF ANTHRACITE

At the close of World War II, the young men of Hazleton returned home with profound pride in their country's response to the challenges of global warfare, and to the human issues of freedom versus totalitarianism. What they discovered when they returned, however, was a region in deep decline. Northeastern Pennsylvania was depressed economically; the area was becoming depopulated; and communities, families, and individuals were in states of disorganization and demoralization. Although the causes seemed obscure and remote to the local citizens, the decline of the anthracite industry reflected the energy transition.

Bitter indictments of the anthracite industry had been expressed through the twentieth century (Jones 1914; Nearing 1915). These only partially penetrated the deeper problems of the economy's growth and the energy transition. Morris Ernst, in his investigative Coal Commission

Report, claimed that the reason for the decline of anthracite coal since 1917 could be explained thus: "Anthracite has not met the challenge of other competitive fuels in this country" (1937:8). He then analyzed the railroads that held monopolies, the labor situation, and the production and distribution processes, and he concluded, "I am persuaded that the decline in the consumers' market is more a reflection of deficiencies in the structure of the industry than of any other factor, and may be corrected in substantial degree through the removal of those deficiencies" (1937:14). He was right; anthracite could not compete in the relatively uncontrolled market situation where oil and electricity systems were more rewarding to investors and convenient to consumers. But it was not the structure of the industry alone that accounted for its demise. Post-mortems of the industry continued until the 1960s, and the late ones included the observation that the coal industry spent insignificant amounts on research and development, as opposed to other industries. "Before 1951, it is doubtful that expenditures for coal research amounted to as much as 0.5% of annual sales volume at any time" (Shapp and Jurkat 1962:5). What these analyses and critiques have missed are the secular causes of industrial decline found in the energetic shifts of the larger industrial system at the world level.

For the people of Hazleton, the declining mine production added insult to injury. The strong ethnic communities with their powerful family ties witnessed the brief return of children who would have to turn around and leave the region again to find employment because even the older workers were being laid off. The figures for all the anthracite fields corresponded to the subjective sense of the citizens (table 7).

The temporary boom of production during the war years was over, and, from 1940 to 1950, the decline in direct employment affected more than 15,000 men. The drop in employment was a regional fluctuation that could not be absorbed by other regional industries. Every community in

T A B L E 7
Production, Employment, and Fatalities in
the Anthracite Fields 1920–50

Year	Production (net tons)	Employment	Fatalities
1920	89,636,036	149,117	490
1930	68,776,559	151,171	444
1940	51,526,454	90,790	182
1950	46,339,255	75,231	86

SOURCE: Pennsylvania Department of Mines and Mineral Industries, Anthracite Division, Annual Report, 1968. Harrisburg, 1969

Jeddo-Highland Coal Company stripping operation at Jeddo. Jeddo-Highland is the largest coal company in the anthracite fields and the large stripping machine, which is mining the Mammoth vein, was the largest mining machine built at the time. Usually these machines are given names like "Anthracite King," but this monster has no nickname; perhaps it is too large. (Photograph courtesy of CAN DO)

Abandoned breaker and culm banks. The devastation of the coalfields is certainly a reason why there is no tourism in the hard coal country. These culm banks also represent ecological devastation, for they continue to leach acids into the ground and surface waters, and they are extremely slow to acquire vegetation. There has been almost no cosmetic reclamation of the anthracite fields. When abandoned mines are reclaimed it is for an airport or shopping mall or some other commercial construction. (Photograph by the author)

the anthracite region was changed, and these conditions persisted in the following years. In April of 1962 Luzerne County registered 10.5 percent unemployment, and, during the 1950s, unemployment in the region had never fallen below 10 percent. In 1962, two analysts observed, "Unemployment compensation is the major single source of income for the Scranton-Wilkes-Barre district, totalling $28,500,000 in 1961" (Shapp and Jurkat 1962:31). It is impossible to estimate accurately the social service costs to the public of the decline of the private sector in this region. This type of accounting, however, should become a matter of public record and subsequent energy extraction policy; it is not at all clear how the costs of an extraction industry are distributed. Decline wounds most deeply the local people, although the rest of the society also pays through the tax system.

The atrophy of controlling mechanisms, formerly associated with the trusts held by the Morgan interests, is also very much in evidence. The Morgan capital was invested in other energy (Derganc 1979:50–59) and resource sectors, and the anthracite situation deteriorated. As the old line companies drifted into receivership, small owner-operators bought land and equipment. In decline, the anthracite fields went from the large-scale controlling corporations in New York and Philadelphia to a greater number of smaller operators. One Department of Energy official characterized the present ownership situation in the coalfields as mere cottage industries. These remain viable due partially to the technological advances that have substituted capital and sophisticated machinery for labor. An interview from the fieldwork provides an illustration.

> Mr. Pagnotti is a second-generation member of the family which bought the coal lands administered by the trusteeship of the Daniel Coxe estate. Jeddo-Highland Coal Company was incorporated in 1964 to exploit the coal remaining on these lands, which all had previously been surface- and deep-mined.
>
> In 1966 Jeddo-Highland procured their present complement of heavy dragline equipment, including a mammoth 85-cubic-yard machine equipped with a 300-foot boom. This $8 million machine has 400 feet of cable and 350 feet of drag. It has enabled them to effectively revolutionize the strip mining process in the anthracite fields. With previous generation machinery (approximately 25 cubic yards), the stripping process followed the outcropping vein downward until the depth of the overburden made it uneconomical to proceed deeper. This produced a typical pattern of longitudinal strip cuts paralleling the strike of the coal basins. High piles of overburden material were an unavoidable consequence of this process. This level of technology also prevented the miner from reaching the rich Mammoth vein which was 25 to 40 feet thick over most of the field and in places reached 100 feet.
>
> Equipment of the 85-cubic-yard magnitude has permitted exploitation of the coal remaining in the Mammoth Vein, and in some situations the Buck Mountain Vein, lying 125 feet deeper, can also be mined. Mining in this manner will result in the most complete

removal of available coal reserves. In fact, the sum total of all the coal being mined is the polar and barrier remnants of the previous deep mining operations (the residual 35 to 50 percent of the vein left to support the surface).

With larger equipment, the mining is done in a transverse fashion across the coal basin. The dragline sits in the bottom of the pit. As it removes overburden lying above the vein (up to 400 feet deep), it rotates 180 degrees and drops the spoil material behind. The result can be near-concurrent backfilling—as the cut is opened in the direction of stripping operations, a relatively flat terrain is left which poses less of an erosion problem.

Although the Jeddo-Highland Coal Company is the largest regionally, in 1974 the company payroll was only 3 million dollars; there were 350–400 employees, and there were approximately 600,000 net tons produced. The whole Hazleton mountain coalfields may not have had 600 mine workers at that time. The veterans of the war, including the workers, the local professionals, and businessmen, could find no future in anthracite and related industries or services. It seemed that all too many of those remaining in the region were suffering from black lung disease or were widows of those who had died from it.* The employment that remained was in the labor intensive, female-employing textile plants, and the pull from the southern United States, Taiwan, and Latin American development platforms was already being felt as companies were moving.

The landscape was visually devastated by overburden. A degraded environment limited some alternative possibilities for the region, such as tourism. Ecological destruction has attended the mining of anthracite, often in ways that could not have been foreseen. Unlike some of the bituminous fields, the anthracite fields have no large mine reclamation projects despite enabling legislation and the promise of money from the state and federal agencies. Subsidence has continuously plagued the coalfields, a remnant of deep mining. In recent years the built-up areas have experienced fewer cases of houses and cars disappearing into deep holes that suddenly open. The U.S. Bureau of Mines has taken preemptive measures to abate subsidence by flushing. They have had to fill mines with culm, particularly under Scranton, to prevent catastrophic collapse beneath residential areas.

One unforeseen problem may be the most serious: mines have recently become the favored dumping ground for extremely toxic chemical wastes. Due to the large number of chemical firms and the high cancer rate in New Jersey, the New Jersey legislature has enacted stiff penalties for illegal hazardous waste disposal. Because Pennsylvania does not have comparable penalties, chemical disposal companies truck the residue to the relatively isolated, orphaned coalfields and dump the waste into the

---

*This observation is based on interview material. The data on black lung payments to the Hazleton region recipients were unavailable in 1979 because the federal agency in charge of payments was being reorganized, and the offices were being physically moved.

abandoned mine openings. Most of the coalfields were, like Hazleton mountain, tunneled early in the century to lower the water table and to permit deeper mining. Now the industrial wastes move rapidly through the geological formations in the coalfields, through the abandoned mine tunnels and into the streams that drain the region.

In terms of ecological-human damage, the most severely impacted natural resource may be the Susquehanna River. The Susquehanna is an extensive watershed that stretches from the fingerlake region of New York to the Chesapeake Bay, the largest estuary in the United States. Because estuaries are the most productive natural areas in the world, and because the Chesapeake Bay, already suffering from the effects of industry and shipping, is a major source of shellfish and crab on the eastern seaboard, disasters on the Susquehanna can directly affect the quality of marine life downstream. Recently toxic chemicals from an unknown location were released from mine drainage tunnels into the Susquehanna and formed an extremely toxic and potentially explosive slick thirty-five miles long. Workers attempting to clean up the hazard had to wear protective gear. Some of the chemicals, including dichlorobenzene, were found in the drinking water of the river towns. It is not the individual incidents of human-induced ecological disaster that cause outrage; it is their additive nature, which contributes to the dramatic increase in human cancers, social disruption, and ecocatastrophe.

CHALLENGE OF TRANSITION

The long Kondratieff wave in the advanced industrial economies is a critical fluctuation that responds to the periodic transition from one complex of energy sources and technology to another. The transition is in response to scarcity or replacement of energetic sources on which the production systems of the core, developed areas of the world-system depend. [Adapted from chapter 1]

World War II was anomalous to the pattern of the Kondratieff wave, for when the long fluctuation should have reached the trough, the world plunged more deeply into war, thereby stimulating production. Despite this aberration in the cyclical behavior of the world-system, the postwar period realized the more expected peacetime upswing. (See figures 9 and 10.)

The rise and decline of anthracite nicely coincides with the third great cycle in the modern capitalist period. Taking anthracite in the economy as one sector of the energy-technology complex, there is an obvious relationship between the rise of anthracite production and consumption, its subsequent decline, and the third Kondratieff wave. This tends to confirm the hypothesis that heads this section that the wave is a response to the changing energy-technology base of the production system and that the decline of anthracite reflected the transition.

At the local level, the transition was characterized by turbulence and a search for means of reversing failing fortunes by members of the con-

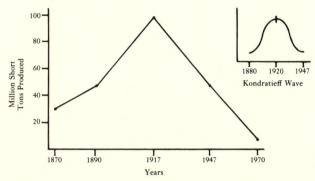

Figure 19. Anthracite production and the Kondratieff wave

trolling institutions, such as the Chamber of Commerce. With the withdrawal of anthracite production, much of the social power of the region eroded. The company towns were no longer owned by the companies because the old coal companies no longer existed. In the case of the severe decline faced by this region, it became a question whether or not ways could be found to reverse the catastrophe of massive unemployment and lack of opportunity. The social power that remained in the coalfield communities at this time lay concentrated in the urban places—such as Hazleton, Wilkes-Barre, and Scranton—and among the remaining banks, businesses, small manufacturers, and service firms. Adams has commented, "The establishment of concentration of power at higher levels of organization is a direct way to harness and release ever greater amounts of energy" (1975:121). With the coal companies effectively gone, the local community, which had been evolving since the nineteenth century, often in conflict with the economic hegemony of the coal companies, was thrust suddenly into prominence. For the first time in the Appalachian mountain hard coal country there was not that powerful brooding presence that defined the lives of its inhabitants. The challenge that faced the businessmen of the coal cities was to step in and concentrate the power they did have at higher levels of organization or else disband. They had to pick up what the exodus of king coal had left in the aftermath. In Adams's phrase, if they were able to organize at higher levels they would be able to harness and release ever greater amounts of energy.

Adams defines social power in terms of energy, and it is appropriate in examining Hazleton to employ his definition. He explains, "Social power, the ability to get somebody else to do what you want him to do through your control over energetic processes of interest to him, is the central issue in all these organization processes" (1975:121). When I use the words "controlling institution," I mean a locus where social power has accumulated. The business people of the anthracite cities, particularly those offering goods and services directly to households, began to integrate at higher levels of self-consciousness and organization. Through their organizational achievements and their self-awareness, a kernel of consolidated social power emerged. In the Hazleton interviews, it became evident that the business people realized there would be no households to sell services and commodities to if they did not organize to find employment for those who were out of work. After World War II, the local business people of city after city in the anthracite region moved to acquire social power by controlling specific energetic processes, in efforts to maintain their own position and consolidate it.

By acquiring new job sources, they generated sources for their own social power over consumers of the region. The new burst of postwar economic growth was in the air, but those returning to Hazleton were faced with a history of dissolution. The local decline was a marked contrast to the new set of expectations rising to match an incipient upturn of the economy.

All the segments of the regional social system were challenged by the permanent erosion of the coal mining way of life with its unmarketable resources system, outmoded technology, obsolete controlling institutions in the form of the large line corporations, and a rapidly changing community organized structure which was disorganized in part through out-migration.

This challenge confronts all resource extraction regions at some time, as well as those industrial areas associated with that particular resource. It is particularly acute at present in Wales, where deep coal mining has exhausted reserves (Rees 1978). The western coal lands and the Texas oil fields promise one day to become declining regions, subject to similar dramatic population shifts and community disorganization. The decline will occur as the particular technology-energy system that in the main generates the settlements in those regions is rendered obsolete or exhausts the resource.

Communities, too, are dissipative structures, and as the energetic sources available to them are reduced, the effects will be manifest in unemployment and disorganization of local institutions. Old elites slough off, settlement patterns are modified, and the land uses undergo transformation. These processes are presently occurring in the United States in steel towns and in cities whose economies are dependent on automobile assembly lines.

1947–1955

By 1947 the business leaders of Hazleton were convinced that the anthracite industry was not going to recover, that other options had to be sought, and that they were the people who were going to have to do it. Their vehicle was the Chamber of Commerce, an institution that had been incorporated in the United States since 1912 with the explicit goal of encouraging business and manufacturing in the local communities. The Chamber is designed organizationally along the lines of a trade association. There are chapters in most American cities that contribute dues to the national umbrella organization that coordinates the local organizations, sets goals, serves as an information conduit, produces public relations and advertising, and, most importantly, represents the interests of Chamber members in lobbying efforts in the U.S. Congress. Its political and economic impact is great at the national level; and, at the local level, the Chamber often plays the vital role of protecting a community's economic interests when they are threatened. When new possibilities arise, the local chapter can quickly mobilize to seize the day if it is aggressive.

So it was the Hazleton Chamber of Commerce that monitored closely the changing economic conditions after World War II. Because they were in the communication network of a national organization, local members were very much aware of the emerging possibilities for economic growth elsewhere in the country. Their first major institutional effort after the war was to capture new facilities being planned by major corporations expanding to meet increasing peacetime market demand. The Hazleton Chamber heard that Electric Auto-Lite, a midwestern corporation, was going to be adding facilities in the East, and they sent a delegation to interview the president of the company and sell him on the advantages of moving to Hazleton. The Hazleton businessmen described their predicament eloquently:

> The Hazletonians soon discovered, however, that they were apparently in a most disadvantageous position. Hazleton was located in the center of a mountain wilderness, Hazleton was *not* a main rail line; Hazleton was *not* on a main highway artery; Hazleton was *not* a port or on an inland waterway; Hazleton was *not* on a scheduled airline route. In fact, Hazleton seemed to be one of the least likely places for a manufacturer to place a plant. [CAN DO 1974:5]

These points were made painfully clear to the Hazleton delegation by the executives of the Auto-Lite company. The delegation responded by pointing out the immense regional pool of labor; it was the one major resource that they could guarantee. The company bargained hard and suggested that, despite the disincentives of no roads, rails, waterways, or airplanes, they would seriously consider locating there if the Chamber raised half a million dollars toward the cost of a new plant. In turn, it was projected that Auto-Lite would employ about 1,000 workers. This prospect looked extremely promising to the Hazleton business people, and they returned determined to launch a fund drive to raise the money for payment to Auto-Lite.

In their exuberance, the fundraisers exceeded their goal by $150,000 and created the Hazleton Industrial Development Corporation on a nonprofit basis, to administer the additional money. With it they launched a new industrial development program. They returned to Auto-Lite with the half million dollars, and the company agreed to locate in Hazleton if their specifications for a new plant could be met. The Hazleton money, in the form of a gift to the company, provided the down payment on the new facility. The remainder of the $1.6 million project was financed by local banks. The project nevertheless ran into many difficulties: the deed to the property took eight months to clear; the architect had no experience with a project of this scale; the workmen were not properly coordinated; Auto-Lite altered its own design criteria twice; and when Auto-Lite moved into the plant, fewer than 300 jobs were created. The feelings of the local business people were documented:

> While Auto-Lite became a solid member of the economic base of the community, contributing a million dollars a year in payroll and direct expenditures in the community, it had been so enthusiastically oversold as the salvation to Hazleton's unemployment problems, and had taken so long to get into operation, that the disappointment of the people became a disillusionment that lasted for nearly a decade. [CAN DO 1974:6–7]

This brief case illustrates the rising and falling expectations that are an integral part of the turbulence of transitional periods. The experience with Auto-Lite was discouraging, and the next six years, until 1955, witnessed further regional decline. A mood of desperation hung over the coalfields and their cities. Efforts continued but were more muted and in different directions. Through lobbying efforts, Chamber members were able in 1955 to acquire an airline route in Hazleton—Allegheny Airlines. This success was mitigated in August of that year by an unpredictable and wholly unexpected ecocatastrophe. Hurricane Diane struck, flooding the remaining deep mines; as a result, they were abandoned by the companies and permanently closed. In the devastation 179 people were killed, 6,992 were injured, and in Pennsylvania alone, 88 died and 94 suffered major injuries. More than 800 homes were destroyed in the Northeast, and in Pennsylvania it was estimated that $70 million damage was inflicted. The American National Red Cross responded with aid given directly to 14,723 families and insurance companies reported property claims for 1.5 billion dollars (*New York Times*, 31 October 1955).

Local catastrophe often has one of two major effects. Either it destroys the remains of a community and its integrity, or it offers a powerful challenge for the creation of new efforts, new community structures. In the wake of either human-induced or nature-induced disasters, new organizations are brought to life that later become integrated into the community as an ongoing component of its organizational structure.

Ecocatastrophe can be a triggering mechanism that stresses existing community social formation and demands a new self-organizing response. The people of Hazleton responded after witnessing in the winter of 1955 the ghost town appearance of the city with its vacant storefronts and proliferating For Sale signs. Again, it is worth quoting CAN DO to see its members' vision for the community.

> But a small corps of merchants and professional men had faith that somehow by working through the Chamber of Commerce, they could turn the tide. After a careful review of the situation, it was determined that the first priority should be to obtain land that could

be developed for industrial use. At the same time, it was determined that all of the people of the community should become active participants. It had to be a true community effort. [CAN DO 1974:7]

The membership of the Chamber formed a project called Operation Jobs-Dime-A-Week Fund with the goal of creating an industrial base in an industrial park to replace the moribund anthracite industry in the Eastern Middle coalfields surrounding Hazleton.

Operation Jobs got started despite a community-wide pessimism about the benefits of fund-raising, for the modest Auto-Lite contribution to their economy was very much in everyone's memory. It had become obvious that the community could not afford to raise and spend $500,000 per industry with uncertain benefits accruing. But it seemed that there was no other way to turn around the economy of the region, given the constraints of the closed coal mines and the opportunities presented by the rapidly growing, decentralizing industrial firms seeking to locate along the megalopolitan corridor near markets.

Several methods were used to capture public consciousness for the fund drive. Public places were used to collect money in lunch pail collectors, the local newspapers and radio stations publicized the efforts, and the associations of the city were all canvassed for donations. People placed their collected dimes on the center strip of the main street and created a dramatic mile of dimes. It was an emotional time in the region. Committees were formed by the Chamber members to insure that public places had coin boxes for donations, and that associations were contacted. The media ran stories and insured that the whole campaign was foregrounded in the public consciousness. The structure of the effort is diagrammed in figure 20. The flow of information as meaningful messages moved from the regional business and professional elite outward to com-

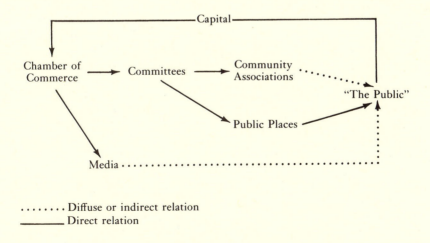

Figure 20. Capturing public consciousness

munity organizations that in turn contacted their constituents, who were in fact the public that the media captured with their publicity. The owners of the media were Chamber members, and there was a common interest among members in seeing the success of the fund-raising campaign.

Eight percent of the regional population were actively registered as having donated to the Dime-A-Week campaign, and as a result $14,000 was raised. The money was allocated to purchase a plot of ground for an industrial park. A public meeting was called and the plans discussed; the audience overwhelmingly approved the purchase of 500 acres for industrial development purposes. Thus the Chamber was able to organize information, capital, land, community support, and *esprit* for the purposes of exchanging local labor for industrial firm employers.

Two points can be made that illustrate the theory being applied:

1. The Hazleton region can be understood as a dissipative structure far from equilibrium, requiring constant inputs of energy (employers) to keep from disintegrating, and, in effect, dying as a sociocultural entity.
2. The Chamber of Commerce, by acquiring social power, acted as an emerging control mechanism to direct new flows of information and energy. It organized segments of the community into a structure to function for the purposes of creating capital, land, and labor resources that could be exchanged outside the system for new energy inputs (industrial employers). These efforts illustrate the self-organizing feature of living systems.

To refer again to Prigogine, as the system was challenged, it organized itself to respond in new, creative, and unpredictable ways. This act of self-organization has been called autocatalysis and autopoesis, the act of self-making.

In 1956 the major search behavior in the system had reached a turning point. Rather than spend time in casting about for ways to revive the region, the Chamber members were on the verge of an organizational breakthrough developing around a firm goal, to create an industrial park employment base. All the work to achieve that goal had yet to be done, but the broad outlines were discerned. The city and its immediate hinterland were now at a threshold: money could still be raised, the community could be organized, land was available, and firms could be recruited.

There were several features that had to be changed before the threshold could be crossed and the new system organization realize the fruit of its efforts:

At this time, industrial development activity of the Chamber and HDIC continued primarily as a salvaging operation. A textile firm and an apparel manufacturer were saved from "moving south" by loans for plant rehabilitation and with the cooperation of the business community and labor organizations. HDIC purchased sewing machines and made possible facilities for the retraining of unemployed coal miners to operate modern sewing equipment. [CAN DO 1974:8]

They had to move beyond salvage operations, and they had to have a permanent organizational apparatus to insure the resources of land, capital, community support, in addition to the labor to exchange for inmoving industries with their salaries, local taxes, and local purchases. This organizational component had to be constructed in direct response to new energy conditions that it was being designed to exploit. As it was historically constituted, the Chamber of Commerce did not provide this structure. With such an apparatus the Chamber members could consciously intervene in the viability of their region; unattended, the region would have become more ghostly. This intervention process was quite complex and took place entirely within the ideological framework of the capitalist, free enterprise system. The next section takes up the structure, functioning, and fluctuations in the new system that emerged in numerous communities in the anthracite region, but, in many ways, most successfully in Hazleton.

STRUCTURE

The year 1956 witnessed the coalescence of the organizational structure that had been evolving to capitalize upon the shift in the energetic bases of society. It was called CAN DO—Community Area New Development Organization—a name that was found for the acronym after the acronym was coined. CAN DO stood for self-help and self-organizing efforts and was consciously designed to express the strong intent and powerful community efforts to achieve a new economic base for the area. The Chamber of Commerce had provided an institutional collective memory and learning system for monitoring the economic climate for possibilities after the war. Through a series of self-help attempts, it had learned as a body much about methods for achieving its goals. In general systems theory, the Chamber of Commerce was the black box, a guidance system that attempted to get the local economic system on a new course and keep it there. In energetic terms CAN DO was organizing at higher levels of integration to direct and release ever greater amounts of energy. Chamber members' knowledge of where energetic sources were had increased, and they were developing institutional forms and strategies to manipulate them.

The CAN DO people were made up of a part of the regional elite. In general terms they were the most active Chamber members who had offices and firms selling directly to the public. The major organizers were members of the medical and legal professions, small manufacturers, contractors, bankers, large merchants, media people from radio and newspaper, and executives from utilities and services. As part of their corporate duties, these executives were expected to be good corporate citizens and to do everything in their power to help local communities achieve economic growth, thus providing customers for the corporation. Local segments of the city and region who were not included in Chamber activities were the remaining coal company owners, smaller merchants, and public officials from the city or minor civil divisions. Thus it was the private sector, directly involved in sales to the public, that acquired the necessary social power to organize at this new, higher level of integration.

There was no real internal competition evident between sectors of the city business people; there was rather an air of cooperation. At the very worst there was indifference to the CAN DO efforts. The real competition lay between cities. Intercity rivalry is old and very real in the United States, and it has an economic and environmental basis. The economies of cities depend on attracting and keeping industry or other energy bases such as government regional offices—hence the rivalry (Love 1977: 33, 39). One informant from CAN DO reported that for each corporation seeking to build a new factory or relocate there were ten other communities competing for the facility. The competition by local communities for energetic sources is illustrated by this observation. One of the nearby competitors for economic growth was the other small mountain city of Freeland to the east of Hazleton. Freeland had been the other free town on Hazleton mountain during the heyday of the coal companies. Freeland, too, attempted to adopt the Hazleton strategy embodied in CAN DO, but it failed. A much more direct challenge to the Hazleton strategy came from Wilkes-Barre, north across the Nescopeck Mountain, and from Scranton to the northeast. The business people of these cities had diagnosed their problems similarly and were attempting similar self-help efforts that would enable them to meet the challenges of the new energy resource period.

The strategies that CAN DO was evolving to attract employers for the regionally unemployed—so that customers would be provided to purchase the goods and services offered by Chamber members—was designed entirely within the prevailing folk model. A folk model is the set of assumptions about the way the world works which is held by the people whom the social scientist investigates. Rappaport makes a similar distinction in ecological anthropology employing the term *cognized models.*

> I have suggested elsewhere that two models of the environment are significant in ecological studies, and I have termed these the "operational" and the "cognized." The operational model is that which the anthropologist constructs through observation and measurement of empirical entities, events, and material relationships. . . . The cognized model is the model conceived by the people who act in it. The two models are overlapping, but not identical. [1968:237–38]

The CAN DO version of itself and its activities is a folk model that includes a cognized model of their environment, the native view, so to speak. The operational or social scientific model used here to analyze and explain CAN DO strategic behavior and accomplishments is not the model it would employ. This distinction is very important, for to confuse folk and scientific models of description, analysis, and explanation can only lead to disorientation and misunderstanding. Anthropologists, perhaps more than other social scientists, are careful to make this distinction and are extremely careful to construct or take into account insofar as possible the interior, native standpoint, the folk models of their subjects, for purposes of theoretical explanation. Rappaport makes an additional valuable analytical point: "I shall therefore only suggest here that if cognized models are important components of control mechanisms their consideration in evolutionary as well as functional studies is warranted" (1968:241). CAN DO represented a control mechanism that developed strategies to keep the regional economy of Hazleton within a set or range of values while capitalizing on new energy sources after the war. Two of the values, from the standpoint of the business people, were a capitalist desire for profits and the preservation of community.

The strategies of the CAN DO men were initiated within a prevalent, pervasive folk model; it was rational from the perspective of the business people of Hazleton. Their folk model might well be termed a capitalist-development growth model. The model was culture-specific; it was particular to the United States and to the history of experience that Hazleton had undergone through a century and a half of growth and decline. It must be emphasized that the men of CAN DO were not seeking political alternatives to the economic or political system. They perceived the possibilities for economic development offered within the system and made decisions to maximize their place within it. Given their collective history on Hazleton mountain, they could not create a new political force, resembling socialist or communist alternatives, such as a system of collectives, nor could they withdraw from the political economy as a utopian or religious movement; there was no utopian movement and there was no religious group either strong enough to cut across the many ethnic cleavages or inclined to innovate that type of framework. The postwar period was characterized by newly evolving institutional structures at the state and federal levels, and the men of CAN DO made a strong, concerted effort to identify these and to manipulate them in their best interests.

CAN DO acquired social power for its members and for itself as an institution that outlived a given membership. This was accomplished by constructing a new component in the social order in the orphaned coal-field settlements. It was not created out of whole cloth, but on the tradition of economic development established at the turn of the century by members of the business community. The goal of the local merchants had always been to develop a regional economy independent of coal mining, and after the war the possibility and the necessity confronted them unequivocally.

In the spring and summer of 1956 CAN DO reviewed the success and failure with Auto-Lite, observed that other anthracite communities were stepping up efforts to recruit "footloose" industries into the region, and posed a question to the members of the community associations. The question was: "How should the money be raised to construct full shell buildings to attract industries?" The answer they got was that there should be a double attack on the fund-raising: "One campaign would seek direct cash contributions from banks, retail stores, utilities, service businesses, professional people and others who should obviously contribute directly to the improved economic health of the community" (CAN DO 1974:11); and a second campaign would attempt to get every worker employed to purchase a $100 bond that would pay 3 percent interest and would be redeemable in fifteen years. Money would not be given directly to a firm as with Auto-Lite; rather it would be used to purchase buildings that would then be sold or leased to the incoming operations. A revolving fund was to be set up that would underwrite future construction of the industrial buildings. There was a final coda or two: no small contributions were to be taken, and the drive was to be kept short-term.

Social structural features were involved that made the highly publicized effort possible. The CAN DO members were a face-to-face network: they all knew one another, and this acquaintance was aided by proximity. The buildings housing the Chamber headquarters, doctors' offices, law firms, banks, and many large retail firms were literally within one block of one another. As in Benjamin Franklin's Philadelphia, everyone could meet for lunch, or a hurried meeting in passing, or a gathering on the spur of the moment in someone's office. This high level network cross-cut the religious affiliations of Protestant, Catholic, and Jewish members. Despite the apparent unity, underlying differences remained obvious; for example, there were twenty-six languages spoken in the county in 1970. This indicates that the region remained heterogeneous half a century after the great migration was officially halted. In a city as polyglot as Hazleton and as large, there are many power bases and many influentials—among members of an occupation, among the clergy, and others. In CAN DO were represented the three major American religious groupings, but, with the exception of the Jewish members, the largest and most successful business people in the region had English or German surnames. It is as if at the very top of this particular base of power the descendants of the first settlers had risen and capitalized on the newcomers by providing them goods and services (Hechter 1979:119). There were no large merchants, doctors, lawyers, or manufacturers of Polish descent, for example, in the original CAN DO organization. Although the Polish migration commenced forty years before the Italian, the Poles were the largest segment of the population speaking their native language. The folk model of the CAN DO organization was that it was indeed representative of the people of the region. But in a strict representative sense, its corporate body did not reflect the proportions of the ethnic groupings; there were so many ethnicities that it could not have.

With the advent of the fund-raising campaign with its goal of $500,000, the new structure finally came into being that was to transform the regional employment picture.

At the final public session on organization [*sic*] the method of fund raising, it was decided that a separate non-profit corporation should be formed to handle the newly raised fund. Its board of directors would be composed of the five incorporating officers of the Chamber of Commerce, the president of the Jaycees (Junior Chamber of Commerce), two representatives from labor unions, two representatives from the Hazleton Clearing House, and, finally, one representative for each $25,000 raised by an organization. The final provision for representation on the board of directors was to be the incentive for competition between organizations to raise the funds required. [CAN DO 1974:11]

The community organizations—Kiwanis, Lions Club, and others—were to be the vehicles for the fund-raising effort. The whole process occurred within the culturally coded methods of capitalism: incentives were offered for the successful, and competition between segments of the community, the community service organizations, as to which could raise the most funds, was chosen as another means to insure success.

These successfully realized activities established CAN DO as an autocatalytic device to assemble and control energetic resources (capital, labor) and to reorganize the local system for these purposes. It was a small dissipative structure within the modern world-system of like structures. The structure of CAN DO also made it able to handle transformations from one energetic form to another. Adams, in an abstract passage, explained,

It is common in human behavior that individuals and societies reconceptualize, reevaluate events that form part of their environment, and that they can and do mix mass phenomena with energy phenomena. Understanding human behavior requires that we deal with this apparent muddle. *The object is not to analyze human behavior into categories of mass, energetic, and informational components, but rather to be able to handle transformations from one of these areas to another with at least the same facility as, but hopefully more systematically than, human beings do in their daily life.* To focus on the mass-energy-information complex is to focus on a material world, to insist that, whatever it is that the social scientist may study, that thing must be of the world, or it cannot be studied. [1975:111, italics added]

The following model is constructed to understand the transformations that social structural components, such as CAN DO, are designed to make. Such processes include the effort to transform a local potential labor pool into a resource that will appear attractive to an industry seeking inexpensive, reliable, and even eager laborers. Whereas an industry took electrical energy, labor, raw materials, and other supplies and transformed them, by means of a production process, into consumables, CAN DO employed capital, labor, land, information, and political influence to transform a liminal section of the old industrial belt into a contemporary, middle-class community. That, in a sense, was the final outcome of their efforts.

The structure, then, was designed to control a catastrophically large fluctuation, a major shift in the regional economy, based on new energy sources. The fluctuation was most evident in the decline in employment, in out-migration, and in community disintegration. CAN DO was designed to reverse these entropic processes and thereby became an important component of the larger regional dissipative structures. The official design of this structure can be seen in the Appendix: the CAN DO organization chart and committees. One highly placed informant shed light on the particular organization of CAN DO. He said that, unlike the other nonprofit corporations that emerged at about the same time in the anthracite region, CAN DO drew from all segments of the highly organized and powerful local social system and did not omit or alienate any. Professionals in other communities, such as doctors or lawyers, tended to steer clear of community involvement. CAN DO, by contrast, incorporated both, as well as others, into the structure through its organizational efforts.

A word must be said about culture in the sense that Goodenough has used the term. This CAN DO piece of social organization is innovative, but it is also culturally adapted to fit entirely within the existing system of social organization. It is cultural in that CAN DO is not transportable to countries that have radically different laws, procedures, expectations, ideology, and social organization.

Because social organization is culture-specific, the modeling of social system–ecosystem relations ought to be done where new interventions are attempted, particularly if they are stimulated from the top down. There is evidence that the World Bank is moving in this direction in forming policy for making loans to the less developed countries. Their goals are increasingly to make investment decisions where the local sociocultural organizations and the appropriate technology are fitted well enough to one another and to the local ecosystem to insure success on returns (Weiss 1979:1083–89). This is indeed delicate and sensitive business, and insures a demand for social science-trained ecologists and other scientists in ongoing industrial development situations whether in the developed countries or the less developed countries.

FUNCTIONS

The functions of the CAN DO organization were multiple and cannot be exhausted by analysis. The interview data shed much light on the local people's perceptions of its role:

1. Male-employing industries were sought, so a major function of CAN DO was to provide the industrial base that would realize that.
2. There was a strong desire to find a diversified industrial base that was not dependent on a single industry in the way that the region had been dependent upon coal.

3. It was also strongly felt that industries which were not beholden to a powerful union would benefit the region. This feeling was voiced against the memory of the ceaseless coalfield turbulence caused by competition between the workers and the owners over wages, supplies, ownership of the factors of production, safety, and benefits.

One cannot help but observe that a new dependence was substituted for an old one: although the old dependence had been upon coal, the new one was upon cheap petroleum, which fueled the trucks that carried goods, fueled the physical plants of the industries, fueled many of the utilities, and formed the basis of the chemical technologies that were used by firms in the industrial park to make foams. I do not think that this perception forms a part of the CAN DO cognized model.

Analytically it appears that the essential function of CAN DO was to arrange an exchange: an exchange between the labor pool of the region and the employing industries desiring suitable locations close to the megalopolitan markets. The men who made up CAN DO articulated one further interest that suggests the classical social contract between the governing and the governed. The contract was that CAN DO and the Chamber of Commerce would make the effort to organize the community to help raise the capital to attract industries which would hire the out-of-work kinsmen of those who were already employed locally. It is the kind of private contracting that goes on in the United States but is largely absent in countries where centralized planning and economic revitalization are all advanced by the public sector.

The social organization of CAN DO represents a process of centralization (Flannery 1972) where a new, higher level subsystem is initiated that takes over several functions previously distributed at a much lower level of integration. The lower level of local business organization existed

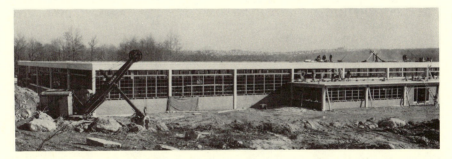

The first industrial park shell building for the General Foam Company, 1956. While CAN DO had problems with this building, they acquired badly needed experience on how to build well and please their clients. The completion of this structure was a proud moment, one of many for CAN DO. (Photograph courtesy of CAN DO)

during the height of anthracite production. CAN DO was the highest level of community organization in the petroleum period, but, during the height of the anthracite period, it was the banks and railroads and "line" companies. Companies had formerly owned the town, store, and services; had hired the police force; and had instituted other, less formal methods of control. The CAN DO community centralizing process increased the involvement of other members of the community, especially those in the men's service clubs. Part of the success of the union of these interests lay in the obvious fact that the Chamber members were not the primary employers of the region, and certainly not a monopolistically controlled industry. They were viewed by many working-class members as serving worker's interests.

In an interview, one of the founding CAN DO members remarked,

> I do feel that the nucleus of volunteers who worked so very hard was extremely important—in other words—this couldn't have flown without the leadership factor, the nucleus of people willing to spend innumerable hours, all of their time really, seven days a week, week after week, month after month, not only just in planning for it and raising money, but afterwards trying to determine what to do with it and so forth.

Thus, in the centralization process, it was locally perceived that leadership was an ingredient in the successful economic recovery of the region. The idea of community leadership and the part it plays was widespread among members of the business community.

TRANSFORMATION STRUCTURE

> Americans of all ages, all conditions, and all dispositions constantly form associations. They have not only commercial and manufacturing companies, in which all take part, but associations of a thousand other kinds, religious, moral, serious, futile, general, or restricted, enormous or diminutive. The Americans make associations to give entertainments, to found seminaries, to build inns, to construct churches, to diffuse books, to send missionaries to the antipodes; in this manner they found hospitals, prisons, and schools. [Tocqueville 1945:114]

I postulated that control mechanisms are widely dispersed throughout the capitalist world-economy. The local community is a subset of the world-economy with its local resource base, its position in the energy conversion process, and its location within the world-market. The local community and local industries have varying degrees of control over their immediate natural resources, and varying degrees of power in community life and in culture, and, to some limited extent, over the way they will articulate with the extra-regional economy. The community and its industries compete with other communities and industries—either close by or on the opposite side of the earth—for their place in the global energy conversion process. This kind of shifting competition is characteristic of the advanced capitalist economy and is the cause for many of the fluctuations that local communities must confront as old industries become uncompetitive and die, as local resources are exhausted or become obsolete, and as new industries start, importing new populations to the locality.

The term *community* is used in its widest sense to include the local social system and political economy. The accumulation of social power in a locality makes it one of the billions of world-system control mechanisms that affect the specific energy conversion processes of a particular place. A control mechanism is a regulator that, in terms of the theory, manipulates the flow and transformations of energy—goods and services, personnel, money, and information. An adequate regulator of a system —a local community—must, in the terms of Conant and Ashby, be a model of that system. The model or models must adequately represent the environment, including the major energetic inputs into the community (Conant and Ashby 1970:89–97). A system regulator, according to these authors, does not have an option as to whether or not to model the internal system and the environment; it must do so in order to satisfactorily survive. The word *adapt* seems appropriate here. Adaptive systems are those which do the best job of modeling system and environment and behaving accordingly (see also J. G. Miller 1978:67).

The physicist Howard Pattee, who has devoted a recent article to complex systems (as opposed to simple systems), argues,

> There is, of course, an enormous gap between a model of single-cell behavior and a model of an ecological, economic or social organization. My point is, however, that all these higher systems are no less self-descriptive than the cell. In fact inherent in all biological systems are their internal linguistic models of themselves and of the external world. Biological evolution can be characterized by the increasing elaboration of internal descriptions and models. We usually call these models by other names—goals, plans, policies, strategies, etc. —but they are only higher levels of self-description in a linguistic mode. [1977:265]

It should be emphasized that complex systems such as Hazleton contain internal linguistic models of themselves and their external world. The adequacy of these descriptions is again a necessary condition of appropriate system behavior; those communities which accomplish the most complete descriptions and can act successfully on them are the most adaptive. The control mechanism which evolved in the Hazleton community, the CAN DO structure, not only made adequate descriptions of a very large external system but was able to use inputs from the larger system to help self-organize to transform internal possibilities into resources usable by other entities outside the system. They were able, in effect, to place themselves in the "environments" of corporations and political structures outside the boundaries of their region. The data suggest that

Hazleton was indeed the most successful of the anthracite coal communities in this regard.

Pattee developed the theory that complex systems are linguistic systems that describe themselves and their environments, that issue linguistic commands from a control center, and that have the executor of the system (the Chamber of Commerce) interpret the linguistic commands. That this was done is evidenced by the CAN DO and Chamber of Commerce recruitment of a new industrial base, which was designed to sustain the viability of the local community, and the efficacy of the control mechanism, the regulator, within it.

Although Pattee may be using linguistics metaphorically, the business leaders of Hazleton operate very much like this. The leadership from CAN DO contacted all the organizations of the area and spoke to any community organization that would place them on the agenda. The evolving regulator, CAN DO, could thereby facilitate a two-way linguistic flow, from the business people outward and from the voluntary association members inward. In this way the linguistic descriptions of the system developed more highly and were made more effective, more "real."

The business communities in American cities are generally well integrated through their respective Chamber of Commerce chapters and other business groups. They develop good internal and external linguistic models, as do trade organizations and community associations. The ordinary talk among members at business gatherings is scaled from international newsworthy events relevant to the economy, through national concerns, the business climate, and to personal business problems, such as pending transactions, deals, and recent successes and failures. Economic, political, religious, and other topics, especially technical ones relating to one's business, are discussed in highly patterned but informative ways. By these rapid internal communication flows, aided by inputs from television, radio, popular and trade magazines, and personal experiences on the road, the segments of a business community can compile an internal linguistic description of itself and its environment in much the way (though in a more complex manner) that Pattee describes for complex systems in general.

The informational, communicative process is the symbolic means by which the local energy conversion processes are guided and the means by which the local political economy can be made to articulate with the world-economy. Both symbolic communication and the exchange of energy and material through world markets mesh the local community with the larger system. The business and professional men of Hazleton had to assemble internal resources, such as labor, capital, land, communications and influence, existing social organization, and public symbols, and they had to acquire external resources in order to self-organize at a new level of integration. By accomplishing this they could preserve and advance the community built during the coal era that now faced the challenge of the petroleum period.

Assembling Internal Resources Once the CAN DO operation was formalized as a part of community structure, the task that lay before the members was to take the existing organizations of the region and activate them, insofar as they could, for a single purpose. This was, however, only generally formulated. These existing organizations included such associations as the Kiwanis, League of Women Voters, and the local churches. CAN DO was a single-purpose organization, to be sure, but its scope had to be community-wide. The new organization was designed with a double edge to it. Its internal operations had to be designed to operate within the community, and its external features had to be fashioned to deal in a systematic way with resources for the community that existed outside community boundaries. CAN DO became a hinge that moved between the local associations and the external structures of government and industry.

The first order of business was that of transforming various components of the local social-economic system into a package of resources that could then be offered to outside manufacturing firms. The effort would have to be great, for the liabilities that Auto-Lite had pointed out to the Chamber delegation in the late 1940s still held true in the mid-1950s.

In the literature of social science, it has often been noted that charismatic leaders play, at times, catalytic roles in their organizations or communities. Hazleton, fortunately, had one such person. Like Anouilh's Becket, he took up the role reluctantly, but, once in it, he performed far above anyone's expectations. The man's name was Edgar Dessen, an M.D. trained at the University of Pennsylvania, and a native of Hazleton. Dessen's father, originally from Philadelphia, had taken his practice to Hazleton in the early part of the century because it was a boom town. Edgar was born there in 1917, the year of peak tonnage production. His father's career spanned the demise of anthracite, and Dessen could have been expected, like his father before him, to move to a more promising location after medical school. Like many other professional people who were natives of the anthracite region, Dessen had a deep and positive identification with the area. My field notes give a brief, informative glimpse of the man:

> My first impression was the office itself, not the man behind the desk. The cramped office had also been his father's. The office was a personal toast, a testament to his public life, for on the walls were plaques, awards for his life of public service. He had been given commendations by the state, the service organizations, Chamber of Commerce, labor organizations, foundations, and more. The pictures of his family graced the walls: father, son, daughter, and family pictures of them, his wife, and their white dog. He was a public man and a family man. His medical degrees were hung along with his father's; both had graduated from the University of Pennsylvania medical school. Dr. Dessen was a short man, not physically imposing, with a smile playing around his lips. He is sixty-one, quite bald on top, and he moves his hand to his head as if to push back imagi-

nary hair. We had given him a list of questions to read over and answer at his discretion. He took a quick look and said immediately, "I'll answer them all." He began, not so much hesitantly as just not warmed up to his subject.

As the interview matured—he gave us two hours—he laughed and smiled as he recalled various facets of the resurgence of Hazleton. He was solemn as he admitted that, for the last two years, no new companies had moved to Hazleton and other companies had left. What was completely absent from Dr. Dessen was any tone of self-congratulation. And he maintained the tone of friendliness one comes to associate with small towns and small cities. He said that the air of friendliness which he exuded was something that all the men of CAN DO were able to project authentically to the company people that chose Hazleton. It was one of the amenities not found elsewhere. In the two hours of the interview, it was easy to understand how Dr. Dessen could have sparked CAN DO to bring a region alive. His calm, thoughtful, competent, positive manner inspired confidence, and there was something more: he understood how the local system worked, the way it was organized, and the way in which local people responded.

Two aspects of Dessen's life are particularly relevant to his role in community redevelopment. The first is that he had a systematic overview of the whole community and its particular predicament; the second is that he moved easily among the regional elite and served in a number of responsible public and private positions.

When in 1953 Dessen reluctantly accepted the presidency of the Greater Hazleton Chamber of Commerce, he began seeing for the first time, from a kind of sociological bird's eye view—from the top of the community hierarchy down—the details of the deep economic crisis that was gripping the anthracite region and Hazleton in particular. His great skill was that he could turn his perception of the challenge into active means for meeting it. Because of this ability he was the organizer and first director of CAN DO. The long interview with him amply documents the consumate expertise with which he guided a successful fund-raising effort which created in its wake an almost religious desire on the part of the local communities to turn a bad situation around.

His ability to move easily among the influential people in the anthracite area extended to the University of Pennsylvania, to his professional associations, to the governor of Pennsylvania's offices, and to the local banks and corporations that conferred upon him at various times board memberships and other honors. This large network outside the immediate area, as well as within it, served to underline the fact that the CAN DO association and its members were inward-facing to community and outward-facing to the larger organizational fabric of the larger society. Sociologically, these perceptions made effective a double vision of community and the place of community in regional, state, and national polity and economy. Hazleton was a liminal area, but it was connected by networks of people of vision to nonliminal, central areas. This is the classical relationship, it should be noted, between city and hinterland, from the hinterland perspective.

The structure of CAN DO, despite the tireless and imaginative efforts of one person, was very much a group project. It was often referred to as a team effort; the idea of team, borrowed from sports, is very pervasive in the business community. Several people distinguished themselves, some eventually giving up their businesses to devote all of their time to tasks of industrial recruitment. The CAN DO structure was initially open enough to incorporate those social service bodies and individuals who distinguished themselves on the fund drive. The most aggressive were awarded board memberships. Labor, capital, and land had to be firmly in place before Hazleton became competitive in attracting new industries, and these were in part acquired thus: (1) by employing a complex of communication-information-influence as means; (2) by contacting existing social clubs, organizations, associations, and churches; and (3) by manipulating the symbols of community.

Labor The labor leaders in Hazleton were consulted for their inputs into the CAN DO efforts, and a member of the local United Labor Council chapter is always represented on the CAN DO Board of Directors. The labor force itself was not represented, nor could it be expected to be, for a variety of reasons: people were leaving the area; people were changing jobs; men were staying home to care for their children while their wives worked in textile plants; and some men commuted great distances, coming home only on weekends. No labor union represented out-of-work laborers. There was a sense of urgency in the area, extending to other businesses outside Hazleton as well, because it was feared that the area would soon become too depopulated to attract industry. Nevertheless, the labor force was the major medium that CAN DO had to exchange for outside employers.

A generation before, the newer immigrants, largely Slavic and Polish, had been the subject of much resentment and ridicule. By the time CAN DO was advertising the Hazleton region to outside firms, their cultural conservatism and reputation for hard work had become an eminently salable image.

Two features of the Hazleton labor force gave it special qualities that CAN DO was able to use in their promotional campaign. The mine workers had a reputation for being hard-working and only a generation or two away from the old country. The ethnic picture is much too complex to justify this as a uniform reality, but it was, nevertheless, a useful stereotype that CAN DO could portray to prospective industrial park companies without fear of falsification. The other feature of the labor force that CAN DO could broadcast was their general low level of skills. The labor pool of the region was unskilled and semiskilled because they had worked the mines; those jobs were gone, and they had not been retrained. In the 1970 U.S. census, more than 25 percent of the male labor force were still classified as operatives. The kinds of laborer that industries were looking for seemed to reside in Hazleton. If they were unskilled the companies would not have to pay premium wages to attract them, and if they appeared work hungry—as they indeed were in the region—the companies could expect a low absentee rate and few labor problems. There is another fact that should be pointed out: the incoming employing industries did not need highly trained laborers; therefore, their demand for labor skill levels was the same as the mining companies'. The largest number of employed male and female laborers in 1970 were in the operative category. This reflected the large employment in low skill level jobs in both the industrial parks and in textiles.

Capital The industrial firms that were attracted enjoyed a sellers' market. For every firm that needed new facilities, there were ten communities seeking to attract it, according to the CAN DO Industrial Director. With this kind of competition, Hazleton had to develop financing. "A prime inducement of these projects was CAN DO's 100 percent financial package. This consisted of first mortgage by local banks of 50 percent at prevailing interest rate; second mortgage of 30 percent by Pennsylvania Industrial Development Authority at 2 percent, and the final 20 percent of risk money by CAN DO at 2 percent" (CAN DO 1974:16). Hazleton's CAN DO mounted three fund-raising drives and, by 1963, had 2 million dollars in a revolving fund. Their efforts were aided by the Pennsylvania Industrial Development Authority, which increased its share of plant financing from 30 to 40 percent. That reduced the amount of capital CAN DO had to provide by 10 percent.

   The local banks of Hazleton were involved in providing capital for the incoming companies, thereby complementing the public funds available. Although the local banks were not uniformly backing the early CAN DO efforts, it did not take long for the board members and officers to realize that their interests were also served by regional redevelopment. During the fieldwork an analysis was made of the composition of the bank boards. Boards invariably included a member of CAN DO or the Chamber of Commerce; this indicates that the local sources of capital were influenced by those who had inputs into decision making, and the input was provided by the advocates of the CAN DO campaign.

Land In addition to financial support, CAN DO developed its own industrial park that included the necessary roads, sewer, water, electric and other utilities. They backfilled a strip mine to reclaim cheap land for the site. This required donated capital, labor, expertise, and machinery. The incoming corporations were to be presented with a complete package that included financing, a built shell to house their plants, and a variety of personal services on the part of CAN DO members for finding housing, advice about schools, and related matters. This total service gave Hazleton a competitive edge on a number of communities.

Communication-Information-Influence These three elements of human interaction need to be considered together in the energy conversion pro-

From the press release of the Pennsylvania Department of Commerce, 19 October 1973: "The Pennsylvania Industrial Development Authority (PIDA) recently was made self-sustaining by legislation signed into law by Governor Milton J. Shapp before members of the PIDA board and representatives of local industrial development groups and industries that have used PIDA low-cost loans to expand production and jobs in the Commonwealth. From left are: Joseph Yenchko, industrial director for the Greater Hazleton Area New Development Organization; Fred Buff, president of the General Foam Company, Hazleton; Governor Shapp; Michael Dunawick, general manager of General Foam Company plant; and State Commerce Secretary Walter G. Arader, Radnor." (Photograph by PIDA, courtesy of CAN DO)

cess. Information is not abstract but must be meaningfully conveyed. Facts and figures, while used by CAN DO recruiters to influence prospective clients, never were presented in the abstract and expected to stand on their own. If only for that reason, a richer definition of information had to be employed. The three terms are not mutually exclusive, and, in fact, communication carries information, information is communicated, and both are designed to influence the recipient. Communication, taken as the broader term, may be defined as the sending of meaningful messages, designed for a recipient (or recipients) with the intentions of the sender embedded in them. The reason for this definition is to convey the political nature of it. For if sender A intends an outcome, and sender B intends one as well, and they do not coincide—

and they seldom do—then this is the heart of the political process.

The media, newspapers and radio, did not have to be courted by CAN DO because the owners perceived quickly that it was in their best interests to have clients, listeners, readers, buyers of messages. For these reasons they carried news reports on the campaigns and presented talk shows on the radio, all geared to the fortunes of CAN DO and its fund-raising and industry-recruiting successes. Donors were listed in the newspapers and announced over the air. Politically these communications influenced the citizens of the region, urging them to respond to the plea for funds. The belief was fostered that they could turn the region around for themselves and their relatives. It is difficult to quantify the role of the various media in American life, but they are very much a part of the culture of freedom that Americans enjoy.

Tocqueville's observations on the power of the press give insight a century and a half after they were made. They apply analytically to the use of the press and radio in Hazleton.

> When men are no longer united among themselves by firm and lasting ties, it is impossible to obtain the co-operation of any great number of them unless you can persuade every man whose help you require that his private interest obliges him voluntarily to unite his exertions to the exertions of all the others. This can be habitually and conveniently effected only by means of a newspaper; nothing but a newspaper can drop the same thought into a thousand minds at the same moment.
>
> The effect of a newspaper is not only to suggest the same purpose to a great number of persons, but to furnish means for executing in common the designs which they may have singly conceived.
>
> In order that an association among a democratic people should have any power, it must be a numerous body.
>
> Consequently, there is a necessary connection between public associations and newspapers: newspapers make associations, and associations make newspapers. [1945:119, 120]

Without a media system, the CAN DO strategy would have been quite differently constructed.

Existing Social Organization The social organizations of U.S. communities, while often studied in terms of class (Vidich and Bensman 1968), can be nicely complemented by understanding their associational life. Hazleton is no exception, and it was through their associations that the direct organizing for fund-raising was done. Tocqueville, again, made a relevant point.

> Certain men happen to have common interest in some concern; either a commercial undertaking is to be merged, or some speculation in manufactures to be tried: they meet, they combine, and thus, by degrees, they become familiar with the principles of association. The greater the multiplicity of small affairs, the more do men, even without knowing it, acquire facility in prosecuting great undertakings in common. [1945:123]

He claimed, I think rightly, that:

> There is only one country on the face of the earth where the citizens enjoy unlimited freedom of association for political purposes. This same country is the only one in the world where the continual exercise of the right of association has been introduced into civil life and where all the advantages which civilization can confer are procured by means of it. [1945:123]

For Tocqueville, the freedom of the press and the freedom of association are two legal guarantees central to the culture of the United States, and uniquely strong there.

For this reason, I focus on associations which are stratified as well as crosscutting as the fundamental organizing feature of U.S. communities, an aspect that ties the local to the national levels (see also Doyle 1978). Although class exists, and always pervasively, it has to be teased out of the data by the social scientist. Class was not much of a viable folk model in the Hazleton region; people, even from the working class, consider themselves middle class.

Associations are one of the most visible, taken-for-granted organizational structures in any American community. Although it is not known how many persons lie outside all associational life in communities, the number must in fact be relatively small.* Associations are indeed pervasive; it is this very pervasiveness that makes them empirically accessible to the investigator. In terms of the native model, the life of the community, in Hazleton and elsewhere, takes place on an organized basis. These organizations are often referred to as voluntary associations, but the term does not capture associational life.

By associational life is meant voluntary associations, professional associations, service clubs, trade associations, religious organizations, ethnic clubs, secret societies, clubs dealing with nature such as hunt clubs for men and garden clubs for women, labor organizations, political parties; the list is extensive and defies easy classification. All of these associations have similar organizational formats: membership rules, a constituency, a charter, a list of elected officers, membership dues, special activities of interest to members, and periodic gatherings. They are finer grain than class, although they are stratified in relation to one another; and there are rankings within each association.

Voluntary associations and trade associations play numerous roles in the social life of a community. From a sociological perspective they are crosscutting, meaning they acquire memberships from people who might not associate outside the association. For this reason they are integrative, pulling people into contact with one another. In terms of the theory, the role of the voluntary, but more so the trade associations, is necessary to the energy conversion process, to help guide the production and con-

---

*Zelinsky finds 50 percent of the U.S. population in associations (1974: 149n), while Smith and Freedman report evidence of 80 percent of the population in some organized association (1972:118–19).

sumption of wealth at the local level. By wealth is meant affluence and privilege—at least in the local community—for in cities the size of Hazleton, amassing great wealth is out of the picture. Merchants and lawyers have traditionally been overrepresented in the voluntary associations having to do with business mainly because these institutions provide an arena of economically and politically well-connected people. They are sources of business, long-term clients, and of critically needed strategic information. One of the functions that these associations have is to provide a ready-made institutional framework to which newcomers to the community can transfer their memberships from their community of origin. Trade and voluntary associations are didactic, they are schools of leadership and organizational skills; because every year there is a new set of officers, turnover is rapid enough to accommodate many who want to try their skills. The communication that rapidly flows when they meet is critical to the members of associations; vital knowledge on the business climate is an acquisition that each person seeks to make. Each segment of the business and professional community brings its particular occupational expertise to bear on common issues. During these sessions the subtle work of opinion formation and value formation gets done, with divisions and alliances shifting as constantly as the topics of talk.

Many of the associations found at the local level are chapters of national organizations. The total membership, therefore, is enormous; the associations have bulging budgets and are incalculably powerful politically. These associations are some of the most active segments of American social, political, and economic life. CAN DO turned immediately to the men's service clubs of Hazleton and adjoining areas for support and organizational effort in raising money for the park. By pitting the clubs against one another, they generated a culturally appropriate spirit of competition that, as Dessen put it, had them fighting in the streets to raise money. Dessen's awareness, his use, if you will, of the folk model of organizations allowed him to launch a successful drive. He made himself and others available to talk to any club anywhere on any occasion to garner support. When asked by the author if any segments of the population did not support CAN DO's efforts, Dessen spoke at length of community response. "The ministers and the priests and the rabbis supported us from the pulpit during the drive; they'd give sermons about this thing." He went on to add, however, when pressed about the role of the coal companies and the old coal families,

> The Coxes? This was their area. The Coxes were mostly toward Freeland and this area. That's one place where I did meet a complete failure. Danny Coxe was left here as a representative of all the Coxe heirs, of which there were many. Tench Coxe died intestate, making one of the most complex problems in the history of the country because there are heirs all over the joint. They married into foreign families, Austrians, Spanish—incredible! But he represented the Coxe interests here, of which there were many, including a lot of land. But I got nothing at all from Danny Coxe.

A partial list of Hazleton's clubs demonstrates that they are an extensive source of social organizations that could be mobilized, and that they serve many community interests in their various functions. This listing (see Appendix) omits entirely the trade, labor, and professional associations that are represented in the community and that were among the most aggressive in raising money for the CAN DO drive.

In sum, it was the associational structure of the Hazleton community that Dessen successfully contacted for fund-raising. Without an intimate knowledge of the social structure of a place, it is impossible to organize in this manner. In three fund drives CAN DO had raised $2,285,000 within a region far from affluent through the work of volunteers, using the associations of the community and the media. It was an impressive feat, and Hazleton was awarded a prize in 1964 which it coveted, the All American City Award.

Public Symbols In Anglo-American communities, there are numerous ways of symbolizing community. Hazleton used performance-based and materials-based means of presenting the new order CAN DO was initiating. Parades are major performances that call upon community organization and attract large crowds. Another major means that communities have of projecting themselves, often for themselves, is by fixing up the physical plant through beautification. Community solidarity can be stimulated by planting trees, building an artificial lake, sponsoring home beautification, erecting new YWCAs and YMCAs; these events and the people involved are highly publicized in the local newspapers. These are precisely the choices that CAN DO made in contributing to the physical structure of Hazleton as a means of dramatizing the city's new social organization. It made the city more attractive to outsiders and symbolized the efforts CAN DO had made, leaving a permanent, almost monumental record of their efforts.

One-half of the transformation process has now been developed. The internal resources that CAN DO represented and shaped can be modeled. The diagram (figure 21) represents the various media that could be exchanged for industry that CAN DO brought into coherent form in the community. This is also a partial picture of a control mechanism and the features of the local system upon which it operated in adapting to conditions of changing energy availability. What remains to be detailed are the exogenous resources that CAN DO discovered and deployed in order to attract industry. Hazleton was nested within Luzerne County, the northeastern Pennsylvania region, the state of Pennsylvania, the northeastern United States, the United States, the north Atlantic, and the world; it had to reach the relevant institutions at these other levels in order to realize its new goals.

Manipulating External Resources The men of CAN DO had successfully coalesced the internal resources of Hazleton, and had demonstrated amply that they had more than labor to offer prospective companies.

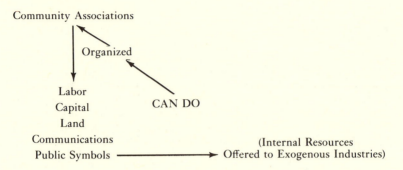

Endogenous Resources

Community Associations

Organized

Labor
Capital   CAN DO
Land
Communications
Public Symbols ⟶ (Internal Resources
Offered to Exogenous Industries)

Figure 21. Transformation process

Again, it should be emphasized that the perceptions of Auto-Lite were still valid. Hazleton was nowhere, particularly in relation to transportation routes. In what was now expected fashion, the Hazleton CAN DO people decided to manipulate the external public and private sectors to increase their attractiveness to industry.

Their greatest achievement, externally, was in acquiring an interstate highway interchange at Hazleton. Without it, the goods of the industrial park factories could not be adequately moved. They had to lobby on a continuous basis to get the highways sited along routes that would bring them through the area. Eisenhower's Highway Act of 1956 created a modern transportation system for the country. It was part of the postwar impetus for growth stimulated by the public sector. CAN DO formed what they called a "road gang" which spent its time acquiring information, making presentations, and helping to organize statewide bodies to lobby for highways near the city.

> The Highway Committee first assembled data in support of the community's needs, outlining its near-isolation by modern transportation standards, enumerating the new plants built in and projected for Hazleton. The group also described the geographic and topographical advantages of routes through the Hazleton area, and assembled stacks of endorsements, support and legal resolutions from adjoining municipalities, from industry, commercial firms, service clubs, civic groups and educational institutions in the region. . . . This material was presented at meetings with the Governor, with legislators, with highway department officials and engineers, and was publicized widely in the regional press and radio, in addition to its presentation at the various hearings which the state had begun to hold as required by the law. [CAN DO 1974:20]

In the United States, one of the major functions of many interest groups is to lobby administrative and elected officials. The executive branch of government is pressured by special interests to tailor its programs and funding to those who knock on its door (Haefele 1973, 1979). There is intense competition among special interests for such necessities as roads. The Hazleton group was simply more energetic and better prepared than many of its opponents.

> The accomplishments of the group can be summed up best by reporting that the original committee slogan "Hazleton—the Crossroads of Tomorrow" which was used during the early days, now has been changed to "The Crossroads of the East" because the intersection of Interstate Highways 80 and 81 at Hazleton is now a reality, putting the community on the most direct route between New York City and San Francisco, and between Montreal and New Orleans. [CAN DO 1974:23]

The constant lobbying for community interests is a fateful and unpredictable enterprise. It is also often highly personalistic. One of the road gang members was a personal friend of a powerful figure, acquired his support, and, so the story goes, gathered enough support at the state level to have the highway interchange sited on the mountain. Departments of transportation in the United States have appeared overly dependent on personalized decision making based on the influence of known, powerful people. The investment in the interstate highway system is comparable in the fourth upswing of the long wave to the investment in railroad trackage in the third upswing. The location of the industrial parks is entirely dependent upon this highway system and upon the trucks which carry goods from point to point in the gigantic national production line and delivery system.

A geographer makes this point eloquently by documenting the succession of the energy bases of society and the associated transportation sectors.

> Many factors have contributed to this decline in railroad freight traffic, one of the chief ones being the increased dependence on petroleum products for heat and energy. National consumption of anthracite and bituminous coal actually declined from 523 million short tons in 1930 to 494 million in 1950 and 434 million in 1957, and this decreased the shipments of what had long been a major freight item for the railroads. The petroleum products and natural gas used in place of and in addition to coal—for transportation, heating, and power development—are carried to a very small degree by railroads in the East. Gas moves by pipelines, of course, and oil and its refined products are carried chiefly by pipeline, tanker, and tank truck. Moreover, much other freight has shifted from the railroads to trucks (which are among the users of petroleum products) because of their greater flexibility.... In passenger traffic the railroads have lost even more heavily, to both planes and motor vehicles, both powered by petroleum products. [Gottman 1961:650–51]

Other programs in the public sector were also manipulated by CAN DO to the group's advantage. As with the highway system, Ha-

Miss Keystone Shortway and staff, 17 September 1970. The civic celebration of the highway opening is personified, perhaps embodied, by a local beauty. Many civic occasions are graced by attractive women, and beauty contests can themselves become the center of civic attention. (Photograph courtesy of CAN DO)

zleton was more aggressive than surrounding communities. As mentioned previously, the Pennsylvania Industrial Development Corporation, the first state industrial development authority of its type in the United States and perhaps one of the most soundly conceived, was another external resource. Between 1956, when it was put into operation, and 1962, nearly 30 million dollars had been loaned in the anthracite area. This represented nearly 50 percent of its loan budget (Shapp and Jurkat 1962:31). Hazleton also received funds from the Economic Development Council and the Appalachian Regional Commission. The annual reports of the Economic Development Council of Northeastern Pennsylvania, a regional economic planning commission, reveal that Hazleton is the most aggressive fund-raiser in the anthracite area. Hazleton also acquired approval and funding from the federal Department of Energy for an anthracite coal gasification plant and is currently building it with much public attention.

Although it has been difficult to acquire data on the public costs of private enterprise, a full study should be made of the welfare needs of declining extraction-industry communities, for this would register not

Interstate interchange, industrial park, and Hazleton looking south, 1971. The highway interchange did more than symbolize the achievement of CAN DO; it made their economic revitalization efforts possible. (Photograph courtesy of CAN DO)

only some of the suffering involved that needs amelioration, but it would also more accurately reflect the true costs of certain fuel resources.

Potential industrial park inhabitants were contacted by CAN DO through both public and private means. The Pennsylvania Department of Commerce was a major source from the public sector. From the private sector, Pennsylvania Power and Light, the largest corporation in the anthracite region after the demise of the Morgan interests, also has had an industrial recruitment program since the 1930s. The left-hand column of figure 22 represents the internal transformations that had to be made, and the middle section represents the exchanges or transactions between the local community and the larger political economy.

The very dramatic successes of Hazleton are reflected in the charts that show the rise from 1956 to 1974 in the annual payroll from the industrial park and in the number of employees. In 1974 the annual payroll from Valmont Industrial Park was close to $45 million, and there were 8,000 employees. The very remarkable growth in employment ac-

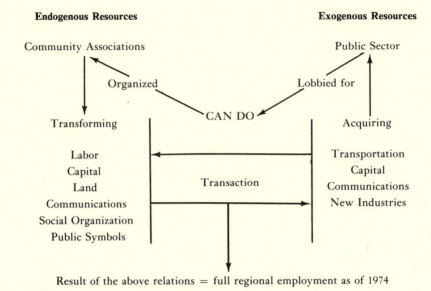

Figure 22. Transformation of community and transactions with exogenous sources

cording to CAN DO figures showed that there was full employment in 1974 in the Greater Hazleton area (figure 23). People were voicing concern that there would be an embarrassment of riches, that Spanish and Afro-American workers would hear the news and begin arriving for new jobs.

The demographics show that Hazleton as a region stabilized although the city continued to lose population. This was now a function of the suburbanizing process, not of massive out-migration from the region (figure 23).

Three major types of industries settled over the years in CAN DO's Valmont Industrial Park. The major category was a complex of petroleum-reliant operations making plastics, polyurethane, and other chemical products. Metal fabrication was the other large category, while the third was more textile-related firms. While the men of CAN DO had wanted male-employing firms, the industries employed both men and women. There were a very few food-processing plants, some services— such as computer services—and several warehousing companies. The companies in the park were close-to-market industries, far from extraction sites, and in terms of the model far down the line in the energy conversion process. However, the firms that employed the most people were not the most numerous. Petroleum-based products require disappointingly few workers.

Pennsylvania censuses (Statistical Abstract, 1973) registered Luzerne County as second only to Philadelphia County in the amount of Pennsyl-

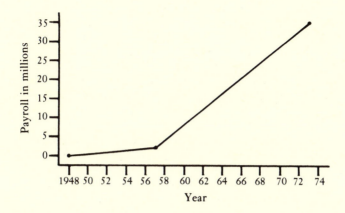

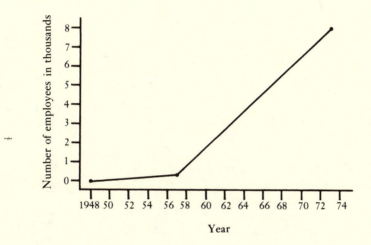

Figure 23. Payroll in millions and number of employees in the CAN DO industrial park. The dramatic increase in employment in the CAN DO industrial parks is a function of the relatively labor-intensive industries that moved in.

vania Industrial Development Authority Loans it had received for fiscal year 1971–72. Such figures reveal the aggressive strategies and strong efforts of the CAN DO group. Further evidence is provided in the report that, with the exception of Pittsburgh, Luzerne County had received the largest number of grants from the Appalachian Regional Commission in the state between 1966 and 1973. Despite these efforts and successes, the major employer in Luzerne County remained textile and apparel firms.

At the level discussed so far, CAN DO was the control mechanism that had emerged, as an autocatalytic device to transform energetic sources—labor, capital, land, and community—that were becoming increasingly dependent on an oil-fueled economy, particularly in the areas of home heating and transportation. The successes of this controlling device in dampening the fluctuations in population out-migration resulting from a shift in the energy base has been documented. Attention has been paid to the internal structure and functioning of the controlling institutions and to the transformation into real assets which was made of potential local resources. The purpose of the transformation was the stabilization of the region. A result was that the interests associated with CAN DO acquired increasing amounts of social power and personal affluence.

CAN DO activity can be understood against the larger fluctuations. The increases in both employment and annual payroll (figure 23) are late phenomena closely related to the rise of the Kondratieff wave during the postwar era from 1947 to 1970 (see figures 8 and 9). By the time of our interviews in 1979, the industrial park was losing firms, employment in them was dropping, unemployment was again climbing toward 10 percent, and CAN DO had overbuilt its industrial park. The group had not leased an empty shell in three years. This decline in industrial park

Shopping center and Valmont Industrial Park, 1977. Commercial, residential, and industrial land uses are in close proximity and have in common the fact that they lie outside the city limits of Hazleton. The industrial park is built on land once stripped for coal. (Photograph courtesy of CAN DO)

occupancy was registered in the Hazleton area and through the whole anthracite region. Firms were once again on the move, and newer companies were not locating there as they once had in the 1950s and 1960s.

The reasons why companies left the industrial parks, according to one local expert on these matters, were several:

1. As the labor force matured at any factory, the company had to pay more every year for wages to workers who gained seniority and required raises. The incentive was to move to a cheaper labor-source region of the country.
2. After long occupancy the companies could no longer depreciate equipment and buildings. Since new capital investment was needed, it was cheaper for the factory to move elsewhere, receive subsidized credit, and invest in new buildings and equipment.
3. Energy costs in the Northeast, particularly for electricity, were higher than in other locations.

The "footloose" industries of the industrial parks really were fickle entities, CAN DO found, and the incentives to move were often greater than those for staying.

In purely economic terms, but addressed to the Kondratieff cycle, Forrester explained this phenomenon by positing that there is, in an upswing of the long wave, an overexpansion of the capital sectors (1976: 183); companies in the park could be considered to be suffering from this. So was CAN DO, as illustrated by its expansion, when CAN DO built the ill-fated Humboldt Park, its second industrial park (figure 24).

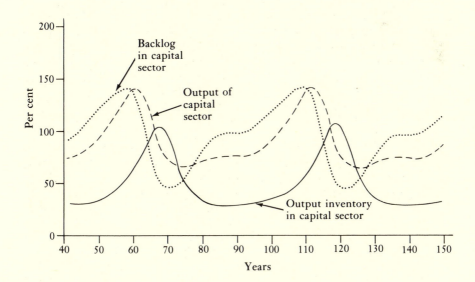

Figure 24. Behavior of the capital sectors in the Kondratieff wave. SOURCE: Forrester (1976:182).

Despite the selling of community friendship, the professed personal interest in the fortunes of the companies that came to Valmont Industrial Park and the small-community approach, the economic realities of the late 1970s—the specter of another energy transition comparable to the substitution of oil for coal and the attendant economic downturn—were forcing the men of CAN DO to face the fact that their successes were not immutable. They were in fact a part of the larger economic forces in the world-economy, a fact that they, in their own way, understood.

It can be predicted, following the pattern of the wave, that there will be increasing decline in employment in the industrial parks and an exodus of plants from the anthracite region until the 1990s when, presumably, a new energy source will kick in and a new growth period will push the regional economy to new levels of productivity and wealth.

IMPACT CHAINS

Impact chains* are the traceable linkages of effects through several interdependent systems or subsystems as the result of a major change or disturbance at some point in the larger system. In economics, a term of art, the ripple effect, is used to explain to lay audiences how price increases in one sector affect prices or employment in another sector. In human ecology an impact chain—which is something like a ripple effect—may begin as a natural disaster affecting the ecosystem, then affecting a local economy, and eventuate in the dissolution of a community. Volcanic eruptions, floods, and hurricanes are the obvious natural catastrophes that provide dramatic examples. On the other hand, economic conditions, such as the demand for oil to power automobiles, create situations where the number of autos is so great that air quality degenerates, causing increased incidences of respiratory diseases and premature deaths. In human ecology an impact chain is unlike a ripple effect because changes in a natural system can be shown to affect both economic and social systems, and modifications in these human systems can be observed in natural systems. One of the most dramatic energy-related chains of impacts is the one seriously noted by the political leaders of the developed Western nations. At the Tokyo Economic Summit of June 1979, the heads of Canada, Germany, France, Italy, Japan, the United Kingdom, and the United States met and agreed that "the oil shortage is permanent, regardless of the effect rising prices have on demand, and that energy is the key to every other economic problem, including inflation, economic expansion, unemployment, trade and currency values" (*New York Times*, 30 June 1979). The ripple effect of oil shortfalls, due to petroleum dependency in the contemporary world-system, is now becoming clearer to heads of state, reporters, and citizens of the developed countries. Ecologists have observed and modeled these linkages for a decade (Odum and Odum 1976),

---

*This concept has been developed by John Bennett in an unpublished work, and it fits within his ideas of decision making and adaptation.

and the economists, politicians, and industrialists are belatedly beginning to make statements that exhibit their growing awareness of the interdependencies.

In human ecology, impact chains exhibit critical relationships and must be modeled, for they link various subsystems with limited control units to one another in specific qualitative and quantitative ways. At the local level, the Hazleton region was first impacted by coal mining, in both natural and social systems; then it was impacted by the decline of anthracite production and the development of industrial parks and the infrastructure that served them. Impact chains are neither good nor bad in the abstract, although they can be evaluated in negative, positive, and mixed terms. Once impact chains are systematically documented for human ecological systems, they should provide a knowledge of relevant connections between the parts so that those who wish to intervene may anticipate the consequences of intended actions on the subsequent behavior of the affected components. The controlling mechanisms in a large system usually take into account at some level of sophistication what the outcomes of their activities will be and will anticipate future modifications to their course of action. Those that anticipate successfully are considered to be adaptive; and those that do not, are not. Turbulent conditions, naturally, offer constant surprises and test the best-laid plans, and conditions and responses are often unpredictable and barely planned.

The major positive impact of the CAN DO efforts was to create full employment in the adjoining area by 1974. By accomplishing this the CAN DO controlling mechanism achieved an expressed goal. Its efforts were integrative, in a sociological sense, leading the local community to new levels of collective effort and self-consciousness. The integration was offset, however, by the spatial diffusion made possible by the oil-based automotive economy in general and by CAN DO's efforts in particular. CAN DO helped set into motion forces that created a city outside the city of Hazleton and decentralized the settlement pattern. The decentralization of the factors of production and of the settlement patterns in relation to working space has been common in industrial societies dependent on the automobile and truck. It has been especially true of the megalopolis; the settlement patterns have been largely a function of the energy base of society.

Forces inside and outside the region contributed to the diffusion of communities on the landscape, but a deep irony haunted the success of the Hazleton decision-makers. One of the major problems they sought to avert was dependence upon a single industry; the memory of the regional reliance on coal was too vivid. In accordance with their interests, they were also afraid of a large union presence as monolithic as the industry they opposed. Mining unions were still receiving a portion of the blame, albeit rather naively, for the demise of the industry. The irony was that the industries in the parks were primarily chemical processing plants and that the decentralization of industry and the transportation networks that facilitated it were ultimately based on inexpensive oil, as Gottman observed in 1960. In a very deep sense, the control over the factors of production remained outside the region in company headquarters just as it had been during the height of the coal mining period when owners lived in Philadelphia and New York and ownership had been in the hands of large railroads and banks. The men of CAN DO did not own the major regional factors of production, and this is a significant structural feature of the locality. The local bourgeoisie thus did not own the means of production, by and large, but they did control much of the means of consumption: local manufacturing, services, and retail for local use.

Three major economic shifts directly affected settlements as a result of CAN DO successes in building the industrial park and attracting tenants. Industry, retail services, and communities moved or located outside the city of Hazleton. The industrial park was built on reclaimed coalfields outside the city limits, a decision that kept the city from realizing taxable income. Retail services, particularly large department stores, furniture, and dime stores *cum* discount outlets, left the city. As a result downtown Hazleton became something of a ghost town once again, with the center of the city left to minor shops, banking, and empty buildings. By 1979 this exodus had become a painful reminder to many of the Chamber members of their failures as well as their successes. Moves were already underway to build new YMCA and YWCA recreational centers in center city. Two publicly subsidized housing units for the elderly had been constructed, and the largest hotel in the city had been converted to an apartment complex for the aged. Rather than the sight of coal trucks, the major vision when driving through Hazleton on a sunny day is of the elderly sunning themselves on benches along the main street. The decline of the downtown area—while a result of CAN DO and developmental efforts—reflects the national economic and spatial trends associated with the auto from 1950 to 1980.

Communities were primarily affected in one of two ways: working-class villages were stabilized, and the elite of Hazleton moved out of the city to the Conyngham Valley seven miles to the north. The exodus to the bucolic valley of the newly affluent—well rewarded for their acquisition of social power—had the effect of splitting the region: a gentrified local, mainly Protestant, elite inhabited a rural setting; the city was left to the largely Jewish and Catholic populations who had arrived last in the region. The city dwellers were left mobility routes via politics and small businesses, while the valley dwellers achieved their mobility via larger businesses and the professions. The incoming managers of the factories in the industrial park were recruited to the valley, where new housing was available and where the prized visual amenities were the highest. Despite their proximity many of these people did not know what a patchtown was, a testimony to the fact that local affiliation was entirely absent. There was a further division between the affluent newcomers and the affluent natives. The factory managers, though they share many of the same tastes and lifestyles as the local elite, have not become integrated

into the community associations. They do not acquire strong local affiliations and identities. This is partially due to their own mobility and
aspirations, since the industries in the parks are merely a step on a career
ladder. The manager or executive expects to stay for a few years and
move to a better position in a better location. The locals have no such
orientation or intent.

With the building of new, large houses in the valley townships, the
county tax assessor felt forced to reassess property values. One of the
major impacts of valley residential development has been the increased
valuation of property, forcing an increase in taxes. This impact has particularly hurt the resident elderly who have fixed incomes; many have
challenged the assessment in the courts to redress the problem.

Two major changes in settlement pattern in the Conyngham Valley
affect, mainly, prime agricultural land. The old agricultural service vil-

Hazleton and the Conyngham Valley looking north. The valley, which is seven
miles north of Hazleton, is a source of pride and amenity to those who live on
the mountain. The visual dullness of the coal fields is offset by the visual beauty
of the undulating shale valley. Topography and society are neatly bifurcated by
mountain zone and valley zone. (Photograph by Ace Hoffman, courtesy of CAN
DO)

lage of Conyngham has been surrounded by suburban development, where whole tracts have been built in the cul-de-sac style of platting. Another, more haphazard, pattern has developed as farmers have sold off corner lots and acreage facing the valley roads. The desultory strip development conflicts with agricultural viability, and, as a result, there is not much farming adjacent to the most built-up village areas. These changes have resulted from the growth of population and the availability of the automobile. Other social distances have emerged as well. Before and immediately after World War II, the villages of the valley and those of the coalfields were engaged in a friendly, aggressive intervillage baseball rivalry. With the increasing reliance on the auto and the growing affluence of the valley dwellers, baseball fell by the wayside. The valley Conyngham Rubes no longer challenge the mountain Jeddo Stars where in residual eastern European accents baseball players once cursed or praised the results of their turn at bat. In Conyngham, sports have taken a more private turn, away from baseball and community, toward tennis, swimming, and jogging by individuals.

Among the working class, flag football, said to be imported from California, has caught on. The game was modeled after regular American football, but each player has a handkerchief sticking out of his hip pocket. If a person has the ball during a turn at play and an opponent captures the handkerchief, the play ends at that location. There were twelve teams in 1974, the games were played on Sunday just as was professional football, and the players were working-class men just out of high school. Football has largely supplanted baseball among the young adult workers in popularity, and the Little League and Babe Ruth League baseball organizations have died in the working-class villages as a result of lowered birth rates and the absence of gradeschool-age children.

There are numerous, nonobvious effects of the industrial park development on the settlement patterns and communities of the Hazleton region. I conducted intensive interviews among some of the industrial park workers, and one of these interviews was conducted in Rock Glen. This is an unincorporated village sited next to an acidic stream that drains Buck Mountain, on which Hazleton is situated. Not only was there acid mine drainage in the creek, but it was an open sewer for the patchtowns located on its banks. The village is directly beneath two mountains. On one there was active coal mining, and on the other the derelict machines used for timbering were rusting in the secondary growth. The houses were wood frame, not built to endure, and most were sided with a tarpaper designed to resemble bricks. This gave the illusion of permanence and good construction, but it was merely an illusion. The village had grown up with the Gowen Mine, where many of its inhabitants had worked, and with the Pennsylvania Railroad, which had built its tracks just above the town. Its deteriorating appearance was accentuated by the abandoned and inactive railroad bed. The nonobvious effect that the industrial parks had on this settlement was that they stabilized what had been a dying town; because the people who lived there could commute in twenty minutes, if the roads were not ice-covered, to Valmont Industrial Park. The stabilization effect was widespread among regional settlements and was a function of the decentralization of industry and the automobile, in which one could commute long distances to work.

As a result of interviews with the workers, I came away with several strong impressions which have been validated by other experiences and not falsified by any of the statistics available for the region:

1. The workers were relatively underemployed. The direct meaning of this is that a young head of household could not afford to support spouse and children and purchase a home on a single, unskilled worker's salary.
2. There had been a lack of upward occupational mobility among many workers over a long time period in the region. The length of time was 100 years, and the occupations included semiskilled and supervisory positions in: carpentry, building, driving, steelworking, farming, butchering, mining, telegraph operating, and railroading. Many of the current workers in the industrial parks held positions similar to their great-grandfathers'.
3. There was a great deal of geographical mobility for work. Before the auto, people moved repeatedly from house to house and settlement to settlement in the region. After the auto, people moved from job source to job source while remaining in the same house and settlement.
4. There were many family members in the region and in the same settlement. The extended family was invaluable in easing the stresses of lateral mobility and underemployment.
5. The workers—both female and male—used multiple employment strategies through the course of their lifetimes to adapt to different and evolving laboring opportunities in the region. The people did not hold the same jobs through a career and were self-trained in several semiskilled occupations.

During the course of the interview in Rock Glen, I was able to elicit the employment history of a family who traced their ancestry back more than 100 years. In one house an industrial park worker in his twenties was married and had one child. He had moved his family into his grandmother's house to care for her. He was to inherit the house upon her death in exchange for the care he and his wife gave. His mother and father lived up the street, and he had aunts, uncles, and siblings in the village as well. In order to acquire enough income for what he perceived as a middle-class living standard, he had learned upholstering by mail order. He and his wife, who also cared for the small child, did contracting for upholstering. He had just negotiated a contract with the largest department store in Hazleton to do custom upholstering, a kind of steady piecework that was particularly important to him. The family vehicle was a pickup truck that he used to commute to work and to pick up and deliver the upholstery jobs. His occupational career was initiated by a combination of cottage industry and wage labor. This combination was common among workers in the village; others, for example, had auto repair shops in their garages; one was a taxidermist.

Long commuting to work was common in this village, and one worker reported that he had commuted 120 miles a day for twenty-five years to work in the steel mills. His particular choice after the war had been to remain a resident of Rock Glen and to drive long distances to work.

Although working-class people had only praise for the efforts of CAN DO which resulted in more local employment opportunities, they acknowledged stresses as well. The most painful was the problem of low wages. Underemployment had in fact been endemic to the region since the nineteenth century; periodic strikes, layoffs, and firings had been common in the coalfields. It seemed that the workers expected employment uncertainty and had developed effective strategies to deal with it. The interview with the Websters of Rock Glen and the view of their living arrangements, their care for one another during periodic illnesses, layoffs, and unemployment, revealed the powerful role the family played in alleviating some of the structural problems of these liminal, predominantly working-class regions. The unions were fragmented among the different occupations represented in the industrial park, and the men of CAN DO realized de facto their wish for ineffectual union presence.

In administering the Cornell Medical Index (CMI) to a sampling of people on the mountain and in the valley, it was discovered that both populations suffered from stress diseases. Formerly, mine workers were afflicted with mine-related pathologies, such as black lung, blindness, and the loss of limbs. The present population shares more equal participation in the etiologies resulting from a consumer-oriented society (Gori and Richter 1978:1125). The current disorders included the classic stress diseases, such as cancer, ulcer, heart disease, hypertension, and overweight. In addition, the CMI results indicated that many people in the region may be suffering from medically significant emotional disturbance. The study suggested that, as mining has declined and the region has acquired the consumer lifestyles of contemporary society, Hazleton is becoming more like the rest of the United States and becoming less anomalous. Since the CMI is widely used by physicians in order to develop general medical information, it was not considered definitive, and the results acquired were not statistically significant. As a tool it was meant to convey an overview, and that is how it has usually been deployed.

When asked in 1974 what the greatest social problems were in the region, people responded—with much agreement among themselves— that they were plagued by inadequate medical facilities, political corruption, lack of educational opportunities and services in the outlying areas, poor public transportation, insufficient facilities for senior citizens, and an absence of recreational activities for children and teenagers. The long-term problems they identified included the xenophobic

fear that new populations of blacks and Hispanic peoples would migrate to the region in search of employment, that children would continue to out-migrate, that agriculture would disappear from the valley,
and that second home development would overrun the area with transient homeowners from Philadelphia and New York. The strengths
they identified as peculiar to the region included ethnic cohesiveness,
strong family bonds, a strong sense of the local community, and a powerful work ethic (Berger 1976: 303).

The public welfare data suggest that the people of Luzerne County
did indeed have strong family ties, as the Hazleton informants had mentioned. Only two counties in Pennsylvania had a lower divorce rate in
1970 than Luzerne County; and while Philadelphia received support for
16.6 percent of its population from the Pennsylvania Department of Public Welfare, Luzerne County by contrast received support for only 4.9
percent (Pennsylvania Statistical Abstracts, 1973).

The fluctuations to which the country and Hazleton both responded
were reflected in shifts in the agricultural picture of the Conyngham
Valley and Luzerne County. Through interviews with farmers, bankers,
and county assessors, we acquired a view of the agricultural situation in
the valley on a farm-by-farm basis. To summarize, the older farmers in
the suburbanizing end of the Valley had sold out and retired, while the
younger farmers remained in the western end of the Valley and were
doing well. There had been a shift in agricultural production from crop
to dairy, and this was reflected also in the scale of operations, which had
increased in recent years. During the 1974 fieldwork period, the farmers
of the valley joined the Philadelphia milkshed. The local milkshed was
thereby transcended, and the increase in scale of operations was reflected
by participation in the larger service area made possible by truck milk
shipping and the larger scale of milk processing and distribution. In
Luzerne County during the twenty-year period 1954–74, the number of
farms decreased from 1,990 to 401 and the amount of acreage in agricultural production plummeted from 130,000 acres to 56,250. The total number of acres fell by more than 50 percent, but the average size of the
remaining farms increased, and thus the scale of operation was larger. As
the small family farm decreased after the war, the ratio of farmers to
nonfarmers in the U.S. population continued its dramatic fall; the region
thus reflected national trends. The ratio of agricultural producers to
consumers in the advanced nations, especially the United States—where
in 1970, according to the United States Census, farmers were 4.8 percent
of the population—is perhaps the best evidence that the Industrial Revolution has increased the carrying capacity of the earth in a proportion
approximating population increase.

Moving with the larger trends in the country, Hazleton increased its
service sector as a key part of a more diversified local economy. A new
vocational-technical school was begun and a two-year college in the
Pennsylvania state system was started. Both schools resulted, in part,

from vigorous CAN DO efforts. These efforts helped erase the differences between the Hazleton average and the state average of years of school completed. The anthracite area had always been lower in educational services and achievement than the rest of the state. The local regional high schools were also consolidated after the war, the result of federal and state policy and funding. The possibility of high school consolidation was generated exogenously, but it required agonizing decisions among the local people. One of these decisions was where to site the regional high school; the question was resolved by locating it on the mountain. Another problem arose, one which often attends the concentration of capital. Since the consolidated school system budget was in excess of $12 million per year, lucrative contracts were awarded for construction and food service. Affluent valley dwellers were distressed over the results of the school consolidation. They felt that the Mafia had acquired access to the school district service contracts and were using extortion and other means to take money. The Federal Bureau of Investigation launched an inquiry; unfortunately, at just that time a fire destroyed the relevant records. A we/them theme developed in conversations with the valley suburbanites, where "we" were the people of the valley, and "they" were the people of Hazleton mountain and city. It was pointed out that there had been sixteen school districts with seven to nine school board directors each serving 8,000 people. In 1974 there was one school district made up of the former sixteen, and there were only nine school board members representing 150,000 people. School taxes had almost doubled as a result of the consolidation, and local people had entirely lost control of the local schools. This loss was widely lamented in the valley. There was neither much discussion nor much awareness of the impact this had on the schoolchildren, but juvenile crime was thought to be on the increase, especially vandalism, resulting, it was believed, from boredom. To the field workers it seemed that the consolidated school provided fewer activities per capita than had the local school. Where there had been many high school basketball teams, there was now just one; this fact alone suggested a reduction of participation possibilities for the students. Advocates of school consolidation point to increased instructional quality, but this was not perceived to be the case by the suburban valley residents who were actively discussing sending their children to private schools. As a result of these and other stresses, greater parental demands were placed on public services in general and on regulated play activity in particular than during any previous period in the region's history.

The major impacts of the postwar growth period were upon the stabilizing and destabilizing of land uses, settlement patterns, and community composition. These consequences were the direct results of local forces, such as CAN DO, and exogenous forces, such as the growth and decentralization of industrial production and the extension of services from the federal and state governments. The particular configurations of both the public and private sectors were functions of a fossil-fuel-based economy. A selection of these impact chains can generally be modeled (figure 25). Much more detailed submodels can be constructed and can aid in understanding the interdependencies of local social and ecological systems.

THE EVOLVING FRAMEWORK OF POLITICAL ECONOMY

The CAN DO experience must be framed within the regional political economy of the petroleum period.* This larger play of forces created the possibility for the creation and success of Hazleton's CAN DO. The country's industries during the petroleum period can be characterized in at least three ways: they became increasingly internationalized, they employed decentralized production processes, and they came to be owned largely by companies which diversified and expanded through takeovers and mergers. At the same time, there was a growth of new institutional forms in the public sector, and, at times, curious fusings between the public and the private, resulting in growth of the not-for-profit sector.

Although I have portrayed much of the interior view of the successful economic development of Hazleton by concentrating on the successful efforts of a not-for-profit, community-based corporation, this organization was merely one of a class. Many of the settlements in the coalfields employed the same strategy, though, as I have emphasized,

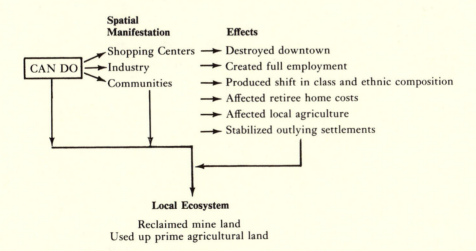

Figure 25. Impact chains

---

*Data in this section are derived from interviews with executives, from public lectures, and from annual reports of companies and councils.

none of the other efforts equaled CAN DO's organizational or economic success in the Hazleton area. Behind all the coalfield community efforts, largely hidden to a field worker absorbed in the communities of the Hazleton region, a presence was dimly reflected in even the most directed interviews. It was that of the Pennsylvania Power and Light Company (PP and L), a utility that monopolizes service to a 25,900 square kilometer area in twenty-nine counties of central eastern Pennsylvania (figure 26). The anthracite region is wholly contained within this company's service area. Coal corporations had accounted for one-third of PP and L's energy demand, in 1947, but the executives of the company had discerned the trend of rapidly declining anthracite production as early as the 1930s. To keep the company viable and growing, policies were devised to disassociate the fortunes of the company from the misfortunes of the anthracite region. A succession of strategies were developed over the years, but two of these directly affected Hazleton. The first was to displace other fuel

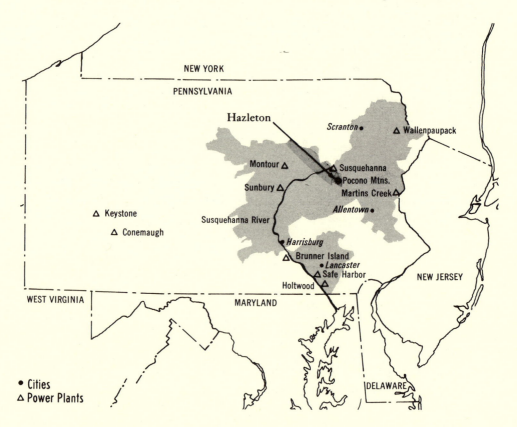

Figure 26. Pennsylvania Power and Light Company service area. Reprinted by permission from Pennsylvania Power and Light Company.

and energy sources with electricity for home heating in the new houses being built throughout the region for the more affluent. This tactic, while important to the viability of the company, provided a thermally inefficient and ultimately expensive home heating source (Commoner 1977). Their second strategy was to recruit new industries into the area on a region-wide basis (25,900 square kilometers), thereby generating new customers with high energy demands. PP and L became the major recruiting agent for industry into the coal country. When CAN DO found new companies, it was through either PP and L or the Pennsylvania Department of Commerce. PP and L was so successful in its sales of home electrical service to new customers and in recruiting new industries into the region that by 1968 it was the second largest utility in Pennsylvania and the twenty-third largest, based on numbers of customers, in the country. The emergence of the power companies closely parallels the rise of oil for use in the internal combustion engine. This is amply documented in PP and L's history; they built their current large-scale operation from 300 small operating companies and 700 nonoperating companies since 1920.

There are numerous linkages between PP and L, various other corporations, state and federal public agencies, congressional representatives, and the local nonprofit organizations such as CAN DO in the anthracite communities. These linkages have allowed PP and L to stimulate the economy of the region by reaching downscale to stimulate the local community and upscale to influence the large corporations and government agencies. The company's strategies for growth after the war included the attracting of industrial customers to the region to replace anthracite mining; substitution of electricity for gas, oil, and coal in home heating; lobbying at all governmental levels; creation of regional public-private, or not-for-profit agencies that would broker for its interests; and creation of local-level responses to the specter of economic decline. PP and L trained its local executives, especially regional vice-presidents, in the economic arts of community leadership. One of these vice-presidents was headquartered in the Hazleton regional office. To help accomplish its goal the company developed a slogan, "Area development is everyone's responsibility," and constructed a handbook—"The Bible," it was called—full of ways to initiate economic action at the community level. PP and L urged its executives to become involved in local Chambers of Commerce and social service clubs. In effect the firm built a constituency among local business club members with the long-range aim of stimulating the formation of nonprofit community organizations which would attract industry. It is not clear whether CAN DO members perceived PP and L's larger role in the region in just these terms, but the founders of CAN DO speak only with admiration of the role that PP and L and its executives played in fund-raising and in giving large donations to fund-raising drives. In addition, PP and L bought land along the interstate highway routes—routes that they had been influential in realizing—and sold the land at cost to the nonprofit community groups who wanted the sites for industrial parks. CAN DO bought such a parcel for Valmont Industrial Park. The large-scale corporations in the United States operate at a level beyond the local community and are more firmly niched into a national economic community than the local business people could ever be. PP and L's role in the state and in the region, and those of similar corporations elsewhere, cannot be underestimated. These roles are extremely important in terms of regional economic growth and political leadership. This complex of relations deserves further study, particularly with regard to its impact on regional ecosystems.

PP and L's fortunes in the region are a function of their relation to the Kondratieff wave. During the upswing of the wave from 1950 onward, the company enjoyed an annual, predicted, and planned growth rate of close to 12 percent. In the early 1970s during an updating of long-term projections based on evaluation of future economic trends and regional growth, the power companies formulated new predictions and set goals that would take them to the end of the twentieth century. From 1975 to the year 2000, the company expects to grow at the much-reduced rate of 2 percent annually, with inflation taken into account. This can be partially understood because the power industry as a whole suffers from an obsolete technology for making steam to generate electrical energy, and the shift to nuclear plants—an all too sophisticated means to make steam —has proved terrifically expensive in time and capital. Nuclear power has also failed to gain public support. The retiring chairman of the board, who was an impressive industry leader, expressed in a public lecture (Busby 1979) that in general PP and L and the other companies of the electric power industry are taking a cautious attitude and will wait to see what new technologies may become available—around 1990—before making more momentous, long-range decisions. The corporate awareness of PP and L fits nicely with the synchronic aspect of the model presented here. The corporation during the florescent period had a rate of growth that mirrored the national economy, so one can only conclude that their careful projections are probably accurate economic and technological assessments of the unfolding long-range downturn facing the economy.

Temporally, the company grew at varying rates for the last fifty years, and structurally it became a thoroughly contemporary large-scale firm. As an energy conversion process PP and L is a vertically integrated enterprise conveniently close to conventional energy sources. While planning for expansion in the 1930s, PP and L executives asked the line companies of the anthracite fields if coal supplies could be guaranteed for power generation. The line companies said they could not make such guarantees. As a result, PP and L turned to the bituminous coalfields for energy supplies for their power plants. Because of their different burning temperatures, bituminous and anthracite require different equipment design for steam-making in the electrical generating process. Despite the existence of millions of tons of anthracite in their service area, PP and L acquired bituminous mines in western Pennsylvania as well as the railroads to ship the coal to their plants in their eastern service area. PP and L thus integrated their operation from mining to shipping to generation to distribution of electrical power. After the war it was listed as a high-rate company because it charged more than many other utilities for its electricity; but PP and L chose a goal of rate reduction through increased economies of scale, and it was this decision that was coupled with a strategy of local community organization and building industrial parks. They introduced the industrial park concept at the local level and offered incentives such as land at cost for the park site, effectively stimulating regional economic redevelopment.

It cannot be stated too strongly that PP and L's interests in the region were a large-scale duplicate of the interests the members of CAN DO had in Hazleton. The members of CAN DO and PP and L *were all directly engaged in selling for a profit commodities or services to regional customers;* any fluctuation in customers immediately affected the viability of the business operation. Examples of operations that were threatened by exactly the same forces include the sale of bricks, newspapers, auto loans, or medical services in Hazleton, and the sale of power to anthracite and other counties. In sum, regional decline was brought about because of the obsolescence of anthracite as an energy source, hence as an employer, and as a market for the energy corporation. The executives of PP and L had acquired social power; had deployed ideas, influence, and direct involvement; and had provided goods (industrial park land), services, and cash grants to CAN DO and other similar fund drives at the local community level throughout the anthracite region. Because their interests converged with community groups like CAN DO, they could provide models for, and stimulus for, acquiring the social power necessary to stimulate increased energy flows in the energy conversion processes of northeastern Pennsylvania.

Some curious institutional entities in the rapidly growing not-for-profit sector (Ginzberg 1976:25–29) emerged in the postwar period. These are the regional nonprofit agencies, neither governmental nor private corporate institutions. One of these, and there are many (see Bezold 1978), was developed in northeastern Pennsylvania, and was appropriately called the Economic Development Council of Northeastern Pennsylvania (EDCNP). Its boundary fell within the PP and L service area and also contained the anthracite counties. EDCNP was proposed by a president of PP and L in 1965 (Busby 1965) and has since worked as a brokerage house for regional development. The original call by the PP and L president had been for an agency with the express purpose of effectively using state and federal aid, promoting land planning capabilities, and publicizing industry and tourism outside the region. The development council has indeed become an effective and successful not-for-profit brokerage organization, receiving 41 percent of its funding from the federal establishment and 26 percent from private contributions. Thirty-six percent of its expenditures go for "technical aid and development assistance to the economic, industrial, and business community." EDCNP reports

Figure 27. Economic Development Council of Northeastern Pennsylvania service area. Reprinted by permission from Economic Development Council of Northeastern Pennsylvania.

reveal that Luzerne County consistently submits the most grant applications for the largest amounts of money and receives the greatest aid; this is attributable to the untiring efforts of CAN DO.

During the three decades after the war a five-tiered public and not-for-profit sector emerged as a resource and stimulus to investment for redevelopment in the anthracite region. The place of PP and L and CAN DO is noted in table 8.

In the energy base transition from the third Kondratieff wave peak in the 1920s to the fourth wave peak in the 1970s, there was a concomitant transition in the ecology, economy, and social organization of the anthracite coal mining region. The older anthracite energy conversion processes guided by the market and the controlling mechanisms of banks, rails, and mining companies deteriorated and left behind a series of settlements, small cities, and outlying villages and towns. The social power of the Philadelphia and New York companies completely deteriorated, and revealed the nascent merchants, small manufacturers, professionals, and media firms of the coal cities. This was the local base of the postwar social order, while the large monopoly companies such as PP and L and the telephone company developed new forms of control and aided the self-organizational efforts of the local community economic revitalization corporations. Federal and state programs for regional redevelopment (such as the Appalachian Regional Commission), for highway building, and for industrial development contributed to the investment resources upon which large-scale and small-scale companies could draw. These institutional evolutions keeping pace with the rest of the country were attended among the people of Luzerne County by changing political allegiances. In 1952 the county had nearly twice as many Republicans as Democrats registered to vote. By 7 November 1972 Democratic registration exceeded that of Republicans by more than 10,000 (Pa. Statistical Abstracts, 1973). These figures indicate that the voting populace was moving toward an endorsement of more public intervention. They voted for

TABLE 8
The Place of PP&L and CAN DO in the Regional Political Economy

1. Nation: Federal congress and agencies: Economic Development Council
   U.S. Dept. of Transportation (U.S. DOT)

2. Macro-region: Appalachian Regional Commission (multi-state region)

3. State: Pennsylvania legislature, Pennsylvania Industrial Development Authority, PennDOT

4. Region: Economic Development Council of Northeastern Pennsylvania (EDCNP)—(PP&L private sector)

5. Local: CAN DO, local ecosystem

the Democratic party, which traditionally was associated with public rather than private intervention. The shift of the Hazleton regional economy from an extraction base to a mixed light manufacturing and service economy parallels closely the direction in which the United States economy has moved.

4

CONCLUSION

What is still missing is an energy policy to guide the transition.
Robert Stobaugh and Daniel Yergin
(1979:233)

We are not at Armageddon. But we are at an important turning-point
in the historical life of the capitalist world-economy.
Immanuel Wallerstein (1979:118)

The transitions in population and mobility are only facets of the grand
transition in human relations with the physical environment. This is
not a single transition, but a great many, involving both natural resources and social structure, the human species and all other species,
the surface of the Earth and the settlement of humans. The ecological
transition is equivalent to the ecological history of humanity; it is also
largely equivalent to what anthropologists have called cultural evolution.
John Bennett (1976:123)

The energy problem over the next two decades should be seen as one
of transition, in which countries need to adjust to higher energy prices
and ensure that their incremental needs can increasingly be met from
sources other than oil.
World Bank (1979)

THE CONTEMPORARY WORLD-SYSTEM

The year 1979 marked the fiftieth anniversary of the U.S. stock market crash of 1929. The columnists of the *New York Times* ran a series of
stories and interviewed a number of noted economists. The central question was whether there could be another stock market failure, and the
consensus was that there would not be a repeat of that stunning financial
disaster to the Western economies because, they explained, the structure
of investment in the stock market and the international monetary system
had been bolstered by new institutions, agreements, and regulations.

There is, however, a different scenario, widely written about in the
business pages of the daily newspapers, the business weeklies, and the

fortnightlies. This spate of fact and opinion addresses the prevailing business climate—the fluctuating attitude business people have toward profits and the expected return on investments at a given point in time —which is, at least at the local level, sober, especially regarding the current energy situation. Rather than a stock market crash, many heads of banks and multinational corporations take the view that petroleum costs will escalate due to periodic and overall increasing scarcity of sup- plies and reserves. The causes are found in the increasing demand for world oil, political instability in the oil-producing countries, and the long-term shortfalls as reserves diminish, which will continue to drive prices inexorably upward.

There are two possible effects from this process that are especially singled out in this literature, and should they be realized, they bode ill for the future fate of the world-economy over the next fifteen years. One immediate and widely felt effect is inflation, which even the most myopic economists are beginning to realize is tied rather closely to the costs of energy. It has been suggested that the rate of inflation could itself bring the Western economies to a real decline in gross national products; in brief, an economic depression paralleling the one following the stock market plunge of 1929. Because the highly productive countries of West- ern Europe, the United States, and Japan are so closely linked in trade and in their dependence on OPEC oil, they are, with Russia, the core of the capitalist world-system. If their economies were to falter, the rapidly developing countries, such as Brazil, and the less developed countries would plunge into economic chaos.

A second effect is no less serious than the first. As OPEC price increases drive up inflation, the oil-producing countries must continue to raise prices in order to sustain purchasing power with their inflated money. This is indeed a deadly spiral. One of the most damaging effects of this feedback loop between inflation and price increases is the eco- nomic squeeze faced by the less developed countries. Already heavily debt-ridden, needing to continue borrowing to industrialize, and de- manding petroleum to run the industries they have and are acquiring, they confront radically accelerating costs, for development loans and for oil, due to world inflation. Many observers fear that if the less developed countries begin to massively default on their loans—which is a real possi- bility—the world monetary institutions—such as the International Mon- etary Fund and the World Bank, and private concerns such as New York City's Chase Manhattan Bank—could not withstand the national bank- ruptcies. Such a chain of events could also trigger a world depression, and the implications of such a prospect are appalling. The quotations at the beginning of this section indicate that a number of learned observers converge in their view that the world is facing a transition of unprece- dented proportions; obviously the energy base of the contemporary world-system is undergoing a massive dislocation. The fluctuations at- tending this passage are evident in the interest rates. Twice in the 1970s, after each of the two OPEC price increases (1974, 1979), the U.S. prime interest rate set successive records for all-time highs. Although the Industrial Revolution began when interest levels hovered at 2 to 3 percent (Ashton 1969), they climbed well above 15 percent in 1980.

The core of the world-system appears to be shifting. It seems inevitable that the economically central industrialized nations cannot sustain their growth rates, particularly with their physical plant overwhelmingly dependent upon imported, high-cost energy resources. Friedman suggests a model that partially accounts for this process.

> Much of the present structural crisis in the world-economy is clearly related to this development—i.e., the tendency, small but growing, for the center as a whole to become a consumer of the products of its own exported capital, while producing less itself, leading to a chronic negative balance of payments. If the model outlined above is applicable to the center as a whole, i.e., a number of competing nation-states, it would seem to imply the long-run decline of the West and Japan and a shift of accumulation to some other area. [1978:145]

To expand his model in terms of the one presented in this case study, it appears that Western nations are exporting significant quantities of capital largely through the purchases of foreign oil. This export of capital to pay for the oil is then recycled back through the monetary system by the OPEC countries, who must reinvest their embarrassingly high capital returns. OPEC reinvests much of the money in banks, which in turn make loans to the less developed countries. The side effect of this energy transition is that areas of the globe that might not otherwise have ready access to investment can acquire it through this mechanism. Thus in this transition, the more marginal parts of the world are in fact increasing their carrying capacity, and hence the carrying capacity of the world through industrial and agricultural development. Friedman's model illuminates what many economic observers are now pointing out: that money spent outside a given country for energy represents capital that cannot be reinvested inside a country for its own continuing development. Money flowing from a nation leads it to stimulate different internal economic sectors to increase exports to offset the deteriorating balance of trade brought about by oil purchases. Oil-dependent countries all seek to expand exports, which crowd markets and lead to de facto trade wars. This effect, of course, is economically and politically debilitating.

In terms of the model presented in this book and in my own sense of the course of the petroleum-dependent world-economy, a world depression after the downturn of the present peaking of the fourth Kondratieff wave is highly likely. I say this because world industry and agriculture are overwhelmingly dependent on oil, and its supply is subject to insoluble structural problems. Unfortunately ready substitutes for the current energy complex have not been sighted on the horizon with any certainty. The transition to a new energy source will prove, I fear, to be painful. In this light the question can be asked: What will happen on Hazleton mountain to the already depressed regional economy, to the social structures that emerged since the war to guide the flows of energy and matter? The answer could be given that, if there is a massive world-scale economic collapse, Hazleton, being insignificant in this process, would not matter. I think rather just the opposite. The world is made up of local places like Hazleton, though each differs from another. These social units are the ones that will be at the forefront of adaptation to and innovation within the emerging world-system that a depression would demand. It is no more certain, however, what path Hazleton and its surrounding villages would choose than whether or not a world depression is imminent. However challenging the petroleum period and its transition may prove to be, the area does now have a tradition of adversity and a strong, positive response to it within the opportunities and constraints of the capitalist economy. There are also vast quantities of anthracite in the ground that become more attractive for recovery as the increasing costs of oil make the anthracite relatively less expensive to mine and use.

POSTSCRIPT ON HAZLETON

Like any other bureaucracy, CAN DO presently has a bureaucratic momentum with large investments in social visibility and a large number of visible and invisible constituents. The overinvestment in industrial park land represents the more tangible side of this built-up motion. This is potentially dangerous for the flexibility of response that is demanded by changing conditions; and, perhaps more seriously, it can introduce possibly damaging features into the regional system in pursuit of its established goals. During an interview with an executive officer, he elaborated at length on the problems of industrial waste disposal and recycling. The conversation built up to the tortured issue of environmental pollution and the growing resistance on the part of some segments of local communities to polluting industries. The officer recounted two such cases and indicated that Hazleton would pursue those industries that other communities had vigorously rejected. One such firm was a lead recycling plant that extracted the substance from old auto batteries, and the other was a new chemical corporation formed to recycle hazardous chemical wastes from existing toxic fill sites and operating industries.

During the 1974 fieldwork it became apparent that CAN DO recruited firms regardless of the potential or real hazards that the workplace might have, displaying a lack of concern for the health of the workers whose disposable incomes they sorely need. The new strategy of recruiting those firms other communities rejected suggests several complex dimensions. It is the case that the wastes of industrial society need proper treatment; the high incidence of cancer in New Jersey, the highest per capita in the United States, is directly related to the large concentration of chemical companies and reflects a flagrant example of this pressing demand. On the other hand the question remains: who will insure that the recycling and waste treatment firms Hazleton recruits will protect those workers involved in the physical manipulation of the toxic materials? There is no adequate answer. The CAN DO members now appear to be trading the health of their regional workers for the pursuit of their own goals. They are, in addition, counting on public support for their moves, believing, perhaps rightly, that the citizenry of Hazleton will not object to hazards in the workplace because they are willing to risk their health and that of their kinsmen for jobs. For a worker this is not a dilemma that readily admits to socially just outcomes. CAN DO is thus counting on the tradition of risk-taking among the descendants of miners, who once worked in the most debilitating and deadly region during the Industrial Revolution.

There is ample evidence of the lack of concern over the well-being and social organization of the labor force on the part of the CAN DO staff and in its recruitment policy. The numerous unions associated with the local industries are considered to be divided, hence good, unlike the monolithic United Mine Workers of little more than a generation ago (there are more than twenty unions, and 90 percent of the industries are now unionized). Labor, like management, is considered by CAN DO to be an internal affair to the incoming company. One officer commented that labor is not always to blame and that poor management decisions have resulted in blatant failure in firms in the industrial park. Despite criticism of management, the indifference toward labor is even more apparent. When asked if Hazleton had labor problems, an officer commented that they had a bit but not as much as the larger cities of the anthracite region. An informal and personalistic relationship between organized labor and CAN DO was revealed, and it speaks to the inadequately understood and far from dominant role labor has played in United States life.

> The only thing that we don't have here is a good, good strong labor leader that could. . . . Back years ago Tom Kennedy was the Vice-President and then eventually President of the United Mine Workers. He was born and raised in Hazleton. He had his home here while he had his office even down in Washington. He was under John L. Lewis; he was Vice-President then. And when there was some union problems in some of the plants, and we could foresee that maybe it would be a week or two or something like that—at least the talk was like that—the company and the union so far apart that very politely we would ask Tom Kennedy,
> "Why don't you pick up the phone and call the union people and find out what the story is?"
> And he would just in his own way with his political pressure ask,
> "Alright what's goin' on and what're ya lookin' for?"
> That's what Tom Kennedy was saying, okay.
> "What're ya talkin' about?"
> And then he would let someone know, and then we'd say to the company,

"Alright, company, let's get off your high horse."
And the first thing you know, the thing was settled. This meant you had a good strong labor leader in the area. There's nothing wrong with that.

The disregard of the labor force, the hazards of the workplace, the further potential ecological degradation of the mountain, and the stagnating regional economy are problems that may prove insurmountable to evolving CAN DO strategies and existing social organization. The stresses in all the anthracite communities are continuously being played out in relation to the world-economy. The fluctuating moods of the Hazleton mountain business people reflect the inadequately met problems of a formerly essential extraction region.

I have two final observations to make, both speculative, one concerning the evolving social organization of the Hazleton region, the other about the long wave in the evolution of the international economy. CAN DO as an entity faces a couple of strong challenges that will change it. The first challenge is the current energy transition that is upon us with the attendant downturn of the economy and the further decline of employment possibilities in the anthracite region. The second challenge that CAN DO must face is the aging and retirement of the postwar generation of men whose vision of a revitalized community was first realized, then disappointingly eroded. Who the next generation of CAN DO people will be and what their perceptions and organizational responses will be is a matter worthy of serious speculation (Haefele 1980). If a high demand for anthracite should materialize along with the predicted greater worldwide use of coal (Wilson 1980), then new organizational structures will rapidly emerge in the coal region once again beyond the reach of the communities, like Hazleton, that now enjoy a prominent position to control flows of energy, matter, information, labor, and capital. CAN DO could be rendered socially obsolete. My own sense is that CAN DO will in fact not outlast this age cohort in the form that can now be discerned.

My second observation is more in the nature of a reflection on some of the implications of the model set forth. I consider the behavior of the long wave, if indeed it does register underlying energy transitions, to be unnecessary. These great fluctuations cause local-level hardships that seem completely unwarranted and avoidable. Although I have claimed that the capitalist world-system is determined at this point in history, I have not succumbed to the fatalism such a view might encourage. Rather, I believe that if the world-economy were perceived to be a function of the adaptation of the human species to the planet by means of energy exchanges, then that awareness would facilitate intervention. Intervention would require that conceptual and institutional means be found to insure a stabilized relationship between world population and world energy supply and distribution. The great fluctuations must be dampened by insuring an energy supply that does not exhaust resources, an

exhaustion that causes the decline in the economy and worldwide depre
sion. The human suffering resulting from these economic vicissitud
could potentially be alleviated. Perhaps the greatest justification for suc
an optimistic view results from the theory of evolution itself. By assur
ing that we are evolving toward greater complexity and are becomir
conscious of this evolution, then the next logical step is to think, as mar
are doing, on where we fit and wish to fit in the continuing process, th
is, the future. Boulding has observed that

> With man, however, comes self-awareness, and not only self-awar
> ness but awareness of a whole system in which the self is embedde
> This can produce conscious effort toward a change in the system (
> the world whether biological, physical, or social. In any huma
> social system, therefore, the image of the world possessed by i
> human participants is a vital element in the over-all dynamics of th
> system. We cannot tell what the system will do unless we know wh
> the people in it think of it, for what they think affects their behavic
> and their behavior affects the system. [1965:158]

With these observations Boulding anticipated the ecological transitio
heralded by Bennett and by Bateson. The challenge is to begin designin
our future while insuring the possibility that we will continue to hav
one. The philosopher Husserl nicely captured (in 1935) the basis of m
expectation, which is rooted in the scientific enterprise:

> Scientific culture under the guidance of ideas of infinity means, ther
> a revolutionization of the whole culture, a revolutionization of th
> whole manner in which mankind creates culture. It also means
> revolutionization of historicity, which is now the history of th
> cutting-off of finite mankind's development as it becomes mankin
> with infinite tasks. [1970:279]

I end on a note of scientific optimism. The local communities that an
thropologists almost invariably study, and often serve as advocates for
suffer or benefit as the result of the hidden machinery of exogenou
forces. By controlling the larger system, the interests of local regions an
ways of life can, it is hoped, be more justly served. One aspect of the
infinite project should be to control the greater system in the interests o
facilitating the lesser systems, on which the greater necessarily depends

APPENDIX

Apostolic
  Apostolic Faith Church
Assemblies of God
  Assembly of God Church
Baptist
  First Baptist Church
  Grace Baptist Church
  Grace Fellowship Church
Catholic—Byzantine Rite
  St. John's Greek Catholic Church
Catholic—Latin Rite
  St. Joseph's Roman Catholic Church
  Holy Rosary Church
  Most Precious Blood
  Holy Trinity Church
  Mother of Grace Church
  St. Gabriel's Church
  SS. Peter and Paul Roman Catholic Church
  Holy Trinity Slovak Church
Byzantine Catholic
  St. Mary's Catholic Church
Christian Science
  First Church of Christ, Scientist
Jehovah's Witnesses
  Kingdom Hall of Jehovah's Witnesses
Episcopal
  St. Peter's Church
Lutheran
  Christ Lutheran Church
  St. John's Lutheran Church
  SS. Peter and Paul Lutheran Church
  Trinity Lutheran Church
  West Hazleton Trinity Lutheran Church
Polish National Catholic
  St. John the Baptist Polish National Catholic Church
Presbyterian
  First Presbyterian Church
Salvation Army
  The Salvation Army
Synagogues—Conservative
  Agudas Israel Synagogue

Synagogues—Reform
  Beth Israel Temple
Ukrainian Catholic
  St. Michael's Ukrainian Catholic Church
United Church of Christ
  Christ Memorial United Church of Christ
  Emmanuels United Church of Christ
  Grace United Church of Christ
  St. Paul's Reformed United Church of Christ
United Methodist
  Diamond Methodist Church
  St. John's PM Church
  St. Paul's Methodist Church
  Salem United Methodist Church
  Welsh Congregational Church
  Gospel Chapel
  Zion E. C. Church

CAN DO, INC. ORGANIZATION CHART

Community-Area New Development Organization, Inc.

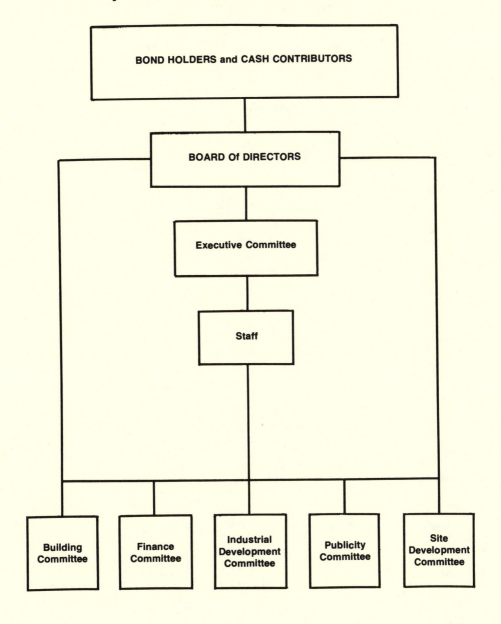

CAN DO, INC.
COMMITTEES—1973-74

NAME	CAN DO FUNCTION	OCCUPATION
	EXECUTIVE COMMITTEE	
Edgar L. Dessen	Chairman of the Board	Medical Doctor
Hugh L. Campbell, III	President	Brick Manufacturer
Louis G. Feldmann	Vice President & Counsel	Attorney at Law
Arthur A. Krause	Vice President & Industrial Development Comm. Chr.	Telephone Company Executive
John Chaplinsky	Vice President	Power & Light Executive
Robert T. Wagner	Secretary	Bank Vice President
Eugene C. Bogdon	Treasurer & Finance Committee Chairman	Bank President
George H. Snyder	Assistant Treasurer	Retired Banker
Robert J. Miorelli	Site Development Comm. Chairman	Building Contractor
Robert Marsilio	Building Committee Chairman	Building Contractor
Martin D. Cohn		Attorney at Law
Carl A. Shermer		Union Official
Eugene M. Dougherty		Vending Service Owner
Joseph Yenchko	Asst. Secretary & Industrial Director	
W. Kevin O'Donnell	Asst. Secretary & Asst. Ind. Director	
	BUILDING COMMITTEE	
Robert Marsilio	Comm. Chr—Exec. Comm. Member	Architect-Contractor
John J. Breslin	Building Committee Vice Chairman	Salesman (Retired)
Allan W. Holman		Insurance Sales (Retired)
Martin Karchner		Trucking Manager
James H. North		Retail Manager
Aloyius Rossi		Retail Manager
Angelo Sacco		Manufacturer
Nicholas Sedon		Union Official
Carl A. Shermer	Executive Committee Member	Union Official
*John J. DePierro		Architect
*John T. Miorelli		Architect
*George Nelson		Engineer
*Edward J. Pittinger		Engineer
	INDUSTRIAL DEVELOPMENT COMMITTEE	
Arthur A. Krause	Comm. Chr.—Exec. Comm. Member	Telephone Company Executive
John Chaplinsky	Comm. V. Chr.—Exec. Comm. Member	Power & Light Executive
Rev. John M. Brndjar		Clergyman
Martin D. Cohn	Executive Committee Member	Attorney at Law
Victor C. Diehm Sr.		Broadcast Company Owner
Eugene M. Dougherty	Executive Committee Member	Vending Service Owner
Louis G. Feldmann	Executive Committee Member	Attorney at Law
Carl E. Kirschner		Attorney at Law
Nicholas Marsilio		Builder
Robert J. Miorelli		Building Contractor
Ramon S. Saul		Newspaper Sports Editor
George H. Snyder	Executive Committee Member	Banker (Retired)
John H. Wright Jr.		Auto Dealer
*Burton E. Schafer		Banker

*Not Members of the Board

FINANCE COMMITTEE

Eugene C. Bogdon	Comm. Chr.—Exec. Comm. Member	Bank President
George H. Snyder	Comm. V. Chr.—	Banker (Retired)
	Exec. Comm. Member	
Robert K. Gicking		Bank President
Roy E. Johnson		Bank Vice President
Robert T. Wagner		Bank Vice President
*George Ernst		Bank Vice President
*Michael Romancheck, Jr.		Bank President
*William J. Simmons		Bank Vice President
*Joseph Weber		Certified Public Accountant
*Paul W. Williams		Bank Vice President

SITE DEVELOPMENT COMMITTEE

Robert J. Miorelli	Comm. Chr.—Exec. Comm. Member	Building Contractor
Henry W. Olewine	Committee Vice Chairman	Equipment Salesman
Frank DeAndrea		Insurance—Real Estate Sales
Robert Justofin		Pharmacist
Emerson Stevens		Manufacturer
Walter Tunnessen		Auto Parts Wholesaler
Thomas J. Wanik		Heavy Equipment Operator
*Robert L. Hillard		Water Company Manager
*Roy Felker		U.G.I. Manager
*Joseph Michel		Engineer

PUBLICITY COMMITTEE

Ramon S. Saul	Committee Chairman	Newspaper Sports Editor
Paul Cerula	Committee Vice Chairman	University Business Manager
Francis X. Antonelli		School Principal
John A. Bobey		Industrial Supervisor
*Dominic A. Antonelli		Newspaper Editor
*James R. Boyle		Radio News Director

*Not Members of the Board

ORGANIZATIONS LISTED IN CAN DO MIMEOGRAPHED MATERIALS

MEN'S ORGANIZATIONS

Barbershoppers
Hazleton Art League Camera Club
Columbus Club
Delta Nu Alpha Transportation Fraternity
Gr. Hazleton Dental Society
Friendly Sons of St. Patrick
Haz. Area Management Club
Freeland Area Jaycees
Gr. Hazleton Jaycees
Valley Jaycees
Kiwanis Club of Hazleton
Conyngham Valley Lions Club
Federation of Men's Bible Classes of Lower Luzerne and Carbon Counties
Lions Club of Drums
Lions Club of Freeland
Hazleton Lions Club
Lions Club of McAdoo
Twin County Lions Club
Lions Club of Weatherly
Lions Club of West Hazleton
Lions Club of White Haven
Rotary Club of Hazleton
Freeland Rotary Club
Weatherly Rotary Club
North Central Penn Safety Council
Swing Club
Haz. Toastmaster's Club #2405
Unico Club of Hazleton
Sheppton-Oneida Area Lions Club

WOMEN'S ORGANIZATIONS

American Business Women's Assoc., Keystone Chapter
Beta Sigma Phi Sororities
    Xi Epsilon Epsilon
    Kappa Upsilon
Bishop Hafey Mothers' Club
Gr. Hazleton Business and Professional Women
International Federation of Catholic Alumnae
The Penna. Guild of Craftsmen, Hazleton Chapter
Hazleton Dental Society, Ladies Auxiliary
Hazleton Garden Club
Drums Garden Club
Weatherly Garden Club
Lioness Club of Hazleton
Conyngham Valley Lionettes
Twin County Lionettes
West Haz. Lions Club Auxiliary
Lower Luzerne County Medical Society Auxiliary, Hazleton Branch

Practical Nurses Association
"Reddy Wives" of PP&L Co.
National Secretaries Assoc., Hazleton Chptr.
Hazleton State General Hospital Auxiliary
St. Joseph's Hospital Auxiliary
The Soroptimist Club of Hazleton
Unico Auxiliary
American Association of University Women
League of Women Voters, Hazleton Area
Hazleton Woman's Club
Church Women United
The First Legislative Democratic Women's Club
Hazleton Council of Republican Women
Freeland Lioness Club
Penn State Women's Auxiliary of the Hazleton Campus

MISCELLANEOUS ORGANIZATIONS

Hazleton Animal Shelter, Inc.
Hazleton Antique Car Club, Hazleton Area Chptr.
Arena Guild
Hazleton Art League, Inc.
Anthracite Motor Club
Can Do, Inc.
Gr. Hazleton Chamber of Commerce
Choralairs
Haz. Community Concert Assoc.
Conyngham Valley Civic Organization
Council on Drug Enlightenment
Haz. Area Educational Assoc.
Gr. Haz. Fine Arts Council, Inc.
Creative Craftsmen of Luzerne County
Hazleton Lutheran Home
St. Luke Manor
Gr. Haz. Senior Highlanders
Highlanders Jr. Drum & Bugle Corps
Independent Insurance Agents of Gr. Hazleton
High-Up, Inc.
Gr. Hazleton Cultural and Historical League
Hazleton Liberty Band
Hazleton Area Film Society
Lower Luzerne County Bar Assoc.
Hazleton Area Public Library, Board of Trustees
Luzerne County Medical Society, Hazleton Branch
Haz. Ministerial Assoc.
Mountain City Ski Club
Haz. Mummer's Assoc.
Nukumer's Club of Conyngham Valley Civic Org.
Gr. Hazleton Oratorio Society
Penn Rod and Gun Club
The Philharmonic Society
Fraternal Order of Police Power City Lodge 18

Executive Committee of the Retail Merchants' Council
Hazleton Sierra Club of Hazleton
All-America Sr. Citizens of Hazleton
Sr. Citizens of the YM-YWCA
Gr. Hazleton Sr. Citizens Services Activities Center
Silver Beavers Drum & Bugle Corps
Hazleton Area Center for Slavic Studies
Sugarloaf Golf Club, Inc.
Tirolesi Alpini of Halzeton
Greater Hazleton Buddy Program, Inc.
United Way of Gr. Hazleton
Valley Country Club
West Hazleton Improvement Club
Hazleton City Civic Organization
M.P.B. Players
Gr. Hazleton Area Polonaise Society
St. Francis Mission Club of Hazleton

BIBLIOGRAPHY

Adams, R. N.
>   1975 *Energy and structure.* Austin: University of Texas Press.
>   1978 Man, energy, and anthropology: I can feel the heat, but where's the light? *American Anthropologist* 80:298–309.
American Ethnologist
>   1977 Human Ecology (special issue) 4:1–206.
Amin, S.
>   1974 *Accumulation on a world scale: a critique of the theory of underdevelopment.* New York: Monthly Review Press.
Anthracite Coal Commission
>   1938 Report of the Anthracite Coal Industry Commission. Harrisburg: Commonwealth of Pennsylvania.
Anthracite Task Force
>   1977 Report. Washington D.C.: United States Department of Energy.
Armengaud, A.
>   1973 Population in Europe 1700–1914. In *Fontana economic history of Europe,* ed. C. M. Cipolla, pp. 22–76. Glasgow: Collins/Fontana Books.
Ashburner, C. A.
>   1884 *Geology of the anthracite coal fields of Pennsylvania.* Philadelphia: University of Pennsylvania Library.
Ashton, T. S.
>   1969 *The Industrial Revolution.* 2d ed. New York: Oxford University Press.
Aurand, H.
>   1971 *From the Molly Maguires to the United Mine Workers: the social ecology of an industrial union, 1869–1897.* Philadelphia: Temple University Press.
Bairoch, P.
>   1973 Agriculture and the industrial revolution. In *Fontana economic history of Europe,* ed. C. M. Cipolla, pp. 452–506. Glasgow: Collins/Fontana Books.
Bakerman, T.
>   1956 Anthracite coal: a study in advanced industrial decline. Ph.D. dissertation, University of Pennsylvania.
Balandier, G.
>   1970 *Political anthropology.* 2d ed. London: Penguin Press.
Baran, P. A., and Sweezy, P. M.
>   1966 *Monopoly capital: an essay on the American economic and social order.* New York: Monthly Review Press.
Barr, Kenneth
>   1979 Long waves: a selective, annotated bibliography. *Review* 2:675–718.
Barraclough, G.
>   1967 *An introduction to contemporary history.* Baltimore: Penguin Books.
>   1978 ed. *The Times atlas of world history.* Maplewood, N.J.: Hammond.
Bateson, G.
>   1972 *Steps to an ecology of mind.* New York: Ballantine Books.

Bennett, J.
   1976 *The ecological transition: cultural anthropology and human adaptation.* New York: Pergamon.
Berger, J.
   1976 The Hazleton ecological land planning study. *Landscape Planning* 3: 303–35.
   1978 Toward an applied human ecology for landscape architecture and regional planning. *Human Ecology* 6:179–99.
Bergier, J-F.
   1973 The industrial bourgeoisie and the rise of the working class 1700–1914. In *Fontana economic history of Europe,* ed. C. M. Cipolla, pp. 397–451. Glasgow: Collins/Fontana Books.
Berthoff, R.
   1965 The social order of the anthracite region, 1825–1902. *The Pennsylvania Magazine of History and Biography* 89 (July): 261–91.
Bezold, C.
   1978 *Anticipatory democracy.* New York: Vintage Books.
Binder, F. M.
   1974 *Coal Age empire: Pennsylvania coal and its utilization to 1860.* Harrisburg: Pennsylvania Historical and Museum Commission.
Blair, J. F., Jr.; Cadwell, G. M.; and Miller, B. E.
   1978 *An analysis of the impacts of the EPA's proposed NSPS SO₂ regulations on the anthracite industry and northeastern Pennsylvania.* Philadelphia: Franklin Research Center, The Franklin Institute.
Boulding, K.
   1965 *The meaning of the twentieth century: the great transition.* New York: Harper Colophon Books.
Braudel, F.
   1977 *Afterthoughts on material civilization and capitalism.* Baltimore: Johns Hopkins University Press.
Brown, L.
   1978 *The twenty-ninth day.* New York: Norton.
Brush, S.
   1977 *Mountain, field, and family: the economy and human ecology of an Andean valley.* Philadelphia: University of Pennsylvania Press.
Bukharin, N.
   1969 *Historical materialism.* 2d ed. Ann Arbor: University of Michigan Press.
   1973 *Imperialism and world economy.* 2d ed. New York: Monthly Review Press.
Bureau of Labor Statistics
   1913 Wages and hours of labor in cotton, woolen, and silk industries, 1890–1912. Washington, D.C.: Government Printing Office, Bulletin #128.
Busby, K.
   1965 The new northeast Pennsylvania. Scranton Chamber of Commerce, Annual meeting at Marywood College, 6 April 1965.
   1979 Future planning. Address to city planning students, University of Pennsylvania.
Caudill, H. M.
   1963 *Night comes to the Cumberlands: a biography of a depressed area.* Boston: Little, Brown and Company.
Cipolla, C. M.
   1973a ed. The industrial revolution. *Fontana economic history of Europe.* Glasgow: Collins/Fontana Books.

1973b ed. The emergence of industrial societies. Part 1. *Fontana economic history of Europe.* Glasgow: Collins/Fontana Books.

1973c ed. The emergence of industrial societies. Part 2. *Fontana economic history of Europe.* Glasgow: Collins/Fontana Books.

1975 *The economic history of world population.* Baltimore: Penguin Books.

1976 ed. Contemporary economies. Part 1. *Fontana economic history of Europe.* Glasgow: Collins/Fontana Books.

Commoner, B.

1977 *The poverty of power.* New York: Bantam Press.

Community Area New Development Organization (CAN DO).

1974 *The CAN DO story: a case history of successful community industrial development.* Hazleton: Community Area New Development Organization, Inc.

Conant, R. C., and Ashby, W. R.

1970 Every good regulator of a system must be a model of that system. *International Journal of Systems Science* 1:89–97.

Cook, E.

1976 *Man, energy, society.* San Francisco: Freeman.

Cottrell, W. F.

1955 *Energy and society.* New York: McGraw-Hill.

Daly, H.

1977 *Steady-state economics.* San Francisco: Freeman.

Deane, P.

1973 Great Britain. In *Fontana economic history of Europe,* ed. C. M. Cipolla, pp. 161–227. Glasgow: Collins/Fontana Books.

Derganc, D. S.

1979 Thomas Edison and his electric lighting system. Institute of Electrical and Electronics Engineers *Spectrum.* February, pp. 50–59.

Diener, P.; Nonini, D.; and Robkin, E. E.

1980 Ecology and evolution in cultural anthropology. *Man.* 15:1–31.

Doyle, D. H.

1978 *The social order of a frontier community: Jacksonville, Illinois 1825–70.* Urbana: University of Illinois Press.

Eckholm, E.

1976 *Losing ground.* New York: Norton.

Ehrlich, P. R.; Ehrlich, A. H.; and Holdren, J. P.

1977 *Ecoscience: population, resources, environment.* San Francisco: Freeman.

Engels, F.

1968 *The condition of the working class in England.* 2d ed. Stanford: Stanford University Press.

Erikson, K. T.

1976 *Everything in its path: destruction of community in the Buffalo Creek flood.* New York: Simon and Schuster.

Ernst, M. L.

1937 Anthracite coal industry commission report. Harrisburg, Pennsylvania.

Flannery, K. V.

1972 The cultural evolution of civilization. *Annual Review of Ecology and Systematics 3.* Palo Alto: Annual Review, Inc.

Forrester, J.

1976 U.S. long-term energy policy in a changing national environment. In *Middle- and long-term energy policies and alternatives,* Committee on Interstate and Foreign Commerce, 94th Congress, pp. 61–191.

Serial No. 94-36. Washington, D.C.: U.S. Government Printing Office.

Freedman, C., and Smith, A.
1972 *Voluntary associations: perspectives on the literature.* Cambridge: Harvard University Press.

Friedman, J.
1978 Crises in theory and transformations of the world economy. *Review* 2: 131–48.

Geertz, C.
1963 *Agricultural involution.* Berkeley: University of California Press.
1973 *The interpretation of cultures.* New York: Basic Books.

Ginzburg, E.
1976 The pluralistic economy of the United States. *Scientific American* 235: 25–29.

Golab, C.
1977 *Immigrant destinations.* Philadelphia: Temple University Press.

Goodenough, W. H.
1966 *Cooperation in change: an anthropological approach to community development.* New York: Wiley.
1978 Multiculturalism as the normal human experience. In *Applied anthropology in America,* eds. E. M. Eddy and W. Partridge, pp. 79–86. New York: Columbia University Press.

Gori, G. B., and Richter, B. J.
1978 Macroeconomics of disease prevention in the United States. *Science* 200: 1124–30.

Gottman, J.
1961 *Megalopolis: the urbanized northeastern seaboard of the United States.* Cambridge: MIT Press.

Gould, S., and Eldridge, N.
1977 Punctuated equilibria: the tempo and mode of evolution reconsidered. *Paleobiology* 3:115–51.

Graham, D. L., Jr.
1977 *Toward a planned society: from Roosevelt to Nixon.* 2d ed. London: Oxford University Press.

Grigg, D. B.
1974 *The agricultural systems of the world.* Cambridge: Cambridge University Press.

Gutman, H.
1976 *Work, culture, and society in industrializing America.* New York: Knopf.

Haefele, E. T.
1973 *Representative government and environmental management.* Baltimore: Johns Hopkins University Press.
1979 Shifts in business-government interactions. Unpublished manuscript.
1980 Societal risk and individual safety. Unpublished manuscript.

Hall, C. A. S., and Day, J. W., Jr., eds.
1977 *Ecosystem modeling in theory and practice: an introduction with case histories.* New York: Wiley.

Hall, C. A. S.; Day, J. W., Jr.; and Odum, H. T.
1977 A circuit language for energy and matter. In *Ecosystem modeling in theory and practice,* ed. C. A. S. Hall and J. W. Day, Jr., pp. 37–48. New York: Wiley.

Handler, P., ed.
> 1970 *Biology and the future of man.* London: Oxford University Press.

Harris, M.
> 1977 *Cannibals and kings.* New York: Random House.
> 1979 *Cultural materialism.* New York: Random House.

Hartman, R. S., and Wheeler, D. R.
> 1979 Schumperterian waves of innovation and infrastructure development in Great Britain and the United States: the Kondratieff cycle revisited. *Research in Economic History* 4:37–85.

Hayes, E. T.
> 1979 Energy resources available to the United States, 1985 to 2000. *Science* 203: 233–39.

Hechter, M.
> 1979 The position of eastern European immigrants to the United States in the cultural division of labor: some trends and prospects. In *The world-system of capitalism: past and present,* ed. W. L. Goldfrank, pp. 111–29. Beverly Hills: Sage Publications.

Henning, B. D.; Foord, A. S.; and Mathias, B. L.
> 1949 *Crises in English history, 1066–1945.* New York: Holt, Rinehart and Winston.

Hjalte, K.; Lidgren, K.; and Stahl, I.
> 1977 *Environmental policy and welfare economics.* New York: Cambridge University Press.

Holland, J.
> 1835 *The history and description of fossil fuel, the collieries, and coal trade of Great Britain.* London: Whittaker and Co.

Hsiang, T-K.
> 1947 Competition of substitute fuels in the anthracite industry. Master's thesis, University of Pennsylvania.

Hubbert, M. K.
> 1977 World oil and natural gas reserves and resources. *Project interdependence: United States and world energy outlook through 1990.* 95th Cong., 1st sess., 95–33.

Husserl, E.
> 1970 *The crisis of European sciences and transcendental phenomenology: an introduction to phenomenological philosophy.* Evanston: Northwestern University Press.

Jansson, A.-M., and Zucchetto, J.
> 1978 Man, nature and energy flow on the island of Gotland. *Ambio* 7:140–49.

Jones, E.
> 1914 *The anthracite coal combination in the United States.* Cambridge: Harvard University Press.

King, A. D.
> 1976 Values, science, and settlement: a case study in environmental control. In *The mutual interaction of people and their environment,* ed. A. Rapoport, pp. 365–89. Chicago: Aldine.

Kondratieff, N. D.
> 1935 The long waves in economic life. *The Review of Economic Statistics* 17:105–15.

Koopmans, T. C.
> 1979 Economics among the sciences. *American Economic Review* 69:1–13.

Kurath, H.
   1972 *Studies in area linguistics.* Bloomington: Indiana University Press.
Leontieff, W.; Carter, A. P.; and Petri, P. A.
   1977 *The future of the world economy: a United Nations study.* New York: Oxford University Press.
Lewis, A. H.
   1965 *Lament for the Molly Maguires.* London: Longmans.
Lewis, W. A.
   1978 *The evolution of the international economic order.* Princeton: Princeton University Press.
Love, T. F.
   1977 Ecological niche theory in sociocultural anthropology: a conceptual framework and an application. *American Ethnologist* 4:27–41.
Lovins, A. B.
   1980 *World energy strategies: facts, issues, and options.* New York: Harper.
Lucas, R. A.
   1971 *Minetown, milltown, railtown.* Toronto: University of Toronto Press.
Luten, D. B.
   1971 The economic geography of energy. In *Energy and power,* pp. 109–20. San Francisco: Freeman.
MacCannell, D.
   1977 The tourist and the new community. *Annals of Tourism Research* 4: 208–15.
McEvedy, C., and Jones, R.
   1978 *Atlas of world population history.* New York: Penguin Books.
Macfarlane, A.
   1979 *The origins of English individualism.* New York: Cambridge University Press.
Macfarlane, J.
   1877 *The coal regions of America: their topography, geology, and development.* 3d ed. New York: D. Appleton and Co.
Man's Impact on Climate
   1971 *Inadvertant climate modification.* Cambridge: MIT Press.
Marx, K., and Engels, F.
   1947 *The German ideology.* Parts I and III. 2d ed. New York: International Publishers.
Mayr, E.
   1978 Evolution. *Scientific American* 239:47–55.
Mead, R. R.
   1935 An analysis of the decline of the anthracite industry since 1921. Ph.D. dissertation, University of Pennsylvania.
Meinig, D. W.
   1971 *Southwest: three peoples in geographical change: 1600–1970.* New York: Oxford University Press.
Miller, D.
   1975 *Leadership and power in the Boston-Washington megalopolis.* New York: Wiley.
Miller, J. G.
   1978 *Living systems.* New York: McGraw-Hill.
Nash, J.
   1979 *We eat the mines and the mines eat us.* New York: Columbia University Press.

Nash, M.
1977a Modernization: cultural meanings—the widening gap between the intellectuals and the process. In *Economic Development and Cultural Change* 25, supplement, ed. M. Nash, pp. 16–28.
1977b ed. Essays on economic development and cultural change in honor of Bert F. Hoselitz. *Economic development and cultural change* 25, supplement.
Nearing, S.
1915 *Anthracite: an instance of a natural resource monopoly.* Philadelphia: John C. Winston Co.
Nef, J. U.
1963 *Western civilization since the Renaissance: peace, war, industry, and the arts.* New York: Harper.
O'Connor, J.
1974 *The corporations and the state.* New York: Harper and Row.
Odum, H. T.
1971 *Environment, power, and society.* New York: Wiley.
Odum, H. T., and Odum, E. C.
1976 *Energy basis of man and nature.* New York: McGraw-Hill.
Oettinger, A. G.
1980 Information resources: knowledge and power in the 21st century. *Science* 209:191–98.
Ophuls, W.
1977 *Ecology and the politics of scarcity.* San Francisco: Freeman.
Orlove, B.
1977 *Alpacas, sheep, and men.* New York: Academic Press.
Pattee, H. H.
1977 Dynamic and linguistic modes of complex systems. *International Journal of General Systems* 3:259–66.
Petrascheck, W., and Petrascheck, W. E.
1950 *Lagerstattenlehre.* Berlin: Springer.
Pierce, N. R., and Barone, M.
1977 *The Mid-Atlantic states of America.* New York: Norton.
Pimental, D; Hurd, L. E.; Bellotti, A. C.; Forster, M. J.; Oka, I. N.; Sholes, O. D.; and Whitman, R. J.
1973 Food production and the energy crisis. *Science* 182:443–49.
Pinder, J.
1976 Europe in the world economy 1920–1970. In *Fontana economic history of Europe*, ed. C. M. Cipolla, pp. 323–75. Glasgow: Collins/Fontana Books.
Powell, H. B.
1978 *Philadelphia's first fuel crisis: Jacob Cist and the developing market for Pennsylvania anthracite.* University Park: Pennsylvania State University.
Prigogine, I; Allen, P. M.; and Herman, R.
1977 Long term trends and the evolution of complexity. In *Goals in a global community*, ed. E. Laszlo and J. Bierman, pp. 1–64. New York: Pergamon.
Rappaport, R.
1968 *Pigs for the ancestors.* New Haven: Yale University Press.
1971 The flow of energy in an agricultural society. In *Energy and power*, pp. 69–82. San Francisco: Freeman.
Raushenbush, H. S.
1924 *The anthracite question.* New York: H. W. Wilson Co.

Rees, T. L.
1978 Population and industrial decline in the South Wales coalfields. *Regional Studies* 12:69–77.

Roberts, P.
1904 *Anthracite coal communities.* New York: Macmillan.

Rogers, H. D.
1838 *Second annual report on the geological exploration of the state of Pennsylvania.* Harrisburg: Commonwealth of Pennsylvania.

Rondinelli, D. A.
1975 *Urban and regional development planning: policy and administration.* Ithaca: Cornell University Press.

Roscoe, E. S., and Thuering, G. L.
1958 The textile industry in Pennsylvania. Engineering Research Bulletin #B–74, College of Engineering and Architecture. Pennsylvania State University.

Rose, D.
1978 Human ecology of mushroom production in southern Chester County, Pa. In *Ethnicity and cultural pluralism in the United States,* ed. T. Ayabe, pp. 113–68. Fukuoka, Japan: Research Institute of Comparative Education and Culture, Kyushu University.
1981 Knights of faith in a Hobbesian world: resource competition in southern Chester County, Pennsylvania. *Landscape Planning,* forthcoming.

Rose, D., and Berger, J.
1974 Human ecology in the regional plan. Philadelphia: Department of Landscape Architecture and Regional Planning, University of Pennsylvania.

Rose, D., and Jackson, J.
1978 Human ecology for ecosystem management. In vol. 1 of *Proceedings of the symposium on technical, environmental, socioeconomic, and regulatory aspects of coastal zone management,* pp. 484–99. New York: American Society of Civil Engineers.

Rose, D.; Steiner, F.; and Jackson, J.
1979 An applied human ecological approach to regional planning. *Landscape Planning* 5:241–61.

Rosen, R.
1974 Planning, management, policies, and strategies: four fuzzy concepts. *International Journal of General Systems* 1:245–52.

Rosenblum, W., ed.
1977 Foreword. In *America and Lewis Hine: Photographs 1904–1940,* pp. 9–15. Millerton: Aperture.

Rostow, W.
1978 *The world economy: history and prospects.* Austin: University of Texas Press.

Schaefer, D. F.
1977 *A quantitative description and analysis of the growth of the Pennsylvania anthracite coal industry 1820 to 1865.* New York: Arno Press.

Schneider, J., and Schneider, P.
1976 *Culture and political economy in west Sicily.* New York: Academic Press.

Shapp, M. J., and Jurkat, E. J.
1962 New growth . . . new jobs for Pennsylvania. Philadelphia: The Shapp Foundation.

Shelford, V. E.
  1978 *The ecology of North America.* 2d ed. Urbana: University of Illinois Press.
Shryock, H. S.; Siegel, J. S.; and Associates
  1973 *The methods and materials of demography.* Rev. ed. Washington, D.C.: Government Printing Office.
Shuman, J. B., and Rosenau, D.
  1972 *The Kondratieff wave.* New York: World Publishing.
Simon, J. L.
  1980 Resources, population, environment: an oversupply of false bad news. *Science* 208:1431–37.
Spooner, B., and Reining, P.
  1979 Desertification and society: a proposal. Unpublished manuscript.
Steward, J.
  1955 *Theory of culture change.* Urbana: University of Illinois Press.
Stobaugh, R., and Yergin, D., eds.
  1979 *Energy future: report of the energy project at the Harvard business school.* New York: Random House.
Strickler, W. M.
  1935 Motor truck transportation and railroad transportation of anthracite coal. Master's thesis, University of Pennsylvania.
Tocqueville, A. de
  1945 *Democracy in America.* Vol. 2. 3d ed. New York: Vintage Books.
Trigger, B., ed.
  1978 Northeast. Vol. 15 of the *Handbook of North American Indians,* ed. W. C. Sturtevant. Washington, D.C.: Smithsonian Institution.
United Nations
  n.d. Concise report on world population situations in 1970–1975 and its long range implications. #E. 74. XIII. 4.
  1975 Task force on integrated ecological studies on human settlements, within the framework of project 11. Man and The Biosphere Programme, Number 31. Paris.
  1977 *Statistical yearbook.* Paris.
Vidich, A. J., and Bensman, J.
  1968 *Small town in mass society.* Rev. ed. Princeton: Princeton University Press.
Wallace, A. F. C.
  1978 *Rockdale: the growth of an American village in the early industrial revolution.* New York: Knopf.
Wallerstein, I.
  1974 *The modern world-system: capitalist agriculture and the origins of the European world-economy in the sixteenth century.* New York: Academic Press.
  1979 *The capitalist world-economy.* New York: Cambridge University Press.
Warner, S. B., Jr.
  1968 *The private city: Philadelphia in three periods of its growth.* Philadelphia: University of Pennsylvania Press.
Watt, K. E. F.
  1978 The structure of post-industrial economies. *Journal of Social and Biological Structures* 1:53–70.
Weinstein, J.
  1968 *The corporate ideal in the liberal state, 1900–1918.* Boston: Beacon Press.

Weiss, C., Jr.
    1979 Mobilizing technology for developing countries. *Science* 203:1083–89.
White, L.
    1949 *The science of culture.* New York: Farrar, Straus and Cudahy.
Whitman, M.
    1979 A year of travail: the United States and the international economy. *Foreign Affairs* 57:527–54.
Wilkinson, R. G.
    1973 *Poverty and progress.* New York: Praeger.
Wilson, C. L.
    1980 *Coal: bridge to the future. Report of the World Coal Study (WOCOL).* Cambridge: Ballinger.
Woodruff, W.
    1973 The emergence of an international economy. In *Fontana economic history of Europe,* ed. C. M. Cipolla, pp. 656–737. Glasgow: Collins/Fontana Books.
World Bank
    1979 *World development report.* New York: Oxford University Press.
Zaleski, C. P. L.
    1979 Energy-choices for the next 15 years: a view from Europe. *Science* 203: 849–51.
Zelinsky, W.
    1973 *The cultural geography of the United States.* Englewood Cliffs: Prentice-Hall.
    1974 Selfward bound? Personal preference patterns and the changing map of American society. *Economic Geography* (April): 144–79.

INDEX